THE

RISINGS OF THE LUDDITES

CHARTISTS AND PLUG-DRAWERS

FRANK PEEL, F.S.A.S.

THE
RISINGS OF THE LUDDITES

CHARTISTS AND PLUG-DRAWERS

BY

FRANK PEEL

FOURTH EDITION

WITH A NEW INTRODUCTION
BY
E. P. THOMPSON

"Fling out the red banner! its fierce front under,
 Come, gather ye, gather ye, champions of right!
And roll round the world with the voice of God's thunder;
 The wrongs we've to reckon—oppressors to smite!"
Gerald Massey.

FRANK CASS & CO. LTD.
1968

Published by
FRANK CASS AND COMPANY LIMITED
67 Great Russell Street, London WC1

This edition copyright © 1968

First edition   1880
Second edition   1888
Third edition   1895
Fourth edition   1968

SBN 7146 1350 9

Printed in Holland by
N. V. Grafische Industrie Haarlem

INTRODUCTION TO THE
FOURTH EDITION

FRANK PEEL's *The Risings of the Luddites* went through at least three stages before it arrived at the present form. It commenced as a series of articles in the *Heckmondwike Herald and Liversedge Weekly Courier*, running from 25th January to 6th August 1878.[1] These were reprinted, with some re-arrangement and additions, in book-form in 1880.[2] The second edition (1888) brought additional material incorporated in chapters 5, 6, 12, 22, and 32 of this edition, and added all the post-Luddite material, from chapters 34 to 41. The third, and final, edition (which is presented here) was published from the *Echo* office, Brighouse, in 1895: it added very little to the 1888 edition, apart from chapter 33 ("Comforting Friends") and some new material in chapter 40 ("The Plug Riots").

Peel himself appears as a characteristic figure in small-town Liberal Nonconformity. Born on 29th May 1831, the son of a small worsted manufacturer at Great Horton, near Bradford, he was apprenticed to a draper, married (in 1856) the sister of his employer, and thereupon went into partnership with his brother-in-law in a linen-draper's business at Heckmondwike. He continued in this business for thirty years: was at one time and another local collector of taxes, a member of the Heckmondwike Local Board, honorary secretary to the Chamber of Trade, and an officer of the local Mechanics' Institute: and was at all times an earnest Congregationalist. He had, meanwhile, written occasionally for the *Dewsbury Reporter*; and he became a founder-member and Vice-President of the Heckmondwike Antiquarian Society in February 1880.[3] In 1886 he retired from the draper's business and became editor and part-proprietor of the *Heckmondwike Herald*, for which he had written occasionally (mainly on local history) since its foundation in 1877. He remained as editor until 1894, using his own weekly newspaper to further his

[1] My thanks are due to the Librarians at Heckmondwike and at Cleckheaton Public Libraries for their assistance; to Mr Geoffrey Ineson of the *Cleckheaton Guardian* for enabling me to consult the files of that paper; and to Mr Joseph Greenald for assistance in consulting these sources.

[2] Frank Peel, *The Risings of the Luddites* ("Herald" Office, Cheapside, Heckmondwike, 1880).

[3] The Objects of the Society included: "(h) The collecting of materials relating to the traditions, manners and customs of the town and neighbourhood." Heckmondwike Library, cutting book, SPE 942 HEC.

researches into local history. Series of articles on "Old Cleck-heaton" (in the *Cleckheaton Guardian*, 25 January to 4 April 1884) and on "Old Liversedge" and "Old Heckmondwike" (*Heckmondwike Herald*, 1887) were gathered together in two further books: *Nonconformity in Spen Valley* (Heckmondwike, 1891) and *Spen Valley: Past and Present* (Heckmondwike, 1893). Peel died at the age of 69, in April 1900.[4]

II

The West Riding was unfortunate in having no Samuel Bamford to chronicle its early Radical history, nor any middle-class historian of radical temper (like Archibald Prentice for Manchester and J. A. Langford for Birmingham) to draw the story together. However, the last decades of the 19th century saw the growth of a vigorous school of local historians—as well as of local annalists and folklorists—distinguished by their preoccupation with economic, industrial and social themes; among the most noteworthy were John James, James Burnley, William Cudworth and William Scruton of Bradford; J. Horsfall Turner and John Lister of Halifax; D. F. E. Sykes of Hudders-field; William Smith of Morley; and Joseph Lawson of Pudsey.

Thus Frank Peel was no isolated amateur, but a representative mind within an efflorescence of historical consciousness within his own community. Undoubtedly these men wrote for an ap-preciative audience: and relations between the historian and his readers were close—when articles appeared in weekly instalments in the local press, it was possible for readers to challenge disputed points (or to add new information) in the next weekly issue. Lawson's remarkable *Progress in Pudsey*[5] first appeared, like *The Risings of the Luddites*, in weekly letters in the local press[6]; and Peel's Luddite articles were so successful that—it is claimed—they were serialised in about a dozen other newspapers.[7] No doubt there may be other important reminiscent articles in the local press of these decades still awaiting discovery by the researcher.

The historical consciousness of this time had two leading characteristics. The first (which concerns us least in relation to this book) was an intense local patriotism, as the Victorian "age of improvement" had come, at last, to a point of poise, or of realisation, and the manufacturing and commercial middle-class wished to celebrate achievement, stability—and continuity. Each town must have its own Town Hall, Chamber of Trade, and

---

[4] Obituary in *Cleckheaton Guardian*, 12 April 1900; T. W. Thompson, *Spen Valley: A Local History* (Heckmondwike, 1925), p. 320; *Heckmondwike Herald*, passim; cutting books in Heckmondwike Library.

[5] Joseph Lawson, *Letters to the Young on Progress in Pudsey during the Last Sixty Years* (Stanningley, 1887).

[6] *Pudsey District Advertiser*, 18 December 1885—27 August 1886.

[7] *Cleckheaton Guardian*, 12 April 1900: I have not checked this claim.

local history; and West Riding historians, piqued by the way in which the industrial north was caricatured in polite London culture as a mushroom-growth of the industrial revolution, were the more anxious to insist upon their own Cromwellian, or Saxon, or Roman antiquities.

The second characteristic is less easy to define. There is a definite sense that, somewhere in the 1870s and 1880s, men became aware that—not this or that particular—but a distinct way of life and a traditional culture had passed away in their lifetime. The Liberal optimism about the march of improvement, the homilies about the benefits of free trade, and the congratulations that the hungry forties had been left far behind—all these are present, but they are modified by a distinct nostalgia and a respect for the culture that has been lost. Again and again this note is sounded by Peel:

We live in a time when all is feverish haste and excitement. Leisure is gone, gone where the spinning wheels are gone, and the packhorses and the slow wagons, and the pedlars who brought bargains to our doors on sunny afternoons. We have been told by inventors that the great work of the steam engine is to create leisure for mankind, but, alas! we fail to realise that it creates anything but a vacuum for eager thought to rush in. Even idleness is eager now . . .[8]

Sometimes the lost values are objectified; descriptions of the old coaching days, the traditional cottages with sanded floors and white-stoned hearth, furnished with the delf case, the carved oak kist, and the shut-up bed.[9] But the actual location of the values was not, of course, in the things so much as in a particular set of social relations which these things called back to mind. And these relations were based upon the "domestic system" or, at least, the very small-scale manufacturing system of the "little makers" which persisted for so long in this part of the West Riding. Here social gradations, between master and skilled journeyman, were gentle, and (with the apprentice or the unmarried worker sleeping in the manufacturer's home or workplace) the "economic family" continued well into the 19th century. The small industrial villages were highly cohesive communities, with the strongest sense of local identity, intolerant of outsiders, united internally by a dense network of kinship. (The reader unfamiliar with the district would scarcely surmise from Peel's account of events at the distinct townships of Littletown, Cleckheaton, Liversedge, Heckmondwike, Robert-

---

[8] Frank Peel, "Roberttown Sixty Years Ago", *Heckmondwike Herald*, 9 September 1887.

[9] Frank Peel, "Old Cleckheaton: V. The Social Condition of the People", *Cleckheaton Guardian*, 22 February 1884: compare *Spen Valley: Past and Present*, pp. 269–76.

town, Hightown, Millbridge, &c., that none of these villages were
more than a couple of miles from each other.) In one of his
articles, Peel explicitly made the contrast;

> There are many people still living who in their younger days
> knew intimately everybody in the village, and could say
> whether they were married or single . . . who they married,
> how many children they had, and all their names and distin-
> guishing peculiarities. The whole population in fact seemed at
> that time to consist of one large family . . . no member of it
> could see any impropriety in discussing the private affairs of
> another in a way which would now be considered not only
> offensive but insulting. This familiarity had, without doubt,
> occasionally an eminently disagreeable side, but it had its
> redeeming features also. Then all the members of the little
> community stood pretty much on a level, and a far stronger
> bond of sympathy existed amongst them than obtains at the
> present time, when people so isolate themselves that they
> scarcely know who are their next-door neighbours.[10]

The same point is made by two other local historians, and
contemporaries of Peel, in the novel *Ben o' Bill's, the Luddite*,
in which they also used the theme of Luddism as a means of
reconstructing a lost way of life;

> Mother had a rare gift that way, knowing the relationship by
> blood and marriage of every family for miles around, and
> able . . . to count up cousinships and half-cousins, and uncles
> and great uncles, till your brain turned round. Except my
> lord's family and the folk at the vicarage, who had come from
> the south, I think she made us akin to all the folk in Slaith-
> waite, Linthwaite and Lingards.[11]

It is, exactly, within such a community that an oral tradition is
particularly vivid, tenacious, and (when used with proper
caution) reliable. It was upon this tradition that Frank Peel
drew.

III

Peel knew what he was at. Where records were available, he
transcribed them accurately and was scrupulous in their inter-
pretation: Cobbett's *Political Register*, Byron's speech, cuttings
from the *Leeds Mercury*, and material from several published
accounts of the Luddite trials (which takes up much of chapters
23 to 31). In the first twenty-two chapters, however, he drew
extensively upon oral tradition; and it is possible, by following up

[10] "Old Cleckheaton", *Cleckheaton Guardian*, 22 February 1884.
[11] D. F. E. Sykes and G. H. Walker, *Ben o' Bill's, the Luddite* (Huddersfield, n.d.).
p. 69. Although the authors claim their novel to be based on the oral record and
papers of a Luddite survivor, it would seem that they in fact lean heavily upon Peel's
account. The novel succeeds better as an imaginative reconstruction of the way of
life, folk wisdom, and dialect of the Luddite community.

the different stages by which he pieced the story together, to note how critically he used this tradition, and how carefully he checked and re-checked one account against another.

When he first came to Heckmondwike in 1856 many eye-witnesses and participants of the events of 1812 would still have been living: a man of 22 in 1812 (Mellor's age) would have been only 66 at that time. But if (as is likely) he only began collecting and comparing accounts in the late 1870s, there would have been very few such survivors. There were a few. The story of Baines, the old democrat, and of the meeting at the Crispin Inn, Halifax, Peel had from an old man—

who had stood as a strippling in the Luddite ranks, and had often joined in their wild defiant songs as they plied the sounding shears, called himself an 'old rebel', and not without cause, for he had been mixed up with every movement against constituted authority that had sprung up in the West Riding during his life-time.

This informant "repeated to me with wonderful fire and energy the impassioned speech made by that staunch old democrat [John Baines]."[12] Other informants can scarcely have been more than children at the time of the events. Thus, he refers at one point to an old lady who, "though she is nearly four score, still retains all her faculties unimpaired".[13] From other evidence, this would appear to have been a Mrs Longley, the daughter of Fearnsides, the foreman at Jackson's workshop, from whom the material on Naylor in chapter 12 will have been gathered.[14] The material on William Hall, and on Wood's and Jackson's workshops, came partly from her, and was supplemented by information from a Mr Dernally of Hightown who, as a youth, had rounds in search for information.[15]

The oral tradition, in such communities of cousinships and half-cousins, is of course especially strong in episodes of "character", dramatic or comic. Mrs Longley is described here (p. 119) as "just one of those garrulous, sharp witted people, full of old world tales and folk-lore, which it delights the hearts of antiquaries to converse with." (Emily Brontë drew upon this same tradition of the shrewdly observant Yorkshire raconteur for the character of Nellie Dean.) No doubt some of these stories were improved in the telling; George Mellor (like Brandreth) became more dominant and more impassioned as the legend was passed down: and Rayner's providential escape through the clock's striking thirteen is a folk-chestnut. And Peel sometimes

---

[12] Preface to 1888 edition. This "old veteran to whom I was most indebted" had died "years since" in 1888.
[13] 1880 edition, p. 61. This "bright eyed garrulous old lady" was still living in 1888 (Preface to 1888 edition).
[14] Frank Peel, "Rambles Round Liversedge, VI", *Heckmondwike Herald*, 29 June 1883: "Old Liversedge", *ibid.* 8 July 1887.
[15] *Ibid.*, 8 July 1887.

nods: Mitchell was from Liverpool, not Liversedge [16]: young Booth may have been a disciple of Tom Paine and—just possibly —of Thomas Spence but not (in 1812) of Robert Owen (p. 14).

But what is remarkable is, not the occasional errors and discrepancies, but the fact that the general account of Luddism preserved in the oral tradition has proved, both in particulars and in larger terms, to be so accurate. In the twentieth century historians tended to discount much of this tradition, and to see Luddism in strictly industrial terms.[17] The Hammonds even discounted oath-taking, and suggested that the evidence of any ulterior political objectives was the work of government spies. But as new documents have come to hand in recent years, so Peel's original picture has been restored. John Baines can indeed be seen as an old Painite "Jacobin"[18], and the revolutionary rhetoric of some Luddites survives in their threatening letters.[19] The portrait of Hammond Roberson, the military parson—who was drawn upon by Charlotte Brontë also in Shirley—is confirmed by his own letters.[20] Cartwright's own accounts of the defence of his mill and of the disaffected soldier who refused to fire upon his own brothers have been uncovered.[21] The evidence as to oath-taking would seem to be indisputable,[22] and documentary sources also confirm Peel's picture of insurrectionary preparations and arms-raids continuing for months after the attack on Rawfolds.[23] The historian is able also to examine the whole series of depositions taken by Joseph Radcliffe at Milnsbridge House through that long summer of 1812, and to realise how richly he earned the respect of his fellow magistrates—and his baronetcy.[24]

[16] In general, the post-Luddite chapters are greatly inferior to the Luddite ones. There are serious inaccuracies in the chapters on Oliver the Spy (35), the Grange Moor rising (37), and events in Bradford in 1839–40 and 1848 are confused (39 and 41). The chapter on the Plug Riots (40) is, however, valuable.
[17] See especially F. O. Darvall, Popular Disturbance and Public Order in Regency England (1934); J. L. & B. Hammond, The Skilled Labourer (1920), esp. Ch. X.
[18] The Crown brief against Baines in the Treasury Solicitor's papers commences: "the elder Baines is a Hatter, a Man notoriously disaffected to the Government": Public Record Office: T.S. 11. 813. 2673.
[19] See e.g. W. B. Crump, The Leeds Woollen Industry, 1780–1820 (Leeds, 1931), pp. 229–30.
[20] See the Radcliffe MSS, published in part in Asa Briggs, Private and Social Themes in 'Shirley' (Brontë Society, 1958) and also drawn upon in chapter 14 of my The Making of the English Working Class (1963), where I offer a general reinterpretation of Luddism in the light of new evidence. Peel in one of his articles quotes from another private letter of Roberson's: "When treating with the poor fellows who were shot at Mr. Cartwright's mill, I could not use roundabout puzzling language, it seemed all I could say was, 'You have broken the laws of God and your country. You are therefore sinners. But Christ is a Saviour. Look to Him.' ": "Old Liversedge", Heckmondwike Herald, 7 April 1887.
[21] See the Hammonds, op. cit. pp. 305–6; H. A. Cadman, Gomersal: Past and Present (Leeds, 1930), pp. 114–16.
[22] See E. P. Thompson, op. cit. pp. 577–86.
[23] Notably papers in the Wentworth Woodhouse archives (deposited in Sheffield Reference Library), especially those cited as Fitzwilliam MSS F. 46 (g) in Thompson, op. cit. p. 572 &c.
[24] P.R.O.: K.B. 8.91. This rich collection of informations and examinations should certainly be studied by anyone who wishes to write a definitive history of Yorkshire Luddism. For Radcliffe's baronetcy, see D. F. E. Sykes, The History of Huddersfield (Huddersfield, 1898), pp. 288–9.

The dying deposition of Horsfall is here, and the record of the successive examinations of the wretched Benjamin Walker. These may, perhaps, throw doubt upon one colouring which the story assumed in the oral tradition, in which Walker was cast as the Judas who betrayed his comrades for £2,000. But they offer an even more realistic insight into his motives. Walker broke down because the net was drawing very tight indeed, and he was afraid for his own life. Already, within a week of Horsfall's assassination, he had come under suspicion. Six months later, on 12 October 1812, he was fetched before Justice Radcliffe again, and was still trying to lie his way out. Questioned about the pistol which Mellor was known to have brought back with him "from the sea", he said he had heard that he had swapped it some time before for some pigeons. The deposition seems to end in mid-sentence. Ten days later the whole story tumbled out.

It was told, of course, in such a way as to incriminate Mellor as far as possible and exculpate the narrator. Walker portrayed himself as a reluctant Luddite. He had moved from Leeds to Longroyd Bridge because he had refused to join the "Institution" (or under-cover trade union) in Leeds[25]. The first night he went out Ludding: "I aimed to have gone to bed that night but he [Mellor] called me a coward so I went to the spot and there was in the course of the night about 45 of us." He did not go about much with Mellor, since Mellor was his master's step-son and was "above" him. Questioned about the attack on Rawfolds, he said: "We durst hardly do any other than obey Mellor, being our Master's Wife's son."[26]

Mellor himself has (like Brandreth) left little to the historian, except his silence. It is clear that he belonged to the élite of the skilled artisans, and depositions confirm that he had worked in Russia. Walker (who himself earned the high wage of 24s. or 25s. a week) claimed that Mellor earned 35s. and, having no family and sleeping above the workshop, could afford to drink freely and to save money (he was rumoured to have £100) as well.[27] There is, however, at least one surviving letter in his hand, written from York Castle while awaiting trial for his life, which enables us to establish his political convictions. The letter asks the recipient to tell his cousin to stick to the evidence of alibi sworn before Radcliffe; and to impress the same upon the servants:

> I hope they will befriend me and never mind their work for if I come home I will do for them.[28] Remember a Soul is of more value than Work or Gold. I have heard you are a Pettitioning for a Parliamentary Reform and I wish these names to be given as follows . . .[29]

[25] See Thompson, op. cit. pp. 527–30.
[26] K.B. 8.91 esp. folios 153, 161, 187, 192, 198.
[27] Ibid, folios 124, 133, 187, 192, 198.
[28] Mellor uses "do for" here, not in its contemporary colloquial sense, but to mean that he will see that if the servants befriend him he will look after their interests on his return. Six servants and apprentices lived in the Wood household: see K.B. 8.91
[29] Radcliffe MSS 126/127A (G. Mellor to Thomas Ellis, copy). There follow the signatures of 39 fellow prisoners.

The snatches of Luddite songs—as well as many important anecdotes—would have perished altogether if Peel had not preserved them. But one or two other songs survive, inferior perhaps, but in the same style as those which Peel records:

You Heroes of England who wish to have a trade
Be true to each other and be not afraid
Though the Bayonet is fixed they can do no good
As long as we keep up the Rules of General Ludd.

As we have begun we are like to proceed
Till from all those Tyrants we do get freed
For this heavy yoke no longer can we bear
And those who have not felt it ought to have a share.

And then they can feel for another's woe
For he that never knew sorrow, sorrow doth not know
But there is Cartwright and Atkinson also
And to show them justice sorrow they shall know.

Though he does boast of the deeds he has done
Yet out of our presence like a thief he does run
It is the laws of England to stand in our defence
If he comes in our presence him we'll recompence.[30]

Thus Peel's account has been, in general terms, vindicated: and since it records, not just an oral tradition but a *secret* oral tradition, which—for reasons which I discuss under the heading "the opaque society" in my *Making of the English Working Class*[31]—only began to break the surface in the 1850s, when the last episodes of "physical force" Chartism were dying down, this book must be considered as, in its own right, an important historical source. Indeed, so much of his account has been confirmed that I am not myself willing to rule out the possibility of the truth of the unlikely story that George Weightman (who was tried with Brandreth for the Pentridge rising in 1817) was a Nottingham delegate at the Crispin Inn, Halifax, in 1812. Some sort of "underground" existed between the disaffected districts, with slender connections backwards to Despard's conspiracy in 1802 and forwards to 1817.[32] We are, by no means, at the end of research into Luddism and its associated movements. The Fitzwilliam and Radcliffe papers only became available in recent years, and there may remain other papers as yet unopened. The Spen Valley figures largely in the Luddite story, not because it was a major Luddite stronghold, but because Rawfolds was in

[30] Preserved with the brief *Rex v. C. Milnes & W. Blakeborough* in P.R.O.: T.S.11. 813.2673.
[31] Loc.·cit. esp. pp. 495–6.
[32] The "underground" of 1802, based on the secret trade union of the croppers, is documented in A. Aspinall, *Early English Trade Unions* (1949), esp. pp. 52–3, and Thompson, op. cit. pp. 474–8. Frank Peel notes that the constables' books provide clear evidence of drilling by night on Hartshead Moor, &c., in 1801: "Old Liversedge" *Heckmondwike Herald*, 1 July 1887, and *Spen Valley: Past and Present*, p. 234. For other tenuous connections, see Thompson, op. cit. pp. 590, 598 and note 3, 668.

its midst and because it found, in Frank Peel, an historian with the patience to tease the story out. The secrets of Yorkshire Luddism at the major centres, Leeds and Huddersfield, still remain to be unlocked, and there is still work for the local historian, following in Peel's footsteps, to do.

E. P. THOMPSON

University of Warwick
January 1968

PREFACE TO THE THIRD EDITION.

The first edition of the " Risings of the Luddites,"
&c., having been sold out almost immediately, a
second and much larger one was issued, but the sale
of this proved to be still more rapid, the whole being
sold, in fact, before it left the binder's hands.   Since
that time orders have poured in continuously,
and at last I determined, in response to many
solicitations, to issue a THIRD EDITION.   As
the book has during the last year or two been also
re-printed as a serial, in some half-dozen newspapers,
it is presumed that the public demand will now be
fully met.

The narrative has been carefully revised, and
several new chapters added.

Heckmondwike, May 20th, 1895.

LIST OF ILLUSTRATIONS.

CONTENTS.

ERRATA.

Page 25, second line, "hearts" should be "hearths."

Page 92, first line on page 93 and the last on page 92 should be transposed.

Page 104, line 2, for "Walker" read "Hall."

Page 122, omit line 5.

Page 308, line 5, after "The" insert "itinerant emissaries, who were afterwards shown to . . ."

Page 337, first line on page 338 and the last on page 337 should be transposed.

The Risings of the Luddites,

CHARTISTS AND PLUGDRAWERS.

◆

CHAPTER I.

JOHN WOOD'S WORKSHOP.
The head-quarters of the Yorkshire Luddites.

Yond Cassius has a lean and hungry look,
He thinks too much : such men are dangerous.
Shakespeare.

The year 1811 came to an end like too many of its
predecessors, amid awful scenes of carnage and confusion. The demon of war which had ravaged for half
a generation some of the fairest countries in the
world, still stalked on unchecked, claiming its
hecatomb of human victims, and blasting and destroying every fair thing in his path. A lurid comet,
which had blazed nightly in the heavens in shape
like a flaming sword was truly a fitting symbol of
the ruthless weapon which throughout the course of
that gloomy twelve months had cut down its ghastly
harvest. Not that the record of that year was much
blacker than that of many which preceded it, but the
misery and wretchedness which inevitably follow in
the footsteps of a long war had begun to culminate,
and the hard pinch of poverty was now felt in many
a dwelling where it had hitherto been a stranger. In
addition to the bloody struggles abroad in which we
had so long been engaged, riots and uprisings were
threatened in several important commercial centres
in the north, and the soldiers who were wanted to
fight our battles abroad had to be retained at home
to keep down sedition and rebellion in our midst.

About three years before the date we have named, an energetic manufacturer, named William Cartwright, had commenced to finish cloth by machinery at a mill driven by water power at Rawfolds, near Cleckheaton, and had excited by that course great resentment amongst the workmen engaged in that branch of business, who had testified their animosity by refusing to work at the new machines, and by covertly injuring them when they had the opportunity. Cartwright was, however, a man of iron resolution, and threats and opposition seemed only to strengthen his determination. His was the only place in this locality at which the hated machines had been introduced, the old method of finishing by hand, or cropping as it was called, being carried on at all the other shops in the locality. These cropping shops were chiefly places of small pretensions, at which three or four men were employed, but there was a much larger one at the top of Aquilla or Quilley Lane, at Hightown, Liversedge, opposite where the Board School now stands, carried on by Mr. John Jackson, a brother of Mr. Abraham Jackson, the currier, where the old system was still adhered to. Mr. Jackson's foreman was an old, trusty servant, of the name of William Fearnsides, a thoroughly reliable man, whose whole energies were devoted to business. Before the advent of Mr. Cartwright's new frames, work was plentiful at Mr. Jackson's shop, and the men received good wages, but, as the machinery began to be used, the little masters who adhered to hand cropping found it more and more difficult to carry on business at a profit, the result being that the men gradually lost their employment, and many of the workshops were, after a struggle, closed altogether. The men watched the gradual decay of their industry in sullen despair at first, but the news of the turbulent demonstrations at Nottingham, where the lace makers had risen against a frame of another character which threatened to destroy their trade, had stirred them strongly,

and the more violent spirits among the local cloth
finishers began to urge that similar measures should
be taken against the cropping frames introduced by
the Yorkshire manufacturers.   The wild idea seems
to have first broached at Huddersfield, but those
who were out of work spread the seeds of disaffection
all round the district, and the men at Jackson's shop
were soon following the lead of their fellow workmen
at Longroyd Bridge.   The finishing shop of Mr.
John Wood, situate at Longroyd Bridge, near Huddersfield, may be regarded as the head-quarters of
the ringleaders of the Luddite disturbances in this
part of the West Riding.   The building still stands
on the water side, not far from the highway, and is
now used as a place for depositing lumber.   Here
worked several of the daring and turbulent spirits
who directed and participated in most of the midnight expeditions undertaken for the purpose of destroying the hated machines, and many a wild scheme
has been planned beneath its old weather-beaten roof.
Mr. Wood, the master of the cropping shop, declared
afterwards, when it was proved that some of these
nefarious plots had originated at his place, that he
was "unaware of any conspiring amongst his men,"
but it is difficult to believe that he did not know that
this was the general rendezvous of the disaffected,
as some men from other shops and delegates from the
surrounding towns were continually in consultation
with his workmen, especially with his stepson, George
Mellor.   It is impossible, in fact, to believe that
Wood did not know or suspect something, for the
simple reason that there seems to have been no particular care taken to conceal the aims and objects of
the reckless band.   But the most marvellous thing
about the Luddite movement is the manner in which
the secrets of the body were kept, especially when
we take into consideration the fact that schemes
for the destruction of the machinery and also for the
destruction of some of the masters who had rendered
themselves obnoxious by their outspoken condemna-

tion of the lawless conduct of the men, were discussed
in the presence of those who were not even members
of the secret society whose doings spread such fear
throughout the whole district.   It would almost
seem sometimes as if the plotters neglected to take
the commonest precautions, but they doubtless were
well aware that many who did not actually join
them, sympathised with the movement to some extent, hoping, unlikely though it seemed, that it
would tend in some way towards the amelioration
of their own hard lot; and with regard to their members, the leaders were well aware that fear of the
consequences which would follow the breaking of the
terrible oath they all took was sufficient to deter them
from breathing a syllable of their secrets.

It is a Saturday afternoon, about the middle of
March, 1812.   Mr. Wood's men have stopped work
for the day, and are now gathered round a young man
who is reading aloud from a newspaper.   The whole
of the group are listening intently, for it is an account
of the daring proceedings of the Nottingham frame
breakers.   The sheet which the youth is reading
is the "Leeds Mercury" which at that day
was smaller than the newspapers sold at the
present time at a halfpenny each.   It was
published at 6½d. per copy, but the sale
being limited and the carriage comparatively
heavy, it was generally sold out of Leeds at 7d.   A
copy was subscribed for at most of the workshops
and was read aloud for the benefit of all.   The day
on which it was issued was looked upon by the workpeople as the great day of the week—the day on
which they stretched beyond their petty surroundings and learned something of the events that were
transpiring in the great world without, and a considerable portion of each succeeding Saturday, and
probably Sunday also, was often spent in discussing
the exciting intelligence with which the columns
of the newspapers were crowded at this eventful
period.

The young man, whose pale cheek flushes as he
reads of the marchings and counter marchings of
the Yeomanry, and the doings of the triumphant
Luddites, is evidently not one of Wood's workmen.
His dress is different, and his appearance is altogether
brighter and more intelligent. In other respects too
he contrasts greatly with his audience. There, close
in front of him, is a young man with square jaws,
and resolute, determined appearance, who is strongly
moved by the news; his eyes shoot forth a lurid fire,
and the veins stand out on his temples like whip-cord,
under the strong excitement which seems to agitate
every fibre of his body, as he listens to the thrilling
account of daring deeds and hair-breadth escapes.
This is George Mellor, a man of iron will and reckless
daring, who dominated strongly over his fellow workmen and forced them into the commision of deeds
which they would have shrunk from if left to themselves. Near him is a fellow workman, Thomas
Smith, a man of much feebler type of character,
the chief expression of whose face is one of sullen
obstinacy. This person works in the same room as
Mellor, and is his right hand man and supporter.
On the other side is a man of a still more stolid
aspect, who betrays no special excitement during the
reading, but stands with eyes fixed upon the reader
in a half dreamy fashion. This is William Thorpe,
who works at Mr. Fisher's cropping shop, just across
the way. These and one or two others completed
the inner circle, while further back were others sitting
or lounging, who were also listening to the reader
with intense interest, as with clear voice and correct
enunciation he made known the startling news from
Nottingham, Lancashire, and other disturbed parts
of the country. The youth who formed the centre
of this interesting group was, we have said, in many
respects very different to the rest. He was evidently
better educated and more refined, although he was
plainly a worker at some handicraft. He was the
son of the Rev. John Booth, a clergyman of the

Church of England, residing at Lowmoor. Mr. Booth was educated at Huddersfield, and when a young man was employed as a cloth cropper. Being a studious, well educated youth, he was taken in hand by the venerable vicar of Huddersfield, who assisted him in his ordination. He was a first-class scholar. The living at Lowmoor being very scanty he went into partnership with another person at Toad Holes, near Oakenshaw, as a cropper. Mr. Booth and his partner kept a bed on the premises, and many a night did the former sit up compiling a Greek lexicon. He put his son apprentice to one Wright, who lived at Huddersfield, to learn of him the art and mystery of saddle and harness making, and also of ironmongery. Young Booth's appearance, while bespeaking a fair share of intelligence, was on the whole rather effeminate; his thin twitching lips and the general expression of his face showing plainly that he lacked firmness and resolution. Unfortunately he had fallen into evil company. His feeble will melted like wax before the fiery determination of Mellor, and he was swept along in defiance of his own better judgment. The opinions of the celebrated theorist, Robert Owen, were about this time making some noise in the country, and Booth had read the writings of that amiable enthusiast, till he had thoroughly imbibed the notion that the whole framework of society was out of joint, and that the nations and governments of the earth required a thorough remodelling. He had endeavoured to make a convert of Mellor, with indifferent success. The processes of Owen were too slow for that fiery enthusiast and he refused to trouble himself to grasp his far-reaching theories. His method in arguing with Booth was to carry the war into the enemy's country, and it is not difficult to understand how an amiable young man possessed with ideas of this kind should fall an easy prey to a resolute and unscrupulous individual like Mellor.

But the reading is now finished, and a stormy

discussion follows, if a discussion it can be called
when all are nearly of one opinion.   Perhaps, if we
follow it, we shall discover still more of the chief
characteristics of the speakers, their opinions, and
the motives that urge them on.

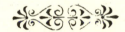

CHAPTER II.—THE OATH.

Persuasion hung upon thy lip;
And sly insinuation's softer arts
In ambush lay about thy flowing tongue.—*Blair.*
Nay, but weigh well what you presume to swear;
Oaths are of dreadful weight! and if they are false,
Draw down damnation —*Savage.*

Mellor is the speaker, and, like the rest, uses the broad Yorkshire dialect, which, however, we shall take the liberty of refining a little, in order that it may be read with more ease. During the reading of the exciting narrative just brought to a conclusion, he has been interjecting fierce comments, and now the account is ended, he gives vent to his pent-up feelings.

"Hurrah! that's right," he cried in a hoarse voice, "the Nottingham lambs are shewing them specials and clodhopping soldiers a bit of real good sport. O, but I wish I was there," he added with a sudden accession of energy, "I wish I was there. It would be glorious to dash them cursed frames into a thousand pieces!"

"Aye," growled Thorpe, surlily, "but wishing's all nowt. It strikes me we've had rather too much of that."

"Thou'rt right, Will," answered Mellor, savagely, "but what can two or three do? What are we doing here? Look at Booth, for instance--he'll come here and talk about the evils under which we working men groan, by the hour together, and air all his new fangled notions that he's picked up through Socialists; he knows very well that machinery is destroying us and nowt but the workhouse will be left for us soon, and yet he's never got farther than talk. Join us, lad, join us, thou'st talked long enough, it's time for action now. Isn't machinery increasing on all hands, and aren't working men half starving and seeking in vain for work? It's true these machines aren't taking Booth's trade out of his fingers, or he'd happen see things in a different light."

"Come, now, George," said a phlegmatic individual at the back, who up to this time had stood with his arms crossed, calmly listening and puffing the smoke at regular intervals from his short black pipe, "Come, now, let's have fair play. Its hardly the thing to set at Booth like that. He's never pretended to be one of us."

Booth listened to the interposition of the last speaker with apparent indifference, but Mellor's fiery appeal had moved him deeply, and his colour came and went rapidly during its delivery. He paused for a little before speaking but at last broke silence :—

"I quite agree with you, my friends, as some of you well know, respecting the harm you suffer from machinery, but it might be man's chief blessing instead of his curse if society were differently constituted. We and other countries are already so placed by it that a very large number of people are thrown idle greatly against their will and they must be supported or starve. We know this is so, but are we therefore to conclude that machinery is in itself an evil? You are all aware that cropping by hand as you now practice it is by no means easy work ; nay, we all know that it is very painful for learners to handle the shears until the wrist has become hoofed. Now look at one of these machines. Observe how smoothly and how beautifully it works! How perfectly it does for the workman the most arduous part of his task. By its aid, as we well know, your task has become chiefly one of care and watchfulness. To say that a machine that can do this for you is in itself an evil is manifestly absurd. Under proper conditions it would be to you an almost unmixed blessing, but unfortunately the favourable conditions do not exist. Society, in the true sense of the word, implies a number of individuals united for the purpose of promoting their physical, intellectual, and moral improvement, individually and collectively,

and if the capitalists and the millions of unemployed
would abandon large towns and cities for communities of moderate size, and were all employed as ec-
onomically as such a union would occasion, in agri-
culture, making and working machinery for the common benefit of the whole, these islands in the course
of a few years would present an entirely different
aspect, and poverty and starvation become utterly
unknown."

"If! if! if!" almost yelled Mellor, "What's
the use of such sermons as thine to starving men?
It's a case, I reckon, of 'live horse and thou'st have
grass.' If men would only do as thou says, it would
be better, we all know. But they wont. It's all
for themselves with the masters. What do they
care if a thousand or two of us are pined to death
if they can make brass a bit faster?"

"Hold!" cried Booth, "No man can feel for the
poor, starving workmen more than I do, but I fear
the course adopted by the Luddites to remedy it
is not the right one. To confess the truth, I am
in a strait. I am afraid your plan will never succeed,
and I don't see much chance of re-organising society
on a better and sounder basis at present, working men
being as a rule almost totally uneducated."

"Feel for them that's starving," shouted Benjamin Walker, another of Wood's workmen and one
of the most violent in the band, "thou'rt either a
liar or a coward. How can thou feel for them when
thou willn't lift up thy finger to help 'em.
Thou should have gone with me yesterday to Tom
Sykes's, and thou would have seen something
that would have knocked all thy grand notions
out of thee. Tom, as you all know, has been
without work aboon a month, and I found that his
wife, a poor, delicate craytur, was just dead—pined
to t'death, they say—and I believe she was. When
I got to his house he was just opening the door and
ordering a parson out, and he called out after him
'I want none of thy sympathy; if it hadn't been for

such as thee, she'd have been alive still.' And there she lay on the bed, poor thing, skin and bone, nowt else."

"I am no coward, Walker, and again I say I do feel, from the bottom of my heart, for you, and for poor Sykes most of all. It is hard for people to starve to death in their own houses in a christian land, but would it not be better to lay these things before the masters and to reason with them, rather than to infuriate them by destroying their machines and—"

"Reason with them," impatiently interrupted Thorpe, "reason with the stones I say, for their hearts are as hard as flint. What's the use of talking about reasoning with a man when his interest pulls all the other way? They'll have these machines if we all clam to death. The only chap that can reason with them is 'Enoch;' that chap is the best reasoner I know of, when he breaks them into a hundred pieces—they understand that!"

"If there was any trade in the country," resumed Booth, in a sad tone, "I should say to you, seek a livelihood by some other means; but this cruel war has drained the very life-blood of the nation, and I know not what to advise or what to say."

"Say thou'lt join us," replied Mellor, "for thou sees with all thy reasoning, as thou calls it, thou can't find us a way out."

"I will join you," says Booth, with sudden resolution, "my head tells me you are wrong, but my heart is too strong for it. Perhaps the masters, seeing you are driven to desperation, will after all be compelled to take your circumstances into consideration."

A murmur of satisfaction arose from all sides as Booth finished speaking, and several stepped forward and shook him heartily by the hand. For many reasons he was a great acquisition to the Luddite ranks, and they were glad he had at last thrown aside his scruples and consented to join them.

"Then," said Mellor, "as thou hast decided to join our cause at last and hast avowed thyself a Ludite at heart, I will now administer the oath of our society and enrol thee a member."

Booth, though still evidently ill at ease, had gone too far to withdraw, and he therefore consented. Immediately there was a stir amongst the little group. Two or three stalwart men planted themselves firmly against the door to prevent anyone from entering, and the rest ranged themselves in an irregular circle round Booth. Mellor, with a New Testament in his hand, then stepped into the middle of the ring and proceeded to administer the terrible

OATH OF THE FRATERNITY.

Standing in the front of Booth and taking his hand, he said : —

" What is thy name?"

" John Booth."

" Art thou willing to become a member of our society and submit without demur or question to the commands of General Ludd?"

" I am."

" Then say after me : —I, John Booth, of my own voluntary will, do declare and solemnly swear that I never will reveal to any person or persons under the canopy of heaven the names of the persons who comprise this secret committee, their proceedings, meetings, places of abode, dress, features, complexion, or anything else that might lead to a discovery of the same, either by word, deed, or sign, under the penalty of being sent out of the world by the first brother who shall meet me, and my name and character blotted out of existence and never to be remembered but with contempt and abhorrence. And I further do swear to use my best endeavours to punish by death any traitor or traitors, should any rise up among us, wherever I can find him or them, and though he should fly to the verge of nature I will pursue him with unceasing vengeance. So help me God and bless me, to keep this, my oath, inviolate."

Booth's voice sounded weak and tremulous in contrast with Mellor's deep, gruff bass, and he hesitated painfully once or twice, but it was impossible to retrace his steps, and when he at last reached the end, he with pallid lips kissed the book which Mellor held towards him. At the conclusion of the ceremony Booth was handed a copy of the oath in writing and he was requested by Mellor to commit it to memory, in order that he might be in a position to administer it to others.

Such was the oath administered to every member of this dangerous society, and it was nearly in every instance strictly observed by those who took it. Even when in prison or at the point of death this oath seemed to close the mouths of all who had taken it.

CHAPTER III.—BAD TIMES.

When beef and mutton and other meat,
Were almost as dear as money to eat;
And farmers reaped golden harvests of wheat
At the Lord knows what per quarter.—*Hood.*

What made the quartern loaf and Luddites rise?
James Smith.

It has been thought by some that the Luddite risings were confined to Yorkshire, but many of our
readers will be aware that risings of a similar character at Nottingham preceded the lawless doings
which took place in the West Riding; the discontent here being fanned into flame by the apparent
success which attended the risings in the capital of
the lace trade, the two being in fact closely connected. In order that our readers may be acquainted
with the widespread character of the Luddite conspiracy, we have thought it better to devote a chapter to a general account of the risings and their
cause. Though this may perhaps not be so interesting as those in which we shall deal with the disturbances in the West Riding, it is still necessary
to a proper understanding of the origin and progress
of the movement.

The witty author of "Rejected Addresses" asks,
in one of his poems, "What made the quartern loaf
and Luddites rise?" We purpose trying to answer
that question first. If any of our readers suppose
that the Luddites were all cloth finishers or croppers
who had been goaded to fury by the rapid introduction of machinery, which threatened to deprive them
of the means of earning a livelihood, they will find,
on investigation, that they are mistaken. That the
leaders of the movement in the West Riding were
chiefly men of that stamp is doubtless correct; and
that their prime object was the destruction of the
obnoxious machines is also true; but there were con-

nected with the risings numbers of weavers, tailors, shoemakers, and representatives of almost every handicraft, who being, in most instances, on the brink of starvation, entered the conspiracy in sheer desperation. The condition of the operative class in this country at the time these risings took place was simply frightful; and if we are to answer satisfactorily the question at the head of this chapter, it will be necessary to enlarge on this point, in order that our readers may understand clearly the cause of the discontent so universally prevalent in the manufacturing districts, and be able to judge if the wholesale condemnation which has been poured upon the heads of these ignorant and misguided men was, in all cases, fully deserved.

Great events were occurring at the time of the Luddite risings. George III. had again succumbed to his mental malady, and his son acted as Regent of the kingdom. Napoleon was at the zenith of his power. A son had been born to him, who was crowned "King of Rome" in his cradle. The struggles between Wellington and the French Marshals in Spain and Portugal were getting more and more desperate. The weary war which the aristocracy of England undertook, to crush French Liberalism and to force a king upon the French nation which that high-spirited people would not have, seemed as far from its conclusion as ever. To crush Napoleon we had not only sent our own armies, but we had also in our pay all the hordes of the despots of Europe. Truly it was a revolting and humiliating spectacle. The hard-earned money wrung from our own working people, till they rose in their misery, and even threatened king and government with destruction, went to be divided among a host of despots and slaves. The commercial difficulties of Britain were such as might have filled the most sanguine with dismay. Closed ports on the Continent, and defective harvests at home, had caused grain to rise rapidly, until 1812, the year when Cartwright's mill was attacked, the

average price of wheat was 155 shillings—a price
which it had never attained before, which it has
never reached since, and in all human probability
will never reach again.   Bonaparte had issued his
famous Milan decree, by which Britain and its islands were declared in a state of blockade, and also
its colonies and dependencies in every part of the
globe.   The mercantile crisis, so often dreaded as
the forerunner of national bankruptcy, had arrived,
and such was the alarming state of commercial and
manufacturing interests that Parliament interposed by
decreeing a loan of six millions to tide over the
difficulty.   Our foreign trade during the whole of
the century had never been so low, and our home
trade had dwindled into the narrowest limits, the
starving population being scarcely able to purchase
enough to keep soul and body together of the damaged
flour at eight shillings per stone, which ran from the
oven as they tried in vain to bake it.   Encouraged
by the high prices of grain, farmers and landlords
speculated largely and gained considerable sums,
but the commercial part of the community suffered
dreadfully, and a more alarming account of bank-
ruptcies was never known, their number amounting
in one year to no less than 2,341, of which twenty-six
were banking-houses.   In the great towns of Yorkshire, Lancashire, Cheshire and Nottinghamshire, the
poor were seeking for work, or failing to obtain it,
were parading through the streets in gaunt famine-
stricken crowds, headed by men with bloody loaves
mounted on spears crying in plaintive, wailing chorus
for bread.   Goaded to desperation, all sense of
loyalty was driven far from them, and they stood at
every street corner with lips firmly set, and with
frowning faces discussing wild, treasonable schemes.
The world had dealt hardly with them, and they
blindly sought to revenge themselves.   They were
too ignorant to understand that if they were miserable and starving, their masters were waging a
great and glorious war.   They knew only that their

children were crying pitifully for bread—the fire had died out on their hearts, and the fire of hope was extinguished in their hearts. Inhumanity had driven out all better feelings ,and need we wonder that they had become a prey to glib advocates of revolution and the dark whisperings of vengeance on their rulers. When trade was prosperous with them, their fare had been poor enough. White bread, which is plentiful now on every working man's table, was only seen on Sundays, and then it was carefully portioned out. Oatcake was then the "staff of life," and oatmeal porridge an article of constant and universal consumption once a day at least, often twice, and not unfrequently three times. Butchers' meat was a luxury in which they could seldom indulge, and then only to a very limited extent. Manufacturers everywhere were availing themselves of the many wonderful inventions that were being brought out for cheapening labour, and as the new machinery threw thousands out of employment when extensively introduced, the poor, misguided wretches, who could not understand how that could be a benefit which deprived them of the means of earning a livelihood and reduced them to beggary, met in secret conclaves, and resolved in their ignorance to destroy them. Had they been better instructed, they would have known that it was their duty to lie down in the nearest ditch and die. The schoolmaster was not abroad in those days ,or they might have read how the British soldiers climbed up the bloody walls of Badajoz and impaled themselves upon the gleaming spikes at the top, until their bodies were piled high enough up to cover the cruel blades, and their comrades could safely creep over them to victory. They had not probably read of this, or they might have learned from it that it was their duty to lie down quietly and suffer themselves to be crushed out of existence by the advancing and unpitying wheels of the Juggernaut of trade in order that the march of progress might not be delayed or obstructed. Had these de-

luded men studied Malthus, they would have at
once discovered that they were indeed altogether in
the wrong in seeking to cumber the earth with their
presence, when they were clearly not wanted; for
the great political economist plainly told them that
" a man who is born into a world already possessed,
or if society does not want his labour, has no claim
or right to the smallest portion of food, and, in fact,
has no business to be where he is. At nature's mighty
feast there is no cover for him!" These men, however, clearly knew nothing of political economy, and
had probably never heard of Malthus, much less read
his famous pamphlet, and being able and willing to
work, and seeing plenty around them, they could not
understand that it was their duty to perish of starvation. Therefore, as we have already said, they resolved to destroy the machines which took away their
daily bread, and before the movement could be suppressed more than a thousand lace and stocking frames
were destroyed in Nottingham alone, and a large
number of cropping machines in the West Riding of
Yorkshire.

Up to the time when the cropping machines were
invented, cloth was finished by a method that was
at once very slow and very costly. The instrument
used was a very primitive one and the whole process
plainly behind the age; when, therefore, the new
machines were introduced, manufacturers at once
realised the great gain in time and the great saving
of money they would secure by adopting them, and
the croppers speedily began to realise also that unless
the introduction of the thrice accursed piece of
mechanism, which did the work so deftly, could be
prevented, their occupation, like Othello's, was gone.
It has been said that the croppers might have turned
their attention to some other method of obtaining a
livelihood, but as we have shown, trade was almost
non-existent, and every occupation seemed to be
greatly over-stocked with hands. Every town and

village was crowded with paupers, able-bodied men
most of them, who would have gladly earned their
living honourably had they had the opportunity. In
Nottingham alone no fewer than 15,350 individuals,
or nearly half the population, were at one time relieved from the poor rates, and though matters were
not quite so bad in Yorkshire, it is well known that
our streets were filled with half starved workmen,
wandering about in enforced idleness. That matters
were bad enough in the West Riding will be evident
when we state that in many towns there were exacted
in that black year four poor rates of three shillings in
the pound each. It was stated in a Parliamentary
return that out of a population of 200,000, in the
manufacturing districts, no less than 50,000 did not
receive more than twopence half-penny per day each
for food.

The croppers had the reputation at this time of
being a wild and reckless body of men ; and the desperate deeds of which some of them were afterwards
found guilty seem to show that the accusation had,
at any rate, a good foundation of truth. It applied
at least to some of the men employed at the finishing
mill of Mr. John Wood, of Longroyd Bridge which
workshop seems to have been the chief centre of the
conspiracy in this neighbourhood, though meetings of
an important character took place, as we shall see, at
Liversedge, also at the St. Crispin Inn, a public house
at Halifax, in and around which towns were a considerable number of members of the secret organisation, which had been for some months engaged in
breaking stocking and lace machines at Nottingham.
Their first object was to destroy all the obnoxious
machinery, but they had also other purposes in view,
such as the coercion, and, if necessary, the destruction
of such masters as made themselves obnoxious to the
society, either by persisting in introducing the
machinery into their works, or by encouraging and
supporting those who did. Condemning as they did
the bloody war that brought them so much misery,

they had also some crude notions about upsetting the Government itself, when their organisation had spread itself throughout the land and they had collected sufficient arms and perfected themselves in military exercises. In order to carry out these aims, every member of the society was required to bind himself by their terrible oath not to divulge any of the secrets of the conspirators, and to aid in carrying out the objects of the association in every possible way.

The system of machine breaking took its rise, as we have stated, in Nottinghamshire, towards the end of 1811, and was directed against the stocking and lace frames or machines which had lately been introduced and are now most common, neither stockings nor common lace being produced in any other manner, except on the domestic hearth by the few who kept up the good old practice of knitting. From Nottinghamshire, Luddism spread into Yorkshire, where the excesses soon rivalled those of the Midland district, culminating in the murder in open day of Mr. Wm. Horsfall, of Marsden, a manufacturer who had often expressed himself violently against the action of the workpeople. The ire of the hand-croppers in this district was directed against a machine termed a " frame "—the shear frame—as was that of the stockingers and lacemen of Nottinghamshire. The shear frame was one by means of which the two hand shears could be worked at one and the same time instead of one by the hand cropper. And with this advantage too that while the pair of cropping shears were working across the length of the two pieces, fixed and prepared on the shear boards, the man or boy in attendance had only to stand and watch the operation until the cut was completed. Then he had to run the shears off the cloth to their resting place on the shear board, unhook the cropped portions of the pieces, pull forward the other portions, hook them to the shear boards, " raise the nap " ready for the shears to cut it down to a certain height for finished cloth, and then run in the two shears again into the position necessary for them to perform the operation of cutting. This, it is not difficult to see, was much easier for the man than if he worked the shears himself by means of the nog, a most laborious and painful operation, especially so, indeed, until the hoof on the right wrist had been formed, by which any cropper of moderate age could be identified, arising from holding the shears and their action to and fro when impelled by the nog. In fact the shear frame served mainly for the relief of the workmen, performing for them a most arduous portion of the work. Still it was a machine and as such was doomed to destruction.

Many of these machines used in this neighbourhood about 1811 and 1812 were constructed by two enterprising and industrious men named Enoch and James Taylor, who had begun life as ordinary blacksmiths, but being of an ingenious turn of mind had gradually developed into machine makers. Their residence was at Marsden and their workshop stood on what is now the site of the town's school. The great hammer used by the Luddites in breaking the frames was always called "Enoch," after the leading partner in the firm chiefly engaged in their manufacture in this locality, the saying being common, "Enoch has made them and Enoch shall smash them."

THE RISINGS OF THE LUDDITES.

CHAPTER IV.

SPREAD OF THE MOVEMENT.

Civil dissension is a viperous worm
That knaws the bowels of the Commonwealth.
Shakespeare.

The 11th of March, 1811, is a notable day in the history of Nottinghamshire. On that day commenced a series of riots which, extending over a period of five years, are perhaps unequalled for the skill and secrecy with which they were managed, and the amount of wanton mischief they inflicted. Trade had been for some time in a very unsatisfactory condition, and as a natural result wages had been considerably reduced. As it was evident to the authorities that mischief was brewing, it was decided to employ a large number of the distressed workpeople in sweeping the streets. But this did not prevent the catastrophe, for on the 11th of March they struck work, and flocking to the market-place, were there joined by a large number from the adjoining country, and being harangued by several fiery orators, they suddenly resolved to revenge themselves on the masters who had reduced their wages. The local authorities, who had been uneasy at the aspect of affairs for some time, summoned the military to their aid at once, and the turbulent population was over-awed and prevented from rioting in the town ; when darkness set in, however, the mob proceeded to the neighbouring village of Arnold, and destroyed upwards of sixty frames. During the succeeding three weeks above two hundred more stocking frames were broken up by bands who seemed to divide and attack many different points at the same time. These

bands it was afterwards discovered were united in a
society and were bound by an oath not to divulge
anything connected with its secret operations. The
names they assumed were "Ludds," "Ludders,"
and "Luddites," and they are said to have derived
them from a youth named Ludlam, a reckless
character, who, when his father, a frame-work knitter,
told him one day to "square his needles," squared
them effectually by taking up his hammer and beating
them into a heap. Whether this youth actually
directed the operations of the desperate bands that
prowled nightly is not positively known, as the secrets
of the society were wonderfully well kept, but it is
not at all improbable, as the proceedings were
evidently planned beforehand, and it is also plain
that the various bodies acted in concert. They were
all disguised when engaged in the work of destruction,
and were armed, some in a primitive fashion, with
clubs, sticks, &c., and others with swords, guns, and
pistols. A number also wielded huge hatchets and
blacksmith's hammers for the purpose of making a
way into the places where the frames were kept and
breaking them quickly to pieces, while their armed
companions kept watch at the doors. On the work
of the night being successfully accomplished, the
party divided and again reunited at a distance, when
the leader called over his men, who answered, not to
names but numbers, and everyone then removed his
disguise and went home. The success which at the
outset almost invariably attended the movements of
the Luddites caused them to be much talked about.
They seemed almost ubiquitous, and as the authorities
could gain little or no information respecting them,
many of the more daring of the working men ventured
to join them, and for a long time they carried on
their destructive attacks with impunity. The frames,
however, as we have already stated, were not the
sole cause of the disturbances; in most cases discontent being heightened or caused by the dearness of
provisions, especially flour. In consequence of the

resistance afterwards made to the outrages of the
rioters, in the course of which one of them was
killed, they became still more exasperated and
violent, till the magistrates thought it necessary to
require the assistance of a considerable armed force,
which was promptly assembled, consisting at first of
local militia and volunteer yeomanry chiefly, to whom
were afterwards added about four hundred special
constables. The rioters were then dispersed and the
disturbances for a time suppressed .

Before the end of November, 1811, however, the
outrages were renewed; they became more serious,
were more systematically conducted, and at length
the disturbances extended to several villages, where
the rioters destroyed the frames, and began at the
same time to collect or exact contributions for their
subsistence, which caused their numbers to increase
rapidly, many joining them being on the brink of
starvation. Early in December the outrages had in
some degree extended into Derbyshire and Leicestershire, where many frames were broken. A considerable
force of cavalry and infantry was then sent to Nottingham, and the commanding officer of the district was
ordered to repair thither. In January, 1812, two
of the most experienced police magistrates were also
despatched to Nottingham, for the purpose of assisting
the local authorities to restore tranquility.

The systematic combination, however, with which
the outrages were conducted, the terror which they
inspired, and the disposition of many of the working
classes to favour rather than oppose them, made it
very difficult to discover the offenders, to apprehend
them if discovered, or to obtain evidence to convict
those who were apprehended of the crimes with which
they were charged. Some, however, were afterwards
proceeded against at the Nottingham Spring Assizes,
and seven persons were convicted of different offences
and sentenced to transportation. In the meantime,
acts were passed for establishing police in the disturbed district to patrol the streets.

The height to which disaffection reached at Nottingham will be seen from an account of the trial of two
men—Glover and Chettle—who were charged with
breaking machinery. Commencing at two o'clock on
a Saturday afternoon the trial continued until two
o'clock on Sunday morning, and is remarkable for
the fact that whilst it was proceeding the judge and
the jury were threatened with assassination. Sutton,
a local historian, says :—" It commenced in the afternoon, and did not terminate until about two o'clock
on Sunday morning." Bailey the author of " The
Annals of Nottingham," says :—" The excitement
among the working class was most intense.
But, strange to say, the very contrary of this feeling
seemed to actuate the High Sheriff and his attendants.
all of whom, as the evening advanced, quitted their
posts and returned to their respective homes, leaving
the judge, jury, counsel, and everyone else connected
with the prosecution, entirely at the mercy of an
organised and infuriated mob." Sutton continues :—
" Mr. Clarke and Mr. Keader were counsel for the
prosecution ; Mr. Denman was sole counsel for the
accused, and added to his rapidly rising reputation
by the ability with which he established the alibi set
up. Fortunately for the preservation of the public
peace the result of the trial was an acquittal. Had
it been otherwise, the most fearful consequences
would doubtless have ensued ; for the body of the
hall was for hours in possession of a number of determined men, who would not suffer a light to appear
in court (there was then no gas, only candles) excepting on the bench and counsel table. It is also
notorious that a number of confederates with loaded
pistols were in the outer hall, and the constables
and javelin men were quite unable to maintain order.
It is understood that had the verdict been adverse
both judge and jury would have been assassinated.
And so serious was the alarm afterwards produced
that it was contemplated to make Newark the Assize
town instead of Nottingham." The court was con-

tinually interrupted by the most threatening and insulting expressions, and on more than one occasion a cocked pistol was levelled at the judge. He was Mr. Justice Grantham, then an old and rather feeble man of small stature. When it was told him that fire arms were in court, and that one had been pointed at him, he paused for a moment, then tapping his snuff box and putting it down he, with the utmost composure, said, "I am informed that my life is threatened, and, indeed, that a pistol has been directed towards me. All that will not intimidate me, nor hinder the course of this trial. I am an old man, and to kill me now could but antedate my death by a very short time. I am here to represent the dignity and majesty of the law, the impartiality of justice; and I can conceive no more honourable death than to die on the judgment seat in the execution of my duty, and in the administration of those laws which the constitution of our country has provided."

The discontent which had thus first appeared about Nottingham and had in some degree extended into Derbyshire and Leicestershire, had also been communicated to other parts of the country. Subscriptions for persons arrested poured in, and anonymous threatening letters became more and more common. At Stockport, shortly after, attempts were made to set on fire two different manufactories, and the spirit of disorder rapidly spread through the neighbourhood. Inflammatory placards, inviting the people to a general rising, were disseminated; illegal oaths were administered, riots were produced in various places, houses were plundered by persons in disguise, and a report was industriously circulated that a general rising would take place on the 1st of May, or early in that month.

The spirit of riot and disturbance manifested itself violently at Eccles, Ashton-under-Lyne, and Middleton. At the latter place the manufactory of Mr. Burton was attacked, and although the rioters were then repulsed and five of their number killed by the military force assembled to protect the works, a second attack was made two days afterwards, and Mr. Burton's house was burnt before military assistance could be brought to the spot. When troops arrived they were fired upon by the rioters, and before the latter could be dispersed several of them were killed and wounded.

There were also scenes of great violence at Stockport. The house of Mr. Goodwin was set on fire, and his steam looms were destroyed. Crowds of men training for military exercise were continually being surprised on the heaths and moors. Disturbances also took place in Manchester, but here the cause assigned was solely the high price of provisions. The people of that city were alarmed by the sudden appearance in the streets of thousands of half-starved looking men from the surrounding places, but on a large military force being paraded, the suspicious looking persons gradually disappeared. Nocturnal meetings were, however, frequent, and arms were seized continually. The manner in which the disaffected carried on their proceedings demonstrated in an extraordinary degree concert, secrecy, and organisation. Their signals were well contrived, and attempts to lay hold of offenders were generally defeated .

The same spirit of disaffection appeared at Bolton-le-Moors. A meeting of delegates was held there, at which it was decided that a manufactory at West Haughton should be destroyed, but finding their purpose was known to the authorities it was apparently abandoned, until the watch being relaxed they accomplished their object. It was known the attack would be made and intelligence was sent to the authorities, but the military force sent to the spot arrived too late ; the rioters had dispersed, and the soldiers therefore returned to their quarters. The mob taking advantage of their absence, returned and assailed another manufactory, set it on fire, and again dispersed before the force could be brought back. Disturbances also broke out in Carlisle and in Yorkshire. At Huddersfield and in the neighbourhood risings took place early in February, 1812, the shearing machines being destroyed in large numbers. The son of an old cropper who still resides at Crosland Moor, in the house where he was born seventy-three years ago, told us that he had often heard his father relate how his fellow workmen at Nab Croft, which is just at hand, boasted how many machines " Enoch " —as the large hammer was then called by them— had destroyed during the night. It was customary, he said for powerful men to cut through the doors with hatchets, and on an entrance being gained, the machines were broken up in an incredible short space of time. Great quantities of fire-arms were seized in the neighbourhood by men with blackened faces and midnight drills were common. A large number of machines belonging to Mr. Vickerman were destroyed in March, and soon after, the destruction of Bradley Mills was threatened and afterwards attempted, but the guard on the spot defeated the attempt.

The authorities at Leeds had been much alarmed by information that attacks were intended to be made on places in the town and neighbourhood, which induced the magistrates to desire a strong military force and to appoint a great number of the respectable inhabitants special constables, by which the peace of the town was in a great measure preserved. Early, however, in the morning of March 24th, 1812, the mills of Messrs. Thompson, of Rawden, were attacked by a large body of armed men, who proceeded with great regularity and caution. First seizing the watchman at the mill and placing guards at every adjacent cottage, threatening death to anyone who should attempt to give an alarm, and then forcibly entering the mill, they completely destroyed the machinery. On the very night following, notwithstanding the precautions adopted, the buildings belonging to the Messs. Dickenson, in Leeds, were forcibly entered and the whole of the goods there, consisting chiefly of cloths, were cut to pieces. Many other firms in Leeds were threatened with similar treatment. The proceedings at this place are represented to have had for their object the destruction of all goods prepared otherwise than by manual labour

At Horbury, near Wakefield, valuable mills were attacked on the 9th of April, by an armed body, consisting of 300 men, and the machinery and considerable property were destroyed. The men who committed the outrage were seen on the road between the two towns marching in regular order, preceded by a mounted party with drawn swords and followed by a similar body of men as a rear guard. They were stated in the official report presented to Parliament to belong to Huddersfield, Dewsbury, Heckmondwike, Mirfield, Halifax, Elland, Brighouse, Morley, Birstal, and Gomersal. The magistrates were unable to give protection by putting the Watch and Ward Act into force, and the working classes, or " the lower orders " as they are called in this report, are represented as being generally either abettors or participators in the outrages committed, or, as being so intimidated that they dare not interfere.

At Sheffield, the store house of arms of the local militia was surprised, some of the arms were broken and others taken away by the mob. Depredations continued almost nightly in this locality, and it was stated in the report that in the districts around Huddersfield, Halifax, Brighouse, and Liversedge, the arms of all the peaceable inhabitants had been swept away by bands of armed men. Respecting the offenders no information could be gained, and it is said that amongst a hundred depositions taken by the magistrates of the facts of robberies committed, the thief was only pointed out in one case.

During the latter part of the period we have named,
that is the commencement of 1812, the districts water-
ed by the Spen and the Calder were especially unsettled and the patrols passing between Huddersfield
and Leeds found the people in ill-affected villages up
at midnight and heard the firing of small arms at
short distances from them through the whole night,
proceeding from small parties who were practising
drill.

Of the brutality of mobs the history of every land
furnishes melancholy proofs. A Spanish auto-da-
fe—a Parisian execution—the British punishment
of the pillory—an Irish rising and a Scotch riot of
past times generally exceeded in barbarity the acts
of still earlier times. But there are differences in
mobs ; a metropolitan one being generally less brutal
than a provincial one. In capitals persons seem to
have a definite purpose, and they can only take means
to effect that purpose, but in provincial riots there is
often a general disposition to violence and brutality,
tending rather to general aggression than to any particular object that can be perceived.

The Luddite mobs were, as we have already pointed out, made up partly of men who did not suffer from
the introduction of machinery—men, who being uneducated and brutal, had a love for brutality and excess : who found it more pleasant to seize by violence
than gain by industry and who finally proceeded to
perpetrate the most dreadful crimes. Considering
what material the local Luddite mobs was composed
of, we are naturally surprised to find that there was
less of brutal excess exhibited in Yorkshire than in
other counties. We cannot enter into detail respecting the outrages in the adjoining counties, which
we have named generally in this chapter, or we might
adduce cases in the Luddite risings involving a much
greater degree of ferocity than any exhibited in Yorkshire.

It is a remarkable fact that throughout all the

cases which Luddism involved we find none in which
the mob had been incited to any violence beyond
that necessary for the completion of their purpose;
that is to say murder was unaccompanied by cruelty;
robbery was unattended by violence; and the destruction of property was not conjoined with the ill-usage
of persons.   This is a peculiarity attendant upon the
Yorkshire riots which no other county possesses.

CHAPTER V.

THE GATHERING AT THE SHEARS INN,
LIVERSEDGE.

" Hereditary bondsmen ! know ye not.—Who would be free,
themselves must strike the blow?"

We alluded in the first chapter to Mr. Cartwright's
Mill at Rawfolds, Liversedge, and to Mr. John Jackson's cropping shop at the top of Quilley Lane, in
the same township. These cropping shops, which
were chiefly places of small pretensions, were pretty
numerous in the Spen Valley and in the intervening
districts, up to Leeds on one side and Halifax and
Huddersfield on the other, about 1810-11, when
Cartwright began to experiment in finishing cloth by
machinery at his water power mill at Rawfolds.
These experiments excited much alarm amongst
neighbouring finishers, and much resentment amongst
the workmen engaged in that branch of business,
who saw that if Mr. Cartwright succeeded in his
effort to introduce his machines their trade would be
seriously affected. The foreman at Mr. Jackson's
shop just referred to, at the top of Quilley Lane,
was an old trusty servant of the name of William
Fearnsides, a thoroughly reliable man, whose whole
energies were devoted to the business. Before the
advent of Mr. Cartwright's new frames work was
plentiful at Mr. Jackson's shop, and the men could
earn good wages, but as frames came more and more
into use the little masters who adhered to hand cropping found it increasingly difficult to carry on business
at a profit, and the result was that the men gradually
lost their employment, and the workshops were one
after another closed altogether. The men watched

the gradual decay of their industry in sullen despair
at first, but the news of turbulent demonstrations at
Nottingham, where the lace makers had risen against
a frame of another character which threatened their
industry, had stirred them strongly, and the more
violent spirits among the local croppers began to urge
that similar measures should be taken against the
finishing frames introduced by some of the Yorkshire
manufacturers. The wild idea seems to have been
first broached at Longroyd Bridge, but those who were
out of work spread the seeds of disaffection all round
the district, and the men at Jackson's shop were
soon following the lead of the Huddersfield malcontents.

William Hall, a native of Parkin Hoyle,
or Parking Hole, as the locality ought to
be called, had learnt his trade at Jackson's,
at Hightown, and had continued to work there
as journeyman for a time after his apprenticeship had expired, but when trade began to
fall off, Fearnsides, the foreman, had been compelled
to dismiss him. Mr. Jackson never liked to part
with men who had been trained at his shop, and he
told Hall that he would try to take him on again if
trade revived at all. Instead of mending, however,
it got worse and worse, and so far from finding work
for old hands the foreman was obliged to dismiss
other workmen whom he held in much higher esteem
than Hall,, who had always been a very unmanage-
able young man, and had given great trouble to
Fearnsides during his apprenticeship. Hall, after
wandering about loosely for some months in the hope
that he would be reinstated in his old position, began
to realise that the prospect grew more and more dis-
couraging, he therefore sought work elsewhere, and
eventually succeeded in gaining employment at John
Wood's workshop ,at Longroyd Bridge, near Huddersfield, but, as he still hoped he might get back to
Jackson's he did not remove thither, but came to
spend his Sundays at Liversedge. Coming thus in
contact with many of his old shopmates he fed the

flame of discontent by the wild reports he brought
home of the doings at Huddersfield. During the
period of his enforced idleness after he had been dismissed from Jackson's workshop, Hall had had all
the strong feelings of his sullen and passionate nature
aroused by the sight of the poverty and destitution
which had been brought upon his fellow craftsmen
and neighbours, and now that he had found himself
thrown into connection with many still more violent
spirits at Longroyd Bridge his strong and vindictive
feelings increased in intensity. Every week when
he returned home he brought exciting reports of what
he called the "stirrings" at Huddersfield and elsewhere, and the discontented croppers of Liversedge
assembled in large numbers at the Shears Inn, the
general meeting place of the craft, every Saturday
night to listen to his highly coloured recitals of the
doings of the workmen in other places. To those
whom he knew could be trusted, Hall whispered the
secret that the men at Huddersfield were banding
themselves together to destroy "the cursed machines,"
and that he had become a member of the organisation
formed to accomplish that object. To Hall's hungry
and desperate companions violent measures seemed
the only likely ones to succeed in stopping the rapid
increase of the hated machinery, and they became
eager to enrol themselves in the secret society which
promised such a summary and speedy redress of their
wrongs, it was therefore eventually arranged that
Hall should ask some one belonging to the organisation to come over with him and meet the Liversedge
croppers to explain to them its objects and methods
of working more fully.

The Shears Inn, at Hightown, which bore and still
bears on its sign-board a representation of the implement used by the croppers in their trade, was, as we
have already stated, a house generally resorted to
by men engaged in that business. A few of the
craft patronised "little Hammond," of the White
Hart, a Crofton man, who had formerly belonged to

the cropper's craft; and a few, James Whitehead,
the jolly host of the Cross Keys; but the popular
gathering place was the Shears That they were
good customers for the landlord's ale when they had
money in their pockets may be guessed from one of
the wildest Yorkshire legends extant, which we will
give as briefly as possible, as it shows what opinions
were entertained of the croppers by contemporaries
before the obnoxious frames were invented, and

THE SHEARS INN.

when they were able to dictate very often their own
terms to their masters when the latter had urgent
orders on hand.   We give it in the words of a most
reliable authority:—" The tradition is, that in consequence of their dissipated and wicked ways all the
croppers at their departure from this world went
to a certain place which, to describe it negatively,
was neither purgatory nor Paradise, and that in the
course of time they became so numerous in that particularly warm region, and withal so very, very
unruly, that the devil was at his wits' end what to
do with them and had no pleasure of his life in their
company.   Get rid of them he could not.   There
they were, and in spite of all remonstrances declared they would not depart nor yet mend their

manners.   One day, while pondering on his difficult
position, a brilliant idea occurred to his Satanic
majesty.   He knew the fondness of the croppers when
on earth for ale, whether good or bad, so he went
to the door of the infernal regions and bawled out
'Ale! ale! ale!' with all his might.   The effect
was magical.   At the joyful sound all the croppers
were seized instantaneously with a burning thirst,
and they rushed out to a man, helter skelter.   No
sooner were they all out than Satan slipped quickly
in, bringing the door to and locking it after him,
shouting through the keyhole to the astonished and
deluded croppers outside, 'Now curse you, I've got
you out and I'll keep you out.   I'll take care no
more croppers ever come in here!'   And that is
given as the reason why no more croppers entered
the infernal regions."

The Shears Inn was at the beginning of the century
one of the most substantial buildings in the locality
in which it stands, most of the surrounding property
being ordinary cottages, although there were a few
good houses, of which Abraham Jackson's, the currier,
was one.   Mr. Jackson was then in a pretty large
way of business, and occupied besides the buildings
round his homestead the old house across the road,
known as Noah's Ark, as a leather warehouse.   The
interior arrangement of the Shears Inn was, at the
period of which we are writing, different to what
it is at the present time.   The bar was then at the
back, at the right hand side of the passage, the other
back room on a line with it being the kitchen, and
over both the front rooms was the club room.   It
was in this large room that the meeting of the croppers
was held at which the delegates from Huddersfield
were present, and which took place in February, 1812.
Although it was still winter according to the calendar,
the morning had been sultry, and soon after midday
the firmament became obscured by black clouds
which rolled up steadily from the south, and an al-

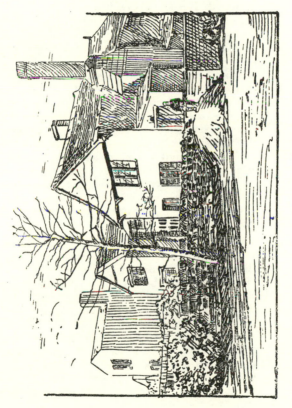

"NOAH'S ARK", OR "EGYPT", HIGHTOWN.

most phenomenal darkness, which was long remembered, set in, continuing for some hours, and was followed by a heavy thunderstorm.   Notwithstanding the
warring elements the gathering of croppers that
night at the Shears was large, and comprised members of the craft from Cleckheaton, Heckmondwike,
Gomersal, Birstall, Mirfield, Brighouse, Elland, and
more distant places.   Had James Lister, the landlord, been aware of the real object of the meeting
he would certainly have placed his veto upon it; for,
although he naturally sympathised with the men who
had been such excellent customers in the sufferings
they were enduring, owing to the introduction of
machinery, he prided himself on being above all
things a law-abiding citizen, and, being a sheriff's
officer, considered himself a sort of Government
functionary, and as such responsible in some degree
for the good conduct of his neighbours.   As we have
said before, however, the house had always been the
chief resort of the croppers, and Lister was not aware
that the meeting was other than a trade gathering
of the fraternity to take into consideration the critical
state of affairs.

William Hall, true to his promise, had brought
with him two of his fellow workmen from Longroyd
Bridge; John Walker, a young man, who was a
true specimen of the old rolicking race of croppers,
and Thomas Brook, a solid taciturn man, who was
in almost every respect the antipodes of his companion, for while Walker was jovially fraternising
with everybody around him, Brook sat stolidly
apart, puffing his long pipe and replying only in
monosyllables to the questions or observations of
the men around him.   The old oak-cased clock in
the corner had long ago struck the hour on its clear-
sounding bell, and a rough looking man had risen
to ask if it was not time to begin the meeting, when
John Walker, who had been for some time imbibing
more of Lister's strong ale than was good for him,
rose from his seat and extending his arms as if he

would shake hands with everyone present, cried out in cheery tones:—"Lads! ah'm pleased to see you all. You muster weel, an ah'm sure by the luke on you there's some true grit in Liversedge. Me an' my mate are pleased to be among you. Ah can promise you 'at we Huddersfield chaps will stand by you shoulder to shoulder till these cursed machines at's robbing us of our trade are sent flying in a thousand shivers an' them 'ats made 'em are sent after them. You've a chap here lads 'at wants straightening up an' wer're ready to help you to do it. We hev his marrow over yonder, but General Ludd is bahn to hev a word with him varry shortly. My mate ahl happen say a few words to you in a bit, but afore ah sit dahn ah'll sing you one of ahr Ludd ditties."

Taking a hearty swig at his mug of ale, Walker then struck up in true ballad patterer's style—

THE CROPPER'S SONG.

Come, cropper lads of high renown,
Who love to drink good ale that's brown,
And strike each haughty tyrant down,
   With hatchet, pike, and gun!
Oh, the cropper lads for me,
The gallant lads for me,
Who with lusty stroke,
The shear frames broke,
The cropper lads for me!

What though the specials still advance,
And soldiers nightly round us prance;
The cropper lads still lead the dance,
   With hatchet, pike, and gun!
Oh, the cropper lads for me,
The gallant lads for me,
Who with lusty stroke
The shear frames broke,
The cropper lads for me!

And night by night when all is still
And the moon is hid behind the hill,
We forward march to do our will
　　With hatchet, pike, and gun !
Oh, the cropper lads for me,
The gallant lads for me,
Who with lusty stroke
The shear frames broke,
The cropper lads for me !

Great Enoch still shall lead the van.
Stop him who dare ! stop him who can !
Press forward every gallant man
　　With hatchet, pike, and gun !
Oh, the cropper lads for me,
The gallant lads for me,
Who with lusty stroke
The shear frames broke ,
The cropper lads for me !

Long before Walker had come to the end of his
song the rolicking chorus was eagerly caught up by
his delighted audience, and when the end was reached
the refrain was twice repeated with extraordinary
vigour, many of the men beating time on the long
table with their sticks and pewter mugs.　If the
object of the singer was to inspire the somewhat
downcast and dejected group with some of his own
enthusiasm he succeeded admirably, as was evident
from the cheering from all parts of the room as he sat
down, and the excitement continued during the whole
of the meeting.

Before the hearty plaudits had died away, Brook,
the other delegate, put down his pipe, rose slowly and
deliberately to his feet and waited with calm self-
possession till the meeting had quieted down sufficient
ly to listen to him.　In appearance, he was, as we
have said, very different to Walker.　No smile
lighted up his sombre, strongly marked features
as in language which showed more education and
refinement, he told his hearers how the Luddite move-

ment had extended to the Huddersfield district and the progress which had been made in the destruction of frames in that locality. "We are playing a hazardous, nay a desperate game, we know full well," he exclaimed, and his dark eyes lighted up as he raised his voice and struck his clenched fist on the table, "We are playing a desperate game I say, but have we not been driven to it? Oppression makes wise men mad, and we refuse to die like dogs without making one bold stroke for the lives of our wives and our little ones, who are starving before our eyes. The masters show us no mercy, no pity. They will not give us a kind word, or throw us a crust of bread. We are clearly in their way, and they would fain thrust us and our misery out of their sight. But we claim a right to live in the land of our birth, and we refuse to be driven out of the country. Curse the machines!" he cried with savage energy, "and curse the men who make them! It cannot be right that we should suffer as we are suffering. It cannot be right that men who are able and willing to work should be thrust out with bitter taunts and scoffs to starve, or that our little ones should pine and wither away before our eyes. We must band ourselves together to sweep the hated frames from the face of the earth. It was a mistake to allow Cartwright to set up those he is working in the valley yonder. You see the result. The other masters cannot compete with the machinery, and all other shops are gradually shutting up. I will tell you something that should interest you. We have heard from our friends at Marsden that two more waggon loads of these frames are coming to Cartwright's place next week. Now is your time men! If you do not want the bread filching from your mouth resolve now that that accursed load shall never cross Hartshead Moor!"

Loud cheers mingled with fierce cries greeted Brooke as he sat down, which had not died away when a tall, dark man rose at the other end of the room. He had a short curt manner with him, and his speech was very brief and to the point.

"Friends," said he, in slow determined tones, "I'll make one to stop any more frames coming here. I think we have too many already." The speaker's name was John Hirst. He was one of Jackson's men, and though he was no lover of violent methods the danger which seemed to beset his craft and the fiery appeal of Brook had stirred even his sluggish nature, and he was eager to take any steps to prevent himself and his comrades from the utter ruin which seemed to him to be certain if the new invention was allowed to spread in the locality.

"Bob Wam, thou'lt go with me," added Hirst, in his short way appealing to a stout, easy looking personage on the other side of the table, who had joined enthusiastically in cheering every utterance of the delegates.

"I will, Jack, I'm sure," was the hearty response of the person appealed to, whose real name was Robert Whitham. He was also one of Jackson's workmen, and resided in a little cottage on Clickem Hill.

"And I'll make a third" cried Jonas Crowther, a determined looking man, with black bushy eyebrows and heavy jaws; and ah reckon my neighbour, Naylor, will keep me company," he added.

Naylor, who was a man of less courageous stamp, was evidently taken aback by this sudden appeal and did not answer for some time; but he also at last fell in with the invitation, though not without some evident misgivings.

So far the volunteers were all Jackson's men, but representatives from other workshops, including Cartwright's, speedily volunteered, and the number eventually included a majority of those present, but the names we have given are all that have been handed down. Walker, who had greeted every accession to the Luddite ranks with loud expressions of grati-

fication, promised that he and their townsman,
William Hall, would also join them with some Huddersfield chaps who would '' bring Enoch '' and show
them "how to go on."

A solemn oath of secrecy was then administered
to all present, and their names were taken down as
they left the room by the vigilant watchmen who had
kept guard at the door.

* * * *

The advice given by Brook was carried out. The
drivers of the waggons bringing Cartwright's machines
were met, as he suggested, on Hartshead Moor, and
the frames were broken to pieces.   It was not known
that there was any organisation of Luddites in Liversedge and the machines were sent, as several had been
sent to Cartwright's mill before, simply in charge
of the waggoners.   They ought to have arrived before night, but the roads being very bad the progress
of the vehicles had been much hindered, and darkness was closing in when they reached the Moor where
the band was lying in ambush.   The drivers, who
were seized by a strong body of masked men, made
no resistance, seeing it would be hopeless to do so,
and suffered themselves to be blindfolded and bound
till the work of destruction was finished.

CHAPTER VI.

MEETING OF LUDDITES AT THE "ST. CRISPIN," HALIFAX.

Fling out the red banner !
Its fierce front under;
Come, gather ye, gather ye,
Champions of right!
And roll round the world
With the voice of God's thunder,
The wrongs we've to reckon—
Oppressors to smite.—*Gerald Massey.*

Shortly after the events recorded in the first chapter transpired at the cropping shop of Mr. John Wood, there suddenly appeared at that establishment a man who, walking quickly up to the outer door of the building, and opening it, passed without speaking to the rest of the men, in to the room where Meilor worked. Mellor happened to be alone at the moment, and a few words were exchanged between him and his visitor, in a low tone. In a few seconds the latter again turned on his heel, made his way swiftly out of the building, and speedily disappeared in the distance. This mysterious individual was the messenger of the Halifax Luddites, and his business was to announce that a delegate from Nottingham would be passing through the town in a day or two, and would meet the leading members or delegates of the various societies in the neighbourhood, at the St. Crispin Inn, on particular business.

The "Saint Crispin," an ancient hostelry which stood not far from the venerable Parish Church, at Halifax, took its name we need hardly say from the patron saint of the shoe makers, and was frequented by many members of the noble craft. The old building was pulled down in 1844, and a new one erected on the site, the title now being "The old Crispin." The customers, at the time of which we are writing, were mostly men of a democratic sort; it was in fact known as the resort of a class who were generally called by the "Church and King men" of the time. "Tom Painers," a name under which it was customary at that day to group all who, professing progressive opinions, did not believe with Pope that "Whatever is, is right." There seems to have existed at this inn at the time of the Luddite movement a democratic or republican club, of which John Baines, an intelligent hatter, and two or three of his sons who were shoe-makers, were members. It has been noticed often that men who work together in groups, at some occupation which allows of quiet talk and discussion, are generally more intelligent and better informed than others who do not follow their avocations under such favourable circumstances, and the number of able men who have commenced life under the auspices of St. Crispin and have afterwards creditably occupied some of the highest positions in the political, literary, and scientific worlds, is a proof of this. The members of the club just alluded to naturally sympathised to some extent with the Luddite movement, knowing well the half-starved condition of working-men generally, and though many held aloof from participating actively in the movement, there were some, and amongst them the Baines family, who actually joined the Luddites, and did their best to strengthen and help on their cause.

On the night appointed for the meeting, the St. Crispin looked pretty much as usual. It was a well-accustomed house, and the inner doors were swinging to and fro in the usual fashion. A close observer who happened to be inside might have noticed that many of the visitors that evening did not enter the ordinary rooms to the left or the right, but went forward up the narrow staircase to the room above. But meetings were common in the club-room, and if any one had seen the men ascending the stairs he

would not have supposed, unless he knew something of their antecedents, that there was anything
unusual or suspicious about them, as they dropped
in, generally, one by one at irregular intervals. Trade
disputes were common then as now, and the un-
initiated observer would naturally conclude there was
some meeting there that night of a trade character.
Had his curiosity led him to endeavour to join the
gathering overhead, he would soon, however, have
been checked in his course. In the little dark room
at the back, the door of which opened at the foot of
the stairs, there was seated a roughly dressed working-
man, who apparently was enjoying a solitary glass
and pipe, but his eye never wandered from the open
door, and as each new comer passed it, rapid signals
were exchanged between him and the watcher. On
reaching the club-room door another sentinel was just
visible in the flickering light of a small candle, sitting
in the small box partitioned off from the adjoining
apartment. As a member of the fraternity passes
the little open window, a peculiar grasp of the hand
is given, some muttered words are heard, the reply
comes as quietly, and he passes in. Entering the
room with him we find there are about thirty persons
present. They are grouped round a long table at
the end of the room and preparations are evidently
being made to commence a meeting. Glancing round
at the company, we are struck first with the fact that
they are nearly all young men. There are not more
than half-a-dozen in the room that we should guess
to be over thirty. One grey-haired man there is and
only one, and they fittingly choose him to preside
over them. This is old John Baines, the veteran republican, to whom we have already alluded as being
connected with the democratic club held at the St.
Crispin. His thin locks and deeply wrinkled face
prove him to be not far from three score years and
ten, but his eye is still bright and clear as he glances
slowly round the little gathering. He is conversing
with a pale, rather intelligent looking man on his

right, the delegate from Nottingham, and as he holds
his hand to his ear to catch the replies we observe
that "old John," as he is familiarly called, is a little
deaf, but his natural force seems otherwise unabated.
On the other side of the chairman are two other men
to whom the reader has been already introduced.
The first, with the gloomy, determined-looking face,
he will recognise as George Mellor, and the other as
his brother cropper Thorpe.   After scanning thought-
fully for some minutes the strangely mingled group
of blacksmiths fresh from the forge, half-desperate
looking croppers, and pale, meagre-faced weavers,
the president thus broke the silence : —

"As the motives that induced me to join the
Luddite movement are probably different from those
which actuate most of you, I should like to have
the privilege of saying a few words to the delegates
assembled before our friend Weightman, from
Nottingham, gives his report from that town and
neighbourhood.   I have been looking round the table,
and think I am safe in saying that my age is more
than double that of anyone in this room.   I am glad
to see so many young men present, and hope their
enthusiasm may carry them right to the end of this
movement."

" Hear, hear," exclaimed the Nottingham delegate,
in a clear ringing voice.

"I say right to the end of this movement," repeated
the president—" and that end, what is it?   Is it the
destruction of the cursed machines that are robbing
your children of their daily bread?   Well, that is one
great object, but, my friends, is that the end?'

" Down with the bloody aristocrats," cried a fair-
haired man at the foot of the table, his light grey eyes
sparkling with enthusiasm.

" Amen !" responded Baines, fervently, and his
raised voice became tremulous with excitement.   " I
too say down with the bloody aristocrats !   Oh that
the long suffering people of England would rise in

their strength and crush their oppressors in the dust!
The vampires have fattened too long on our heart's
blood. Let the people now rise in their majesty and
rid themselves for ever of the vile brood who have
flung upon them the sole taxation of the country and
reduced them to the condition of galley slaves in the
land of their birth. They have filched from us our
natural inheritance, and by usurping the House of
Commons, have got the purse strings of the nation into
their hands also. They have provoked wars and lived
and fattened upon them. They have sent us to fight
anybody and everybody; to crush French liberalism
and to maintain despotism all over Europe. They
swarm over everything and cover it with their slime
—over the state, over the House of Lords, and over
the people's house, over the army and navy, over
everything. All the offices in the land are held by
them and their friends; salaries and pensions are
showered upon them from the national treasury; and
still like the horse-leech they stretch forth the greedy,
ravenous maw, and cry "Give! give!" For thirty
years I have struggled to rouse the people against the
evil and, as some of you here know, have suffered
much for my opinions in body and estate. I am now
nearing the end of my pilgrimage, but I will die as
I have lived; my last days shall be devoted to the
people's cause. I hail your rising against your oppressors and hope it may go on till there is not a
tyrant to conquer. I have waited long for the dawn
of the coming day, and it may be, old as I am, I
shall yet see the glorious triumph of democracy."

The effect of the president's passionate harangue
on the rough group around him was startling. Several
rose from their seats as the appeal grew warmer,
whilst some who were foremost pressed the horny
hand of the old veteran as he resumed his seat. A
brief interval of silence followed, and then the impetuous George Mellor sprang to his feet.

"We'll reckon with the aristocrats in London in
due time," he said "but, friends, is there not some

work nearer home to be done first? I know of no
aristocrats who are bigger tyrants than our .own
masters, and I'm for squaring with them the first."

" Our friend is right," said the Nottingham delegate, and he is also wrong. Right in his longing to
strike down the tyrant who would rob him of his
daily bread and turn him out to starve in order that
the gains may be poured with redoubled speed into
his bursting coffers ; but wrong in thinking he is his
greatest oppressor. What means this cruel war which
is carrying away the very flower of the country to
die and rot in a foreign land? For what are we fighting and what is to be the end of the conflict? Look
at our closed ports, our decaying commerce, our starving workpeople ! Now that we are aware of our
strength and have proved ourselves able to crush our
local tyrants, let us not forget we have other foes
also. Let us go down to the root. Throughout
Nottinghamshire, Lancashire, Derbyshire and
Cheshire, our movement is everywhere powerful. We
have thousands of weapons collected, and we have
strong arms to use them. Our council is in daily
communication with the societies in all the centres
of disaffection, and they urge a general rising in May.
We must crush cur tyrants at home, but remember
also those who have ruined your commerce and destroyed the peace of your homes by this bloody war.
Since John Westley was shot at Arnold, the feelings
against the masters, and their frames has redoubled
in intensity and bitterness, and our men are inspired
with desperate courage. The cavalry and the specials
do their best to put us down or capture us, but we
learn their secrets. The people everywhere sym
pathise with us, and we visit with swift and sure vengeance all who show themselves prominently in the
ranks of the enemy. Many in our body advocate the
policy of shooting such of the masters as are engaged
in hunting and harrying us, but some hardly like
the idea of murdering them in cold blood, and I must
confess there is something revolting to the feelings of
an Englishman about it."

"Let them do what's right then," broke in Mellor, with his usual impetuosity, "if we're to stick at such squeamish nonesense as that there will be nowt done. If they shoot at us, why should'nt we shoot at them? There's two in this neighbourhood that will have to be taken underhand, and at once. I mean Cartwright, of Rawfolds, and Horsfall, of Marsden. Most of you know how these two brag, day after day, at Huddersfield market and at home, and threaten what they'll do with the Luddites if they come near their places. We've sent a warning to both, and the only reply made by Cartwright is to get soldiers stationed in small detachments all over Liversedge and Heckmondwike, and our friends there tell us he still continues his bravado, and is talking about defending his mill. Now, I think it's time he had a lesson."

"To this suggestion there was at once a universal murmur of assent, and Weightman strengthened them in their resolution by saying that it was "best to tackle such troublesome men as Cartwright at once."

"What is to hinder us from attacking Rawfolds Mill next? asked Mellor. "We've done very little round there, and we are middling strong in that neighbourhood."

"There's just one thing to hinder us," said a delegate on the left of the president, "and that's all I know of."

"And what's that, Job?" enquired Mellor.

"We've not so many guns and pistols as I should like," replied the man addressed. "If we're bahn to go at a mill with soldiers inside to defend it, we want something besides a few malls and hatchets. I am sorry to say me and my mates have not been doing much lately. Hartley's poorly again."

"Is he poorly or he's showing t' white feather a bit?" asked another gruffly.

"Nay, he's a true pluck'd 'un is Hartley," replied Hey, "but he's a lot of bairns, six or seven I think, and his wife is a poor delicate thing. Since they found it out that he's joined the Luddites they are sadly again it, altho' they're half starved. However. we'll see about it to-night, Hill. But to give us time to collect some more guns, I think it would be better to put Cartwright's affairs off a bit."

"I think we ought to take Horsfall under-hand the first," said Thorpe. "I am just about sickened with the reports of his brag and threats browt into our shop. Cartwright isn't hawf as bad as him."

Several other Huddersfield delegates supported Thorpe's suggestion, and a division seemed to be threatened as the discussion grew warmer.

"Come," said Weightman at last, "don't let us get into a squabble on that small matter. Spin up a shilling—heads Cartwright, tails Horsfall!"

The suggestion was adopted and "heads" won, so it was settled that Cartwright should be first "tackled."

The next question was the date when the attack should be made, and various times were named and objected to for reasons given.

"Well," said Mellor, "would Saturday, the 11th of April do? We shouldn't be later than that. I shall never rest till the mill is in ruins. If we defer it till then that will give Job and the other searching parties more time, and I don't think it would be right to put it off any longer."

"As the man you speak of is setting you at defiance, sooner you deal with him the better," observed Weightman. "We have inspired such a wholesome dread of us at Nottingham, amongst all classes, that the threat of General Ludd is almost invariably sufficient. Our motions have been so rapid and our information respecting the possession of arms so accurate that few now dare to speak of us defiantly. As usual, rumour magnifies our deeds, and we are credited with much that we never do; but the authorities, I can assure you, are very much dissatisfied with the result of their efforts to put us down. Many who don't sympathise with us taunt them with the little progress they make in crushing us. With regard to the proposed general rising, it will be as well to get together weapons of all kinds as soon as possible, and report to us their number and kind."

A general conversation followed, and all agreed that Saturday the 11th of April would be the best day. Mellor at once arranged the method of attack. The time of meeting was to be eleven o'clock at night, and the place, a field at Cooper Bridge, not far from the obelisk called the "Dumb steeple." Messengers were chosen to carry the decision of the delegates to all the organisations not represented, and after other matters of detail had been agreed upon the gathering was brought to a close.

CHAPTER VII.

A RAID FOR ARMS.

That some mighty griefs
O'erhangs thy soul thy every look proclaims ;
Why then refuse it words ?—*Mason.*

Try courage but from opposition grows ;
And what are fifty, what a thousand slaves,
Matched to the sinew of a single arm
That strikes for right ?—*Brooke*

After the termination of the proceedings at the "Saint Crispin," as stated in the last chapter, the Luddites left the inn in the same stealthy manner in which they had entered it. The dark, moonless night was in their favour, but still they did not venture to leave the house in a body. They knew that the authorities had been warned that illegal meetings were held in some part of the town, and were in consequence just at that time more than usually watchful ; they therefore dropped out singly or in twos and threes, so that no one—even if watching the place—would have suspected anything unusual. As their homes were in many cases widely apart they were soon scattered over all parts of the town, or having cleared the more populous quarters, were trudging along the dark, quiet roads that led into the country beyond. Leaving the rest of the delegates to their own devices, we will follow two who are walking steadily on along the highway and anon through green lanes and fields,' until, after a journey extending over about an hour, they suddenly pause at a very poor looking cottage which stands a little from the main road, between Elland and Brighouse. All appears quiet in and around the little house, and it seems as if the inmates have retired to rest. After

looking at the windows for a short time, one of the
two travellers taps gently at the door. There is no
response, and, after listening for a moment, he knocks
smartly with his knuckles. Still all remains quiet in
the interior for a brief space ; then there is a slight
shuffling of feet, and by and by, a cloth which stops
up one of the broken panes being removed, a woman
in a weak, frightened voice asks,

" Who's there ?"

" Open the door and thou'lt see," replies one of
the men, gruffly.

" What do you want ?" asked the woman timidly.

" We want thy husband—open the door or we'll
break it down."

" William cannot come," said the woman, " he is
poorly to-night."

" Open the door," replied the man savagely, " if you
don't want it sending through in shivers."

" Open it, Mary," said some one inside.

A sob and a faint cry follow, then the door is
opened with evident reluctance, and the two men,
one of them with an ugly oath on his lips, burst into
the room. The place seems almost dark as they
enter, but they can detect the dim outline of a figure
bending over a few red cinders in the grate. They
see that it is a man, and that he is trying to light a
diminutive piece of candle. In a minute or two he
places it upon the little round table at his elbow. It
casts only a feeble, flickering light, but it suffices to
show that the surroundings are wretched in the extreme. On one side is an old carved oak chest which
looks as if it had served the purpose of two or three
generations. This is the only article of furniture on
that side of the house. There had evidently been
pictures suspended on the white-washed walls, but
there are none now. On the right of the fire-place
is a bed, and these, with the table we have named,
six or seven old stools and chairs, and a few kitchen
utensils, complete the furniture, if we except a sort
of table of home manufacture which stands under the

window, on which are a tailor's goose and a pair of
shears, which show what is the occupation of the pale,
serious, looking occupant of the cottage, who having
placed the candle on the table, sinks into his chair
again with a look of mingled despair and defiance,
but utters no sound. The two intruders gazed at
him also without speaking for a few seconds, but they
soon recovered themselves.

"How is it thou hast not been at the meeting to
night, Hartley?" asked the milder looking of the two,
in quiet tones.

"Because he was too poorly to go anywhere," replied the woman instantly, "and if he'd been well he
would have gone to no meetings of yours if I could
have hindered him."

"Silence!" growled the other man, fiercely.

"Silence thyself, John Hill," said the tailor, breaking his strange silence, "is this my house or thine?"

"Well, I've no objection to thee calling it thine,"
replied Hill, glancing contemptuously around at the
squalid furniture.

The unfeeling taunt seemed to agitate poor Hartley
strongly, and he made a hasty movement towards
Hill, but Hey interposed by pacing his hand firmly
on his shoulder, and the woman also rushed between
the two.

"Hill," said Job Hey, sternly, "no more of this.
Is this a time of brawling amongst those who should
stand shoulder to shoulder? Hartley," he continued
in soothing tones, "be quiet. We came to say that
we have orders from the delegate meeting to-night to
collect as many arms as we can, and at once. An
attack on a mill at Rawfolds has been decided upon.
This order requires our instant attention. I command
you on the oath we have all taken to prepare to go
with us."

A mournful sound burst from the woman at this
appeal, and she begun to wring her hands in deep
anguish. Her husband looked at her, and as he looked

the hard defiant expression in his face gradually disappeared and it beamed with tender sympathy.

"He is not fit to go anywhere," sobbed the woman, "he is so weak and poorly. He has not tasted food this day. We had but one small loaf this morning, and he would not touch a morsel of it. God knows what is to become of us. Our poor children have all gone supperless to bed, crying for food and we have none to give them."

"And yet," replied Hey, "you would prevent your husband from trying to remedy this. We live in a land of plenty, and you would pine yourself and all your little ones to death. Do you care so little for them that you can sit and see them droop and die before your very eyes? Here you've been working and struggling to keep body and soul together, while all round you see scores revelling in luxury who never lift their little fingers to do anything. While they have lived in grand mansions, well housed and well clad, you have been forced to exist in this poor miserable hut. And now that you have sold nearly all your furniture to keep the wolf from the door, what is there before you but the workhouse?"

"Nothing, nothing," wailed the woman, "but even that is better than the prison cell. William don't go."

But the strangely silent man had risen to his feet and was preparing to accompany the two messengers.

'Mary," said he, in a low tone, "let me go quietly."

But his agonised wife had swooned in her chair and was happily unconscious. Seeing this, he opened the chamber door and called his eldest daughter. The poor girl huddled on her scanty clothing and came down. As she entered the room below even the uncouth visitors she found there were evidently struck by her rare beauty. Her hair, black as a raven's wing, hung in dishevelled masses down her shapely shoulders, contrasting strongly with her pallid face, and as she stood at the foot of the stairs, with eyes

dilated by fear, she looked like a startled, timorous
fawn. Glancing rapidly at the rough visitors she at
once took in the situation, for none of the secrets of
that sad household were unknown to her. Her dress
was shabby enough and her whole appearance spoke
of deep poverty, but there gleamed through all these
sad surroundings a beauty which was so remarkable
that even the rough visitors were struck dumb and
almost forgot their errand. Crossing the floor to where
her father was standing she whispered in his ear.
Without speaking he kissed her fondly, and, pointing
to her mother, disengaged himself from her clinging
hands and strode rapidly after his friends.

On the morning of the following day the neighbourhood for miles around was startled by tales of the
visit of a band of Luddites to some score of detached
or solitary houses in the valley, from which they had
carried away a great number of guns, pistols and other
weapons.

* * * *

The attack on Cartwright's mill at Rawfolds having
been resolved upon, the Luddite leaders immediately
bestirred themselves to make it a success. Disguised
bands like that of Hill, Hey and Hartley, stripped
the district of arms, and active measures were taken
to secure a good stock of ammunition also. Messengers were despatched to the societies in all the
surrounding towns, and considerable detachments of
men were promised from Huddersfield, Leeds, and
Halifax. Although the members of the fraternity
were not so numerous in proportion to the population
in Heckmondwike, Cleckheaton, Birstall, Gomersal,
and Liversedge as in some of the towns we have
named, still there existed a large sprinkling in un-
suspected corners, and these were also warned to
hold themselves in readiness. Midnight drills were
common, and belated travellers who had to pass near
wild moors and unfrequented places told how they
had heard the word of command and the measured

tramp of many feet; or had seen what their imagination converted into thousands of armed men practising military manœuvers and accustoming themselves to act together.

The man who had rendered himself so obnoxious to the leaders of the Luddite fraternity, and for whose punishment all these preparations were being made, was not altogether unaware of what was in store for him. Mr. Cartwright had had many opportunities of knowing that he was a marked man, and that the Luddites had sworn to compass his destruction; he therefore set about to prepare himself to meet the coming storm. Hitherto the master manufacturers and owners of frames had proved themselves very adverse to the prosecution of the offenders, even if discovered, being manifestly afraid of putting themselves into prominent opposition to a society whose knowledge and strength they no doubt often over rated. They were, in fact, so thoroughly cowed by the bold acts of the Luddites and by their dreadful threats that they hardly dared to lift up their hands to defend their property, and shrunk from giving evidence against any who might be apprehended even in the very act of destruction. Such being the case, it was hardly likely that many prosecutions would, if left in the manufacturers' hands, be carried into effect; it was therefore deemed by the Government absolutely necessary for the public good that the course of justice should be opened by taking the indictments out of the hands of the nominal prosecutors, and accordingly the whole of the cases were conducted by the counsel for the crown. Still it cannot be said that any vindictiveness was shown by the Government at this stage. On the contrary great laxity characterised these prosecutions. At the Nottingham Assizes, which were held just before the attack we are about to describe took place, thirteen persons were committed for offences connected with the disturbed state of the country, but none of them were capitally convicted; and in many cases where they were found guilty of felonies, the punishment awarded fell far short of that which the law authorised. Whether the Luddites in this locality were encouraged by the mildness of the punishments which their confederates received at Nottingham, or by doctrines which were broached at the time casting doubt on the moral guilt of destroying machinery, or from any other cause, certain it is that immediately after the Assizes were over and the visit of the Nottingham delegate to this district had taken place, cases of outrage became more and more common. The discipline of the disaffected was also manifestly improved, and a system of exacting subscriptions was established here after the model of Nottingham.

Mr. Cartwright had often referred in public to what he considered the pusillanimous conduct of the masters, and had openly announced his intention to defend his property to the best of his ability if it should be attacked. Nor did he rest here, but endeavoured to instil some of his own resolute spirit into the hearts of his brother manufacturers. The Luddites, as we have already stated, had been accustomed to carry all before them, and it is not difficult to see how a stumbling block like Mr. Cartwright came to be feared and hated by them. In fact they soon began to regard it as an immediate necessity that he should be made an example of if the prestige of the secret societies was to be maintained.

"I shall never rest until he is punished, his machines broken to pieces, and his mill levelled to the ground," passionately exclaimed Mellor at one of the meetings, and as we have already seen he soon took steps to put this project into practical shape.

It does not appear that Mr. Cartwright was regarded as a tyrannical master; on the contrary he was generally liked by his workmen, and had it not been for his rash manner of expressing himself and his well known character for acting up to his determination, his mill might possibly have escaped, as no violence of that kind had taken place in the immediate neighbourhood previous to the attack on his property.　He had, however, provoked the Luddites beyond endurance, and they fully resolved to punish him.　How they carried that resolve into execution must be detailed in another chapter.

From what we have already said, the reader will be well aware that the times of which we are writing were times of severe trial to the masters as well as the men.　Only a few years before the Luddites arose, the paternal legislators, which had foolishly shackled trade were engaged in the consideration of a bill to repeal certain restrictive provisions which they and their fathers had made law.　There were regulations and orders in various Acts of Parliament relating to the length, breadth, and weight of woollen cloths ; the tentering, straining, viewing, searching, and sealing by officers appointed for that purpose ; the boiling of wool with certain ingredients ; the prohibition of the use of lamb's wool ; the use of gig mills, and the number of looms, etc.　These strange devices by which trade was then crippled are now fortunately unknown, but while they existed they must have cost the clothier more, by limiting his operations in the field of industry, than any damage done by the Luddites.

CHAPTER VIII.

LORD BYRON'S SPEECH.

I could a tale unfold whose lightest word,
Would harrow up thy soul.—Shakespeare.

While Luddism was thus spreading in this district the excesses in Nottinghamshire engaged the attention of Parliament. A bill was introduced by the ministers of the day—the stern and rigid Percival administration—to render frame breaking a capital crime. punishable with death. Against that bill. Lord Byron, the celebrated poet, made his first speech in the House of Lords. His lordship only spoke three times in that assembly and then left the gilded chamber in disgust, never to return to it. At this time he had become famous, for his celebrated poem "Childe Harold" had been issued shortly before he stood forth so nobly in defence of his starving countrymen.

The order of the day for the second reading of this sanguinary bill being read, Lord Byron rose and addressed the assembly as follows :—My Lords,—The subject now submitted to your Lordships for the first time, though new to. the House is by no means new to the country. I believe it had occupied the serious thoughts of all descriptions of persons long before its introduction to the legislature whose interference could alone be of real service. As a person in some degree connected with the suffering county, though a stranger not only to the House in general but almost to every individual whose attentions I presume to solicit, I must claim some portion of your lordships' indulgence whilst I offer a few observations on a question on which I confess myself deeply interested.

THE RISINGS OF THE LUDDITES.

To enter into any detail of the riots would be superfluous; the House is already aware that riot and actual bloodshed has been perpetrated, and that the proprietors of the frames, obnoxious to the rioters and all persons connected with them, have been liable to insult and violence. During the short time I recently passed in Nottingham, not twelve hours elapsed without some fresh act of violence; and on the day I left the county I was informed that forty frames had been broken the preceding evening, as usual, without resistance and without detection.

Such was then the state of the county, and such I have reason to believe it to be at this moment. But whilst these outrages must be admitted to exist to an alarming extent, it cannot be denied that they have arisen from circumstances of the most unparelleled distress; the perseverance of these miserable men in their proceedings tends to prove that nothing but absolute want could have driven a large and once honest and industrious body of the people into the commission of excesses so hazardous to themselves, their families, and the community. At the time to which I allude, the town and county were burdened with large detachments of the military; the police was in motion and also the magistrates, yet all the movements, civil and military, had led to—nothing. Not a single instance had occurred of the apprehension of any real delinquent taken in the act, against whom there existed legal evidence sufficient for conviction. But the police, however useless, were by no means idle; several notorious delinquents had been detected; men, liable to conviction, on the clearest evidence of the capital crime of poverty; men who had been nefariously guilty of lawfully begetting several children, whom, thanks to the times! they were unable to maintain. Considerable injury has been done to the proprietors of the improved frames. The machines were to them an advantage, inasmuch as they superseded the necessity of employing a number of workmen, who were left

in consequence to starve. By the adoption of one
species of frame in particular, one man performed
the work of many, and the superfluous labourers
were thrown out of employment. Yet, it is to be
observed, that the work thus executed was inferior
in quality; not marketable at home, and merely
hurried over with a view to exportation. It was
called, in the cant of the trade, by the name of "Spider
work." The rejected workmen, in the blindness of
their ignorance, instead of rejoicing at these improvements in arts so beneficial to mankind, conceived
themselves to be sacrificed to improvements in
mechanism. In the foolishness of their hearts they
imagined that the maintenance and well doing of
the industrious poor were objects of greater consequence than the enrichment of a few individuals by
any improvement in the implements of trade, which
threw the workmen out of employment and rendered
the labourer unworthy of his hire. And it must be
confessed that although the adoption of the enlarged
machinery in that state of our commerce which the
country once boasted, might have been beneficial
to the master without being detrimental to the
servant; yet, in the present situation of our manu-
factures, rotting in warehouses, without a prospect
of exportation, with the demand for work and workmen equally diminished, frames of this description
tend materially to aggravate the distress and discontent of the aggravated sufferers. But the real
cause of the distress and consequent disturbances
lies deeper. When we are told that these men are
leagued together not only for the destruction of their
own comfort, but the very means of subsistence,
can we forget that it is the bitter policy, the destructive warfare of the last eighteen years, which has
destroyed their comfort, your comfort, all men's
comfort? That policy, which, originating with 'great
statesmen now no more,' has survived the dead to
become a curse on the living, unto the third and
fourth generation! These men never destroyed their

frames till they became useless—worse than useless,
till they were become actual impediments to their
exertions in obtaining their daily bread. Can you,
then, wonder that in times like these, when
bankruptcy, convicted fraud, and imputed felony, are found in a station not far beneath
your lordships, the lowest, though once most
useful portion of the people, should forget
their duty in their distresses, and become
only less guilty than one of their representatives? But while the exalted offender can find means
to baffle the law, new capital punishments must be
devised, new snares of death must be spread for the
wretched mechanic who is famished into guilt. These
men were willing to dig, but the spade was in other
hands; they were not ashamed to beg, but there was
none to relieve them; their own means of subsistence were cut off, all other employments pre-
occupied; and their excesses, however to be deplored
and condemned, can hardly be a subject of surprise.
It has been stated that the persons in the temporary
possession of the frames connive at their destruction; if this be proved upon enquiry, it were necessary that such material accessories to the crime should
be principals in the punishment. But I did hope
that any measure proposed by his Majesty's government, for your lordships' decision, would have had
conciliation for its basis; or, if that were hopeless,
that some previous inquiry, some deliberation would
have been deemed requisite; not that we should have
been called at once without examination, and without cause, to pass sentences by wholesale, and sign
death warrants blindfold. But, admitting that these
men had no cause of complaint; that the grievances
of them and their employers were alike groundless;
that they deserved the worst; what inefficiency,
what imbecility has been evinced in the method
chosen to reduce them! Why were the military called
out to be made a mockery of, if they were to be
called out at all? As far as the difference of the

seasons would permit, they merely parodied the
summer campaign of Major Sturgeon; and, indeed,
the whole proceedings, civil and military, seem to
be of the model of those of the mayor and corpora-
tion of Garratt. Such marchings and countermarch-
ings! From Nottingham to Bullwell, from Bullwell
to Banford, from Banford to Mansfield! And when
at length detachments arrived at their destination,
in all 'the pride, pomp, and circumstance of
glorious war,' they came just in time to witness
what had been done, and ascertain the escape of
perpetrators, to collect the fragments of broken
frames, and return to their quarters amidst the
derision of old women and the hootings of children.
Now, though in a free country it were to be wished
that our military should not be formidable, at
least to ourselves, I cannot see the policy of placing
them in situations where they can only be made
ridiculous. As the sword is the worst argument
that can be used, so it should be the last. In this
instance it has been the worst, but providentially
has rested yet in the scabbard. The present measure
will indeed pluck it from the sheath; yet, had proper
meetings been held in the earlier stages of the riots;
had the grievances of the men and their masters (for
they also had their grievances) been fairly weighed
and justly examined, I do think that means might
have been devised to restore these workmen to their
avocations, and tranquility to the county. At
present the county suffers from a double infliction
of an idle military and a starving population. In
what state of apathy have we been plunged so long
that now for the first time the House had been
officially apprised of the disturbances? All this
has been transacting within 130 miles of London;
and yet we, good, easy men, have deemed our
greatness was a-ripening,' and have sat down to
enjoy our triumphs in the midst of domestic calamity.
But all the cities you have taken, all the armies
that have retreated before your leaders, are but paltry

subjects of self-congratulation if your land divides against itself, and your dragoons and executioners must be let loose against your fellow citizens. You call these men a mob, desperate, dangerous, and ignorant; and seem to think that the only way to quiet the 'Bellua Multurum Capitum' is to lop off a few of their superfluous heads. But even a mob may be better reduced to reason by a mixture of conciliation and firmness than by additional irritation and redoubled penalties. Are we aware of our obligation to the mob? It is the mob that labour in your fields, serve in your houses—that man your navy and recruit your army—that have enabled you to defy all the world, and can also defy you when neglect and calamity have driven them to despair. You may call the people a mob, but do not forget that a mob too often speaks the sentiments of the people. And here I must remark, with what alacrity you are accustomed to fly to the rescue of your distressed allies, leaving the distressed of your own country to the care of Providence, or the parish. When the Portuguese suffered under the retreat of the French, every arm was stretched out, every hand was opened; from the rich man's largess to the widow's mite, all was bestowed; to enable them to rebuild their villages and restore their granaries. And at this moment, when thousands of misguided but unfortunate fellow-countrymen are struggling with the hardships of extremes and hunger, as your charity began abroad it should end at home. A much less sum, a tithe of the bounty bestowed on Portugal, even if these men (which I cannot admit without enquiry) could not have been restored to their employment, would have rendered unnecessary the tender mercies of the bayonet and the gibbet. But doubtless our friends have too many foreign claims to admit a prospect of domestic relief: though never did such objects demand it. I have traversed the seat of war in the Peninsula: I have been in some of the most oppressed provinces of

Turkey; but never under the most despotic of infidel governments did I behold such squalid wretchedness as I have seen since my return into the very heart of a christian country. And what are your remedies? After months of inaction, and months of action worse than inactivity, at length comes forth the grand specific, the never-failing nostrum of all state physicians, from the days of Draco to the present. After feeling the pulse and shaking the head over the patient, you prescribed the usual course of warm water and bleeding—the warm water of your mawkish police, and lances of military—these convulsions must end in death, the sure consummation of these prescriptions of all political Sangrados. Setting aside the palpable injustice and the certain inefficiency of the bill, are there not capital punishments sufficient in your statutes? Is there not blood enough upon your penal code, that more must be poured forth to ascend to Heaven, and testify against you? How will you carry the bill into effect? Can you commit a whole country to their own prisons? Will you erect a gibbet in every field and hang up men like scarecrows? Or, will you proceed (as you must to bring this measure into effect) by decimation? Place the county under martial law? Depopulate and lay waste all around you, and restore Sherwood Forest as an acceptable gift to the crown, in the former condition of a royal chase and an asylum for outlaws? Are these the remedies for a starving and desperate populace? Will the famished wretches who have braved your bayonets be appalled by your gibbets? When death is a relief, and the only relief it appears you will afford him, will he be dragooned into tranquility? Will that which could not be effected by your grenadiers, be accomplished by your executioners? If you proceed by the forms of law where is your evidence? Those who refused to impeach their accomplices, when transportation only was the punishment, will hardly be tempted to witness against them when death is the penalty.

When a proposal is made to emancipate or relieve.
you hesitate, you deliberate for years, you temporise
and tamper with the minds of men; but a death bill
must be passed off hand, without a thought of the
consequences! Sure I am, from what I have heard,
and from what I have seen, that to pass the bill
under all the existing circumstances, without enquiry, without deliberation, would only be to add
injustice to irritation, and barbarity to neglect. The
framers of such a bill must be content to inherit the
honours of that Athenian lawgiver whose edicts were
said to be written, not in ink, but in blood. But
suppose it passed; suppose one of the men, as I have
seen them—meagre with famine, sullen with despair,
careless of a life which your lordships are perhaps
about to value at something less than the price of a
stocking frame—suppose this man, surrounded by the
children for whom he is unable to procure bread, at
the hazard of his existence, about to be torn from
a family which he has lately supported in peaceful
industry, and which it is not his fault that he can
no longer so support—suppose this man, and there are
ten thousand such from whom you may select your
victim, dragged into court, to be tried for this new
offence, by this new law; and there are two things
wanted to convict and condemn him; and these
are, in my opinion—twelve butchers for a jury, and
a Jefferies for a judge."

The effect of this impassioned harangue on the
noble lords who listened to it was. we may well believe, sufficiently startling, and the political opinions
of Lord Byron almost caused as much sensation for a
time as his wonderful poem.

CHAPTER IX.

PREPARING FOR ACTION.

They stand erect ; their slouch becomes a walk ;
They step right onward, martial is their air,
Their form and movement —*Cowper*.
Put on
The dauntless spirit of resolution —*Shakespeare*.

Saturday, the eleventh of April, the day fixed
upon for the attack on Mr. Cartwright's mill, arrived,
and some of the restless spirits at John Wood's workshop waited impatiently for the shades of evening to
close in. Dickenson, the mysterious messenger of
the fraternity, had visited all the centres of disaffection to warn them to be in readiness, and to convey
powder and ammunition to such as required them.
He had visited John Wood's workshop early in the
morning of that day, and having supplied their wants,
had passed on to other places. He arrived at Jackson's shop just as the men were leaving their work
for dinner ; at any rate he was then first seen by
Fearnsides, the vigilant foreman who, knowing the
dangerous spirit that was abroad amongst the men,
would certainly have tried to prevent Dickenson from
having an interview with them if he had come into
the cropping shop, as he was well aware that the
course entered upon by some of his men would
certainly end in trouble. John Hirst, Bob Wam,
Crowther, and some others did not return to their
work that day. They were engaged with Dickenson
in the upper room at the Shears, where he submitted
the details of the scheme for the attack on Cartwright's mill. It was finally arranged that the Liversedge contingent should meet the Huddersfield men
near the Dumb Steeple, and that John Hirst and
Samuel Hartley should act as guides from this gathering place to the mill. Hirst was well acquainted

with every turn of the road, and Hartley's services it was thought would be valuable when the mill was reached in pointing out the most vulnerable places for the attack.

As the hour fixed upon for the general gathering drew near various bands began to make their way towards the meeting place, which, as we have already stated, was a field belonging to Sir George Armytage, at Cooper Bridge, near the "Dumb Steeple." The officers of the Luddites had been very busy all the previous week looking up their men and conveying to them arms of various kinds. Notwithstanding the vigilance of the searching parties they were not however able to supply the whole of their members; they were all warned nevertheless to attend the general rendezvous.

It was arranged that the party should start on their destructive mission before midnight, and the men left their homes singly or in little groups at various times, so as not to arouse suspicion. Soon after ten o'clock some of the more eager spirits were on the ground, and before the hour expired the number had increased to about fifty. They were armed in very motley fashion; some bore guns, others pistols, while many carried only hedge stakes or stout bludgeons of various kinds, and not a few held on their shoulders huge hammers, mauls, and murderous looking hatchets of various sizes. They were nearly all disguised, some having their faces simply blackened and others wearing masks to conceal their features effectually. Many of them were dressed in carter's smock frocks, others had their coats turned inside out, some had put their checked shirts over their clothes, and a few had actually dressed themselves partly in women's apparel. By the time eleven o'clock arrived all the leading men were in the field and amongst them George Mellor, James Haigh, John Walker, William Thorpe, and the young neophyte, John Booth. In another half-hour their number had augmented to about a hundred, and as the hand of

the clock stole upwards towards midnight some fifty
more joined them and then the leaders held a consultation about starting. The last arrivals were the
men from Liversedge, Heckmondwike, Gomersal,
Birstall, and Cleckheaton, under the leadership of
John Hirst. Some of the Liversedge men had been
for meeting the advancing party at Hightown, but
it was finally decided that it would be safest to
have only one gathering place, namely, the Dumb
Steeple. They were still some fifty short of the
expected number, but they must start if the work
was to be done that night, as they had arranged to
meet the Leeds contingent near the scene of action
at half-an-hour after midnight. The men, too, were
weary of waiting, and it was therefore decided that
instant preparations should be made for the march.
The stragglers are called together by a low whistle,
and Mellor's deep voice is heard as he puts them in
order. They form in a long lane, down which the
various leaders walk, calling over their rolls, not by
names but by numbers. This being done, they are
next formed into companies. The men with guns
are called to march first, and Mellor assumes the
command of this detachment. Next follows the
pistol company, headed by Thorpe. A hatchet company comes after, and the rear is brought up by the
men wielding huge hammers, and by those who
carry only bludgeons or are without weapons of any
kind. They are rapidly put through a short drill
and then formed into marching order, John Hirst,
of Liversedge, and Samuel Hartley, of Rawfolds,
who was or had been in Cartwright's employ, being
told off as guides. It is now approaching midnight
and they have some three miles to walk, so no time
must be lost. Before giving the word to start
George Mellor stands in front of the men and endeavours to fire their courage.

"We are all ready now, men," he said, in a deep
clear voice. "You are all aware that we go to-
night to wreak vengeance on the braggart Cartwright,
of Rawfolds, who has so long taunted us and set

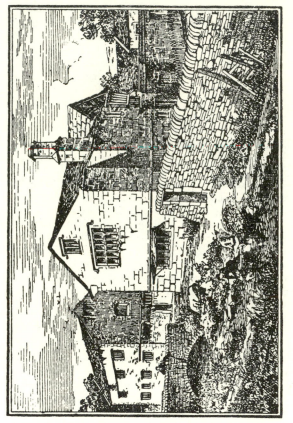

OLD GATE HOUSE.

us at defiance. We know that he has been keeping
guard over his cursed machines for some weeks and
that he has soldiers in small detachments all round
the adjoining villages. He has boasted again and
again how he would defend his mill, and from what
we can learn of him it seems likely he will. Nevertheless we are able to deal with him; we are well
armed and when we are joined by the Leeds brethren
we shall be sufficiently strong to handle him and the
soldiers also. Now, lads, show us you know what
to do!"

Instantly the first company placed their guns to
their shoulders as if about to fire, the next company
held out their pistols as if animated by a similar
intention, and the rest uplifted significantly their
great hammers and hatchets.

"Right, men! cried Mellor, "now march."

The motley multitude, headed by their guides,
marched steadily forward—all but two, William Hall,
of Parkin Hoyle, Liversedge, and George Rigg, who
are ordered to go last to drive stragglers up and see
that none go back. As these two were bringing up
the rear they thought they saw some one mount the
wall and drop quietly over into the highway but
they were not certain, and as the body were now
marching out of the field, they followed, after stopping
a brief period to satisfy their doubts. Stepping
briskly onward they pass along the park wall side,
the old hall of Kirklees, over the corner of the moor,
and through the upper part of Hightown. All the
houses are in darkness, the watch and ward will
allow no one to have a light in their dwellings after
ten o'clock. As the heavy tread of the men falls
on the hard road, many of the sleepers in the houses
are awakened, and rushing to their windows peep
stealthily forth and see the black compact masses,
with the barrels of their guns and the dreadful looking hatchets and hammers gleaming dimly in the
starlight, and then creep back to lay their head on

sleepless pillows, their teeth chattering with fear.
They have heard many frightful tales of the doings
of the dreaded Luddites and now they are passing
their very doors No one wonders respecting their
destination.   They all know that Mr. Cartwright
has long been threatened and the avengers have come
at last to carry out their threats.   The affrighted
imaginations of the startled watchers magnify the
hundreds of the mysterious body into thousands as
they wheel to the left at the hoarse word of command,
near the White Hart Inn to pass down the narrow
lane to the mill in the hollow. The distance is but
short and the listeners strain their ears to catch the
first sounds of the conflict.

Rawfolds mill is before the men at last, and they
gaze with keen interest at the dark object in the
valley which can just be distinguished. A halt is
called, and a hurried consultation takes place amongst
the leaders. "Where is the Leeds detachment?" is
the question they ask of one another, but no one
is prepared with an answer. Scouts are sent forward in the direction in which they are expected,
but there are no signs of the Leeds men.   They
listen long and intently ere they return, but can
detect no sound of marching.   Everything seems
perfectly still, the silence is almost oppressive. An
impatient oath bursts from the lips of the headstrong
Mellor. A brief conference follows; hot, passionate
words are spoken in suppressed tones, and the impetuous leader of the first division has his way as
usual. They will not wait for the Leeds men.
They are numerous and well armed. so they
will begin   the attack, and   their   expected
comrades will hurry to their assistance, anxious
to share in the honour of the victory. Poor
misguided men! The expected aid was not far
away ; it was so near indeed that the approaching
men could soon after hear distinctly the heavy thud
of the hammers and hatchets and see the blaze of
musketry in the valley below as the attack was made,

but instead of rushing forward to the aid of their
brethren, they stood still to listen, and as they heard
volley answering volley their craven hearts failed
them, and they turned and marched home again!
But we are anticipating.

Mr. David Cawthra, an old man of 96, who resided
at Brighouse, and whose father was one of the
" watch and ward " stated a few weeks before his
death (which took place on March 18th, 1895), that
there were many connected with the Luddites at
Rastrick and Elland—not so many at Brighouse,
which was then a very small place of about 300 inhabitants. He well remembered the night of the
attack on Cartwright's Mill. His father was taken
ill that night, and he was sent by his mother to
fetch Dr. Hopkinson. The doctor resided in Daisy
Croft, and, as the lad passed over the canal bridge,
near the Anchor Inn, he well remembered meeting
a party of men who seemed to be coming from Elland
and Rastrick, who had big mauls with them, and
who were no doubt going to the meeting that night
at Cooper Bridge. Elland, Mr. Cawthra said, had
a very bad name at that time, being generally called
" Elland Thief Hoil," and the Luddites were
particularly numerous round that place.

The old historic mill at Rawfolds, which has been
looked upon with interest by thousands, was pulled
down soon after the Luddite attack, either wholly or
partly, and rebuilt much in the same style as
before. That erection also now exists no longer,
having unfortunately been destroyed by fire a few
years ago. The plain and substantial, though by no
means handsome looking building will, however, be
clearly remembered by all who have seen it. At
the period of the Luddite riots it belonged to the
grandfather of the family who worked it up to the
times of its destruction, and it was at that time leased
to Mr. William Cartwright as a finishing cloth mill.
It was turned by water power, and had a large dam
on one side extending the whole length of the

building, and which came within two or three feet
of the wall. The dam stones were then much higher
than they are at the present day, the water being kept
at a depth of three yards or more, and fish were then
very plentiful in the dam and the stream, trout
especially. As we have already stated Mr. Cartwright had been expecting the attack on the mill
for weeks and was fully prepared for it. His defiance of the Luddites was not mere braggadocio as
some of them supposed; he meant all he said. He
was fully determined to defend his property and had
fortified the mill, which was in itself a strong building, and strengthened it in every possible way. The
ground floor and also the room above it were flagged.
The flags in the second floor were of a large size, and
he had rings and pulleys fixed to them, so that he
could raise them to fire into the room below if the
rioters should succeed in getting possession of it.
When the flags were thus raised, he could while
sheltering behind them, also command the front of
the mill by firing obliquely through the windows.
The correspondent of the "Leeds Mercury," writing
at the time of the attack and who saw the mill as it
stood, says, "The assailants have much reason to
rejoice that they did not succeed in entering the building, for we speak from our own observation when we
say that had they effected an entrance the deaths
of vast numbers of them, from a raking fire which
they could neither have returned nor controlled,
would have been inevitable." To prevent any one
reaching the room above, rollers with spikes sixteen
to eighteen inches in length were fixed in the staircase, so that the attacking party would be confined to
the ground floor, where as we have already shown,
they could be picked off by those above at their
leisure. Even if this chevaux de frise had been
surmounted the assailants might still have been held
in check, for huge carboys of vitriol stood at the
head of the stairs ready to be poured upon the heads
of any who should attempt to ascend. Choosing four

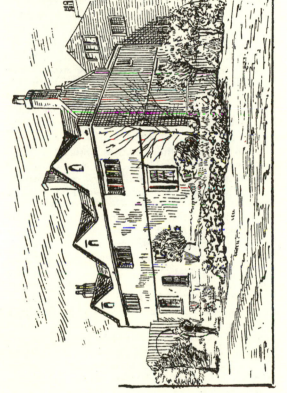

HAIGH HOUSE.

of his workmen in whom he could confide, he completed his garrison by adding five soldiers, and also had two watchers at the gates to give warning of any danger. These last, however, it will be seen proved of no use, and had it not been for a large dog which he kept inside the mill, the rioters would have taken the little garrison by surprise. The doors were made unusually strong by means of huge iron studs and stout bars, and an alarm bell was fixed upon the building to call to his assistance the soldiers who were billetted at nearly all the public houses within a circle of two miles. The watch and ward, and also parties of soldiers patrolled the district every evening, but Hirst and Hartley had ascertained when the coast was likely to be clear.

As the agents of the Luddites were often found tampering with the soldiers, they were constantly being changed, and the Queen's Bays, some Hussars, and a regiment from Stirling were in Liversedge in succession during the time the disturbances continued. The headquarters was at Huddersfield, their commander being Major Gordon. The Scotch regiment were hardy soldiers, and were in the habit of bathing in the water near the mill even in winter when it was necessary to break the ice for the purpose. As has before been said, they were quartered in many of the public houses within a radius of two miles, but the main body was placed in a building near Haigh House, in Hightown, which had been built for a cropping shop but was empty. The commanding officer was billetted in the house itself. There was also a good number quartered in the old building at Millbridge, which stands close to the causeway. Up till within the last few years the names of some of the officers were scratched on one of the window panes, but the windows have now been altered. At Heckmondwike the chief billetting places seem to have been the Woolpack Inn, the Brown Cow, now the Commercial, and the George and Dragon, now the George.

CHAPTER X.

THE ATTACK ON CARTWRIGHT'S MILL.

And such a yell was there
Of sudden and portentous birth,
As if men fought upon the earth
And fiends in upper air.—*Sir Walter Scott.*

We left the rioters about sixty paces from the
mill, resolved to make the attack at once and not
wait the arrival of the Leeds detachment. Mr.
Cartwright had on this eventful evening stationed his
watchmen at the mill gates, as usual, and retired to
rest in the counting-house about twenty minutes past
midnight; four of his workpeople and five soldiers,
which completed his little garrison, taking possession
at the same time of the beds ranged down the side
of the mill, behind the huge flags which were raised
by means of pulleys, as described in the last chapter
All the defences having been, as usual, carefully in-
spected, the men had piled their arms and placed
their ammunition in readiness, and were soon fast
asleep. Mr. Cartwright himself was just about to
drop off into unconsciousness when he was aroused
by the low growling of the dog in the room beneath.
His first thought, as he raised himself on his elbow
to listen, was that the alarm was a false one, as he
naturally expected that his watchmen outside would
have been the first to apprise him of approaching
danger. The low growling of the dog speedily, however, changed to furious barking, and, listening still
more intently, he could hear above the monotonous
booming of the neighbouring waterfall a confused
murmur. Sprinking hastily from his bed, he found
his suspicions confirmed, and immediately rousing
his companions, they at once prepared for the
defence.

The Luddites were well aware that two sentries were posted outside the gates, and had sent forward the two guides, John Hirst and Samuel Hartley, who knew the place well, to seize them. The men executed their mission with great skill and dexterity. Stealing very carefully forward, they pounced suddenly upon the careless watchers and silenced them before they had the opportunity of giving any alarm whatever, and then, by a low whistle, announced their success to their comrades, who at once marched up to the ponderous mill gates. After examining them for an instant. Mellor gave the order.

" Hatchetmen, advance !"

The ranks opened and the stalwart band, bearing huge hatchets and great hammers on their shoulders, advanced to the front.

" Now, men," cried Mellor, " clear the road !" Instantly at the word of command the weapons, wielded as they are by powerful arms, come down upon the gates with terrific force. Soon the heavy woodwork flies in splinters, and anon, with a fearful crash, like the felling of great trees, the first barricade drops prostrate and the rioters pour rapidly and steadily over it into the mill yard. A few paces and they look up at the great mill. Its long rows of windows glitter in the starlight, but all is dark inside, and there are no signs of its defenders. It stands all black and still, and nothing is heard but the furious barking of the dog which has now changed to a frantic howl. But though there are no signs of the existence of the little garrison, they are on the alert. They have not had much time to put on their clothing, but they are ready behind their stout barricade of stone flags. Their muskets, which command the whole front of the mill, are ready pointed through the loop holes and they are waiting for the order to fire. They can hear the trampling of many feet, a confused hum of voices, and then, with a sudden and tremendous crash, hundreds of great stones come bounding through the long lines of windows

RAWFOLDS MILL.

and it seems as if every atom of glass and woodwork
are swept away. Then follows a terrific yell from
the desperate multitude—a yell loud enough and wild
enough to strike terror into the boldest heart. The
echoes of that savage cry have not died away before
the rioters fire a volley through the empty windows.
The signal is now given to the defenders of the mill;
the hitherto silent building wakes up, and a steady
peal of musketry echoes sharply through the valley.
The rioters are half mad with rage; they have never
been so set at defiance before.

"Hatchetmen to the front!" shouts Mellor,
hoarsely.

They march in steady phalanx to the mill door.
It is studded with great nails set so closely that it
seems as if the hatchetmen were hewing at solid
iron. The edges of their weapons are turned, they
can make no impression on the solid mass, and they
fall back to allow the hammer men to take their
places. Down come the great hammers once more
with thundering noise, and the heavy boom almost
drowns the sound of the alarm bell on the top of the
mill, which one of Cartwright s men is now ringing
loudly. In their wild fury the hammer-men strike
not only the door but the stone door posts. The
sparks fly at every blow, but there are no signs as
yet of the staunch door yielding to their frantic
efforts. Mellor and the other leaders are rushing
about like wild men, encouraging the rioters who fire
volley after volley through the yawning windows.
Sheets of flame light up the interior of the mill at
regular intervals, and the frequent groans and cries
which issued from the seething mass surrounding the
walls testify to the accuracy of the aim. Mellor notes
that the volleys come obliquely through the floor
above, and that his enemies are safe behind their
covers. They must try to take them in the rear.

"To the back, lads," he cries.

The defiant voice of Cartwright is heard in reply:

"Come round, we'll meet you."

Some went round to the back, but the proximity of the mill dam deterred them from proceeding far, as they were afraid of falling in in the darkness; one of them indeed, the delegate from Huddersfield, who spoke at the "Shears Inn," Thomas Brook, did slip into the mill goit, and was rescued with some difficulty, losing his hat in the water. Baffled here, the crowd came surging once more to the front.

Again Mellor cries, "To the counting house."

"Welcome! We shall have you there," rings out the defiant voice once more, and the pealing musketry flashed fiercely from the counting-house front as soon as the rioters made their assault there. Mellor, now half wild with rage, again rushes to the mill door. He sees clearly he can never reach his enemies by firing from without, and he is therefore frantic to get into the building before the cavalry come to the rescue. The door has suffered from the tremendous pounding, and Mellor encourages the desperate giant who is now striking at it so wildly to redouble his efforts.

"Bang up, my lads," he cries. "In with you! Kill every one of them!"

The clanging alarm bell on the roof of the mill excites him to madness.

"Fire at the bell!" he shouts, and a dozen voices echo the order. "Shoot away the bell!" "D——n that bell! Get it lads!"

Suddenly the bell ceases, and the rioters again send up a triumphant yell. But it is only the rope that is broken. The defenders of the mill must continue the ringing or the troops will not be aware of their danger; two of the little garrison are therefore sent into the false roof to ring the bell and fire alternately. Cartwright has his attention called to one of the soldiers under his command and immediately changes his own position. All the rest seem to be steadily loading and firing with regularity of clockwork, but this

man is idly playing with his weapon. Cartwright,
who is now next to him, asks if his gun is out of
order.

" No !" sullenly responds the man, without alter-
ing his position.

" Then why don't you fire?" asked Cartwright.

" Because I might hit some of my brothers," replied the miserable traitor, still idly handling his
gun.

The intrepid Cartwright gazed silently at the man
for an instant, his proud lip curling with contempt.
He made no reply, but the traitor was conscious
that that fiery eye took in his slightest movement,
and he knew well that if he ventured to attempt to
betray the garrison his life would be forfeited. The
man had been tampered with by the Luddites, but
he found himself utterly unable to afford them any
active assistance whatever.

The baffled rioters exhibit signs of discouragement
at the stout resistance offered, and they fire with less
regularity. The garrison, however, show no likeli-
hood of yielding, they fire steadily as ever, and the
alarm bell still keeps up its deafening clang. Mellor
rushes about as if he were stark mad. Standing besides the hammer-men, he sees that a panel is broken
at last, and a hole is made in the door about the
size of a man's head. " The door is open !" he yells.
The men crowd around it but they soon discover
that the lock and bars still hold as fast as ever. One
of the garrison in the mill, a soldier it is said, sees
the hole in the door opposite, and taking steady aim,
fires through it. A sharp cry follows, and poor Booth,
the foolish young man who had so lately joined the
Luddites, falls helpless on his face. Again there is
a flash and a report, and Jonathan Dean, who is
plying the hammer, is struck, and the implement
falls from his wounded hand. Affairs are getting
critical, the rioters seem to be baffled at every turn.
" Enoch " has done wonders; it has cleared away

many obstacles, but it fails this time; and the strong men who have wielded it until they can hardly raise it from the ground from sheer exhaustion, lean against the mill-side in despair. The firing has now gone on for nearly thirty minutes; the bell has been heard for miles around, and the flashes of musketry have been seen from Heckmondwike Top; and yet, strange to say, the military have not yet arrived to assist the little garrison. John Walker, one of the most desperate of the Luddites, the man who sang the rollicking ditty at the Shears Inn, has managed to hang by one of the dismantled windows while he takes aim. He is seen from the interior, and a ball is sent whistling through his hat. Once more he catches hold of the stone, and thrusting his pistol through the window, fires at where the flash came from.

"I was determined to do it," he said afterwards, "though my hand was shot off, and hand and pistol had gone into the mill."

The Luddite leaders are now despairing. The steady fire from the mill still continues at regular intervals, the door still resists the ponderous hammers, and the bell still keeps up its clamour. The soldiers must surely be on their way by this time, and the rioters begin to realize the bitter truth that their attack has failed and failed utterly. Their stock of amunition is nearly exhausted, and the firing from their side has consequently nearly ceased. Mellor saw that all was lost, and counselled the men to cease firing. Most of the rioters finding that all was over, sullenly withdrew. Proceeding to the spot where the wounded men lay in the bloody dust, writhing in agony, Mellor discussed briefly with those around the feasibility of taking them away with them. They would gladly do it, but it is plainly impossible. They come to the decision to leave their disabled comrades behind very reluctantly, but they can do no other. The if they were disposed to try issue with them, as

military must be on the way by this time, and even
Mellor boasted at the outset, it was not possible now
as they had used up all their ammunition, and were
practically an unarmed mob. Stooping down to
the poor fellows, Mellor briefly explains the dilemma
and exhorting them to remember their oath, he turns
away with tears of rage and pity in his eyes.

Mellor was the last to leave the spot. He had
come to wreak his vengeance on the man who had
defied the dreaded fraternity to which he belonged,
and he had been defeated utterly. With his black
heart full of impotent rage and fury, he stood alone
in front of the mill, and with an oath, fired the last
shot into the building, and then rapidly retreated
from the spot. He found the rest of the rioters at a
short distance awaiting him; a hurried discussion
was held, and the party then divided, the greatest
number retreating in the direction of Huddersfield.

As the Luddites had up to this time been accustomed to carry all before them their defeat at Rawfolds was quite unexpected and fell upon them with
crushing effect. This was especially the case with
the Liversedge contingent, who now began to realise
that they would be in special danger of detection as
the military and the constables would speedily be
searching every corner of the township and apprehending all who had shown themselves to be in
sympathy with the rioters. Hall fled from the scene
before the attack, which he saw to be hopeless, had
entirely ceased, and keeping to the fields he was able
to reach his lonely home without meeting with a single
person, and his saturnine friend, John Hirst, who
waded through the beck and struck a beeline for his
house at Hightown, was equally fortunate. Crowther, who had taken a prominent position in the
attack, was almost wild with alarm at the perilous
position in which he found himself, and not knowing
where to fly for shelter ran in a purposeless manner
along the sides of the hedge-rows until he found

himself entering Cleckheaton. While hesitating
whether to run through the village or not his eye
fell upon a large building then in course of erection
upon the site now occupied by the Central Chapel,
and he suddenly resolved to hide in one of the flues
until the search had slackened and then to take
such further means of escape as might best commend
themselves to him after careful consideration. Next
day was Sunday, so he knew there would be no
workmen there, but he was not free from alarm nevertheless. Groups of men strolled into the building
at intervals and as they stood there they discussed
the alarming events of the night and referred to the
strict search that was being made for himself. The
day seemed to Crowther the longest he had known
in his life, but the welcome shades of evening fell
at last, and half dead with hunger and cold he
descended and made the best of his way to Leeds,
where he remained in concealment for several weeks
at the house of a relative.

CHAPTER XI.

THE WOUNDED LUDDITES AT THE STAR INN, ROBERTTOWN.

Confess to us, Sir Priest!
Nay, I'll confess to God.—*Bowles*.

'Tis in my memory locked,
And I, myself, shall keep the key of it.—*Shakespeare*.

As the Luddites separated after their humiliating failure at Cartwright's mill, they were advised by their leaders to endeavour to reach their homes as quietly and as speedily as possible. Mellor, though evidently deeply chagrined at his unexpected defeat, exhorted his friends to be of good courage, and raising his clenched fist in the direction of the mill, swore he would yet be avenged on Cartwright, and vowed not only to destroy the machines but the men who owned them.

When the gallant defenders of the mill heard the retreating footsteps of the last of the fierce band that had assaulted it so desperately, they naturally congratulated one another on the success of their efforts. Not that they had at any time felt doubtful about the result, for their position was so strong that it was, as we have shown, practically impregnable. Nevertheless the Luddites had earned themselves such a name for desperate and unheard of deeds, that the little garrison was naturally glad that the long expected stuggle was at last over, and that they had covered with unmistakeable defeat the formidable fraternity that had hitherto been regarded with such abject terror. Now that their victory was assured, their first step was to secure the soldier who had so strangely and so basely refused to do his duty. All seemed still outside the mill, and its defenders could hear nothing except the faint cries of the wounded whom the rioters had not been able to carry away, but Mr. Cartwright, although he was willing under certain conditions to render them assistance, was anxious that the soldiers, or some one who might be attracted by the bell, should arrive and see the actual situation before he opened the doors.

The Rev. Hammond Roberson, a neighbouring clergyman, would probably have been first on the spot but for what we may perhaps call a singular accident. It was well known, as we have before said, that the Luddites had fully resolved to attack Raw-folds mill, and Mr. Roberson, who seems to have been wishful to take part in the affray offered a re-ward to the first who should apprise him when the rioters arrived. A man at Littletown, who was aroused by the alarm bell, and who heard from the firing that the conflict was actually going on, hurriedly dressed himself and ran towards Heald's Hall to apprise the doughty parson. At first the course seemed clear; there was no one stirring in the dark streets, and the anxious messenger heard only the echo of his own feet as he ran, but as he passed the bottom of Listing Lane and dropped into a quick walk in rising the hill, he thought he detected the sound of another footfall in the distance away. The thought instantly crossed his mind—What if it were a Luddite who had noticed him leaving his house and suspecting his errand, had followed to wreak his vengeance upon him? The thought was too much for him; he durst go no further; he would hide behind the adjoining wall and make sure. He did so, and as he crouched in the darkness the second runner came nearer and nearer. As he slackened speed a little in coming up the hill, and gradually drew near to the hiding place, the heart of the first man beat quickly, but no pause was made ; the second man, whoever he was, or what his errand, again began to run, and to the chagrin of the first messenger, sped onward to the hall and won the prize.

Mr. Cartwright was a thoroughly self-reliant man, and seldom felt the necessity of consulting any one respecting the wisdom or otherwise of any course he proposed to take, but there is no doubt that his resolves with respect to the Luddites were at any rate supported and strengthened by his intercourse with Mr. Roberson. A few of our readers may have some recollection of this notable clergyman. In the memory of most he seems to be inseparably connected with a large cocked hat and a grey mare with a long flowing tail. Before coming to Yorkshire he was rector of Caston, in Norfolk, and for many years was accustomed to visit his old flock occasionally, riding when he did so, all the way on his grey mare. Miss Bronte, who it will be remembered makes this strong-minded parson, under the name of Helston, one of her heroes in "Shirley," states that she only saw this remarkable man once, and was much struck by his stern, martial air. She describes him as standing straight as a ramrod, looking keen as a kite, and having far more the appearance of a military officer than that of a minister of the gospel. It is perhaps not difficult to understand how a man hold- ing such strong views as Mr. Roberson should come to be regarded in the unsettled times by one class of the community with such detestation for his high-handed procedure that it was thought necessary for the military to patrol round his house for his protection. Miss Bronte was perhaps right in think- ing that the martial divine would have been decidly more at home at the head of a cavalry regiment than in a pulpit ; but with all his sterness, Mr. Roberson undoubtedly possessed many excellent qualities, and was certainly held in high regard by many of his parishioners. Coming as he did from a people

who are more docile and subservient, the sturdy
independence of the rougher men of the West Riding
would naturally irritate his proud spirit. The difference between the people who would listen to his
admonitions with heads uncovered and those who
doffed their caps to no man, recognising no right of
either squire or parson to question or meddle with
them, was no doubt painfully evident to him, and in
endeavouring to check the unbridled turbulence of
such men as these, he would no doubt be sure he was
doing his duty

While the Rev. Hammond Roberson was preparing
to go to the assistance of his friend Cartwright, and
perhaps to call to his aid the strangely lagging
military, a neighbour of his who had also taken great
interest in the repression of the Luddite movement,
was hurrying to Rawfolds, attracted by the ringing
of the alarm bell. This was Mr. Cockhill, a gentleman of some means, who carried on an extensive
business as a dyer at Littletown. On arriving at
Rawfolds Mr. Cockhill speedily made himself known
to the garrison, and the coast being apparently clear,
the sorely battered mill door was opened, and procuring lights, the defenders sallied forth to reconnoitre
and to render assistance to the wounded men whose
cries had been heard after the departure of the rioters.
The next person to make his appearance was Mr.
Alec. Dixon, the manager of some chemical works
near the mill. Dixon had watched the progress of
the attack from his own house, which was close at
hand, but did not think it prudent to venture out.
Just as he joined the party another person was seen
entering the mill gates. The new comer was found
to be a well-known bon vivant named Billy Clough,
who was carrying out his usual plan of not going
home till morning, when he was alarmed and
effectually sobered by meeting scores of Luddites
running in all directions. He was welcomed by Mr.
Cartwright, who knew him well, and joined in the

search round the building. While they were thus engaged Mr. Roberson, who was armed with a long sword, and a number of others arrived and assisted The mill, with its battered door and door posts and its wrecked windows presented a ruinous appearance and the yard was strewn with broken glass, brick-bats, and debris of various kinds. There were also powder horns, masks, muskets, pickaxes, hammers and other weapons, some of which were broken in the armed attack, while others had been dropped by the baffled rioters, who, finding that their efforts had proved abortive, were anxious to rid themselves of all that would hinder their flight or betray them if they should be captured. There were other sights, however, which met the gaze not far from the door, and soon monopolized all their attention, for there the light fell upon the prostrate form of a young man who was writhing in agony and who implored them piteously to kill him and put him out of his misery. Not far from him was another also prostrate, who asked them feebly for help as they turned the light on his pale face. Dixon at once bent down to assist the poor fellow nearest him, but Cartwright forbade him to do anything towards mitigating his misery until he had confessed who were the leaders in the attack. No reply came from the wounded man except a moan. The low pitiful cry went to Dixon's heart, and he ran into his house and fetched some wine and water with which he moistened the parched lips of the pain-stricken wretch, in spite of Cartwright's cruel words. While this was going on, the other wounded man asked that his head might be raised. Cartwright, in reply, promised him if he would confess he should be taken to his house and everything done to cure him. Again there was no reply. Mr. Roberson looked on in grim silence, but Billy Clough could not resist the cries of the poor choking man; he brought a stone and placed it under his head, amidst the approving cries of a considerable number who had gathered round by

this time. Cartwright noted the indignant murmurs
of the little crowd and deemed it prudent to show
more feeling for the men whose lives were ebbing
away, and they were therefore now, by his orders,
very carefully carried into the building, where they
were made as comfortable as possible until the
medical men arrived. It was soon ascertained that
one of them was Samuel Hartley, of Halifax, a.
cropper, who had formerly been one of Mr. Cartwright's workmen. Hartley was a fine looking
young man about twenty-four years of age, and was
a private in the Halifax local militia, of which body
Mr. Cartwright was captain. The other sufferer
proved to be poor, foolish John Booth, the clergyman's son, who had so recently been drawn into the
meshes of the Luddites in John Wood's workshop,
as recorded in a former chapter. Hartley had received a shot in the left breast while making a blow
at the door. From the agony he suffered in breathing
it seemed as if the shot had passed through his lungs,
and it was evident that his end was near. Booth's
wound was in one of his legs, which had been struck
in such a peculiar way that it was almost shattered
to atoms. From both wounded men the blood
flowed copiously, and by the time the medical men
arrived and bandaged them roughly, they were
suffering considerably from exhaustion.

The wounded men were conveyed to the old Yew
Tree Inn in the first instance, but the crowd began
to gather in such numbers that the authorities had
them taken to the Star Inn, Roberttown. It is
said by some that they were conveyed there because
the people had begun to exhibit so much sympathy
for the deluded men that the military were ill at
ease and were anxious to get them to as great a
distance as possible from the spot. Whatever may
have been the reason, it is an undoubted fact that
the two wounded men were carried as we have stated
to the house of Tommy Sheard, the Star Inn, Robert-

town, much to that good man's chagrin. Tommy
Sheard prided himself on keeping one of the
quietest and most orderly houses in the district, and
was consequently much annoyed when the melancholy procession stopped at his door. The news of
the removal soon spread and thousands assembled in
front of the inn, the horse soldiers being compelled
to ride up and down to keep back the excited crowd
that surrounded the house. Amongst those who
attended the two wounded men at the inn was the,
Rev. Hammond Roberson. Tradition says that he
and others strove hard to persuade them to confess
who were their accomplices and where their arms
were secreted, but that he met with no success
whatever. It is said too that the men were treated
very cruelly, and it seems beyond question that aquafortis was used for some purpose. An old dame who
lived at the Star Inn, as servant at the time, states
that two beddings were destroyed by it and that
Mrs. Sheard, on learning what was being done,
went into the room and interfered, saying she would
have no more of it. The question is—What was the
aqua fortis used for? The old people say to torture
the poor fellows to make them confess! But it
seems altogether incredible that such barbarism could
have been practised by medical men and in the presence too of a minister of the gospel. We would
rather believe that it was used as a styptic to stop
the bleeding from the wounds. Our forefathers it is
well known were in the habit of resorting to extraordinary expedients, and it was no unusual thing
to apply an iron heated to a white heat to cauterise
wounds when other means failed. It was decided
by the medical men to be necessary that Booth's
leg should be amputated, but owing to the great loss
of blood before the surgeons arrived, spasms came on
during the operation and the poor fellow gradually
sank and died about six o'clock in the morning. As
we have just stated, Mr. Roberson had been from
the first anxious to prevail upon the two men to

implicate their accomplices. Hartley appears to have
maintained absolute silence to the end when questioned ; Booth repeatedly regretted that he had in a
weak moment joined the Luddites, but would say no
more. As, however, he lay at the point of death
he signalled to Mr. Roberson, who instantly went
to his side. " Can you keep a secret?" gasped the
dying man. " I can," eagerly replied the expectant
clergyman. " So can I," replied poor Booth, and
soon after calmly expired.

The bullet that proved fatal to Hartley was discovered to have passed through his chest, and was
found lodged beneath the skin of the left shoulder,
from whence it was extracted, with a portion of bone.
He lingered till about three o'clock on Monday
morning, when he fell into an unconscious state and
died soon after. An inquest was held on the bodies
of the two young men, but the proceedings were
very short, the jury speedily bringing in the verdict,
" Justifiable homicide,"—the only possible decision
under the circumstances. Hartley's body was removed to Halifax for interment on the Wednesday
following, with considerable parade. The news of
the Luddite attack had spread widely, and the coffin
was met at the entrance to the town by a multitude
of people. A great many who fell into the procession
wore mourning, and the members of the St. Crispin
Democratic Club, amongst whom were old John
Baines and his sons, wore round their arms badges
of white crape. At Huddersfield the excitement was
so great that the authorities were very uneasy, they
therefore caused Booth's body to be secretly brought
from the Star Inn during the night and it was interred as early as six in the morning of Thursday,
April 16th. It had been arranged that the funeral
should take place about noon, and thousands came
in the early part of the day to see or take part in
the procession, but the hasty proceedings were over
hours before they arrived.

CHAPTER XII.

THE TWO DESERTERS.

Fear sometimes adds wings to the heels.
Montaigne.
I feel my sinews slacken with the fright,
And a cold sweat thrills down o'er all my limbs,
As if I were dissolving into water.—*Dryden.*

It may be remembered that when the Luddites were leaving their rendezvous in the field near the Dumb Steeple, George Rigg, who with William Hall, of Liversedge, had been ordered by Mellor to bring up the rear and make sure that none left the ranks, thought he saw some one mount the wall just as the procession was moving, and drop quietly into the highway. He could not recognise the lithe figure as it appeared and disappeared like a flash of lightning, but he was persuaded that it was one of the Luddites who was deserting at the last moment, and he communicated his suspicions to his companion Hall, who instantly ran to the wall side and listened intently, but, as he could hear nothing, he was inclined to think that his companion had been mistaken. They, however, had not much time for investigation as they could now hear the measured tramp of their companions on the hard road.

"I am pretty positive I saw a man of slight figure vault suddenly over this wall," said Rigg.

"Well, I think you are mistaken," replied Hall." I was as near the wall as you were, Rigg, and I saw nothing. However, he continued, " the men are on the march and unless we follow closely Mellor will perhaps think we have deserted. Let us push on, Rigg."

The last detachment was leaving the field, and
Walker and Rigg had to walk quickly to come up
with them as they reached the highway. Falling in
the rear of the stalwart men bearing the great hammers and hatchets, they marched silently onwards
towards their destination.

Rigg's sharp eyes had not deceived him. A youth,
named Rayner, who resided in the neighbourhood of
Brighouse, and who, like Hartley, had been foolish
enough to join the Luddites on a sudden impulse,
had taken the opportunity of the slight confusion
in the field when the men were separating into companies, to effect his escape in the darkness. Finding himself near a recess in the wall he laid himself
down beneath its shadow till the start took place.
He had come in the company of a neighbour, who
was evidently suspicious of his loyalty to the cause,
for he had called for him at his home, and had never
lost sight of him for an instant after until the order
to separate into divisions came. Rayner then slipped
from his side and stretched himself near the wall, intending to remain behind until the coast was clear,
but, seeing some one approaching towards the spot,
he rose to his feet, just touched the wall with his
hand, and bounded lightly over. Crouching low,
he ran swiftly along the gutter until he had reached
the Dumb Steeple, when darting like an arrow across
the road he was at once lost in the plantation. Here
he remained for a minute or two till the measured
tramp of his confederates died away in the distance,
and then stepped carefully back into the highway.
Rayner was the champion athlete of his native
village, and had proved at numerous festivals his
great fleetness of foot. These qualities were now
to stand him in good stead for what proved to him
a race for life. Buttoning his coat tightly round
his light figure, he started off at great speed along
the highway, which fortunately for him was frozen
as hard as iron. Desperation lent him strength,
and he bounded along the silent road like a deer.

Bye and bye he came to where the road made a
sweep, when, to save time, he again sprang lightly
over the wall and ran in a direct course across the
fields.   He was approaching his native village now,
and he knew every inch of the ground as he bounded
over hedge and ditch, never stopping for breath
till he neared the entrance to the village street. Fearful now of being seen running he changed to a
rapid walk.   He swept quickly past a solitary farmhouse or two, and anon little groups of cottages,
which grew more numerous as the centre of the
village was reached, until the church at last stood
before him.   He had up to this time met no living
thing in his rapid flight, but as he passed the church-
yard gate he heard the heavy foot of the sexton
near the entrance.   Instantly changing his quick
walk into a careless saunter he passed the old man
as he turned the lock in the gate and bid him " good
night."

" Good night," responded the sexton, and then
turning his horn lantern on his companion, he added,
" Oh, Rayner, is that thee?   Good night, lad.   1
have just been into the church to see all was right
before I turned in for the night.   Old Skelton has
been mending the clock."

Just then there was a hoarse whir in the tower
overhead and the clock began to strike the hour.
It was evident that Skelton had not completed his
work satisfactorily for the hammer fell at irregular
intervals.   The sexton counted the strokes.

" Why Rayner," he exclaimed as the last stroke
boomed out with startling distinctness, " it has
struck thirteen !"

" So I counted," replied Rayner, " Old Skelton
will have to come again, John."

" I think so," yawned the sexton as he turned
down the street, " good night, lad."

Resuming his quick step once more Rayner disappeared down a by lane and entering a little cottage

he quietly passed into the upper room and was soon resting his tired limbs on his humble bed. ᵕleep, he could not, till the grey morning broke, the rush of tumultous thoughts banishing for hours all slumber from his eyelids as he tossed his burning and aching head on his pillow. Rayner's aged grandmother, who was the sole occupant of the cottage besides himself, had not noticed his absence, and when he came down weary and languid in the morning her purblind eyes did not detect anything amiss.

As Rayner ate his humble morning meal and reviewed the events of the past eventful ten or twelve hours, he felt thankful that he had obeyed his sudden impulse to fly, and thankful also that he had met no one till he nearly reached his home. The few words he had passed with the village sexton he hardly thought of in his review, but he had good reason to remember them afterwards. Breakfast finished, he passed into the village street to find little excited groups discussing the rumours of another Luddite raid, of which the particulars as yet were only meagre.

Nor was young Rayner the only deserter from the Luddite standard on the eventful night when Cartwright's mill was attacked. The man, Naylor, who it will be remembered joined the Luddites so reluctantly on the direct appeal if his neighbour, Crowther, at the meeting at the Shears, at Hightown, also failed to muster at the rendezvous, although his neighbour had done his best to keep him loyal to his oath. Knowing Naylor's wavering character. and suspecting his remorse and regret for his hasty resolve on the eventful night at the Shears Inn, he had kept a keen eye upon him, and had endeavoured to force him to commit himself to the movement irrevocably. Brook, of Longroyd Bridge, who early discovered the wavering character of his disciple, also visited him frequently and did his best to interest him in the doings at Huddersfield, where the movement was continually gaining strength.

Naylor durst not absent himself from the gathering place of the Liversedge men on that eventful Saturday evening, but as they passed near the fold end which led up to his home a sudden fear seized upon him, and he stole away in the darkness and hid beneath the bed in his own house till, as time passed on, he found that he had apparently not been missed. His absence indeed was not detected till Mellor went through his roll call, and in the excitement of the return journey he was forgotten altogether. As the next hour or two wore away Naylor walked in and out of his house like an unquiet spirit, one moment regretting that he had not joined his companions, and the next feeling glad that he had managed to escape them. His gratification at his good fortune was tempered, however, by a fear of the after consequences. He remembered the fearful oath which condemned him to certain death at the hands of his late confederates, and was ready then to reproach himself with his folly in deserting them and thus rendering himself liable to their vengeance. As the thought of this fearful alternative grew stronger upon him he decided it would be better to rejoin their ranks on their return, and he once more wandered to the fold end to hear if there was any signs of their approach. As he stood gazing wistfully into the darkness, and listening intently for the sound of approaching footsteps, a sudden flash of light was seen in the valley below, and then flash after flash followed in quick succession. The struggle then had commenced—would it not be better for him to join the fray and thus save himself from the traitor's death that awaited him? His doom at the hands of his incensed confederates he now began to look upon as certain, and cursing his folly in not accompanying them, he determined to endeavour to retrieve what he now thought had been a mistake by descending into the valley and joining in the fray. Just then a hand was suddenly laid upon Naylor's shoulder, and turning round he found himself confronted by

Mrs. Fearnsides, his foreman's wife, who had un-
seen been watching his movements for some time.
She saw the critical moment had arrived, and divined
what was passing in the man s mind.

" Naylor," said she, in a low but determined tone,
" get to bed, this instant !"

Naylor, who was startled and overawed, turned
silently into his house and obeyed his mistress's
bidding.   She was a woman of great energy of
character, and her perceptions having been quickened
by what her husband had told her respecting the
ferment amongst Jackson's workmen, she had
observed their proceedings narrowly.   As Mrs.
Fearnsides turned from watching Naylor enter his
house she took a parting glance down the valley in
which the conflict was raging.   She could hear the
heavy thud of the hammers on the stout mill door,
and could see momentarily the buildings as they
were lit up at intervals by the quick discharges of
musketry.

Naylor's wife, who appears to have been a
foolish, gossiping woman, was late that evening with
her household duties. Her husband, who had no
confidence in her ability to keep a secret, told her
none, but she could see by his excited and uneasy
manner that something important was transpiring
in which he was deeply concerned, and she therefore dallied with her work in the hope that she
would get a clue to the mystery.   When her husband
had come into the house and retired to rest she saw
there was little chance of her curiosity being gratified,
so she prepared to retire also. Just, however, as
she was about to leave the lower room she heard
stealthy footsteps, and a minute afterwards a gentle
tap on the door. Opening it she saw standing on the
threshold Thomas Brook, the Huddersfield cropper,
whom she well knew as having often held consulta-
tions with her husband. He had fallen as we have
stated in a previous chapter into the goit during the
attack on Cartwright's mill, and had lost his hat.

When the retreat was made Brooke fled with the rest. As he ran he thought of the certainty of detection if he were met on the highway without hat, and he determined to call at his friend Naylor's as he passed and borrow one. He quickly made known his wishes to Naylor's wife, and she snatched up the hat her husband had just taken off and handed it to him. Brooke promised to return it and then quickly disappeared in the darkness. Could the unfortunate man have foreseen what this transaction would have led to he would certainly have risked the journey home bareheaded. The hat he had lost in the mill goit was found floating on the water next day, and as it became known from Mrs. Naylor's gossip that one of the retreating Luddites had borrowed a hat at her house in Hightown, the authorities were soon on the trail, and the result was the apprehension of Brooke a day or two after. Naylor's hat was, it seems, taken to John Wood's workshop by Brooke, who requested Wm. Hall to take it back to Hightown. This became known to the authorities and led to Brooke's apprehension as just stated.

Mrs. Naylor had hardly recovered from the fright into which Brooke's appearance had thrown her when she again heard a measured tread approaching her door. This she knew was the watch and ward, and she sat cowering over the dying embers of the fire hoping they would march past as usual. They saw however the reflection of the fire through the windows and stopped at the door. One of the constables knew that Naylor was suspected to be a Luddite and he asked his wife where he was. She replied he was in bed, but this answer not satisfying them, she lighted a candle and asked them to go upstairs and see for themselves. They found Naylor there apparently asleep, and seeing nothing of a suspicious character they ordered Mrs. Naylor to put out the light, and left to continue their pursuit of the fugitives.

CHAPTER XIII.

FLIGHT OF THE LUDDITES: LOCAL REMINISCENCES.

In haste he fled and so did they
Each and his fear a several way.—*Butler.*

What is my offence?
Where is the evidence that does accuse me?
Shakespeare.

When it was seen that the attack on Cartwright's mill was an utter failure, the Luddites were not slow to avail themselves of the advice of their leader to disperse as quickly as possible. Many of them threw down their hammers or guns as impediments to their flight and fled precipitately, wading through the beck to save time. Avoiding the highways for fear of meeting the military or the special constables, they spread over the fields in the direction of Mirfield, Hightown, and Roberttown, keeping as widely apart as possible. Many of them were wounded besides those who were left so reluctantly on the ground near the mill, as was proved by evidence given after, and marks of blood were found next morning on the roads leading to Huddersfield for a distance of four miles. George Mellor, Thomas Brook, Joseph Drake, Benjamin Walker, and James Haigh took the direction of Hightown. Brook, who was bruised, and whose clothes were wet from falling into the goit, and James Haigh, who was in great pain from a wound in his shoulder by a musket ball, often lagged behind, but fear of capture urged them onwards, and they sped through the darkness as well as they were able. After calling at Mrs.

Naylor's for a hat, as already stated, they went onwards to Clifton, where they were obliged to slacken their speed from sheer exhaustion. Finding themselves unable to proceed, they, notwithstanding the risk of detection, determined to knock at the door of one of the solitary cottages and ask for some refreshment. The inmate, a widow, was alarmed by the untimely knocking at her door, and was naturally afraid to open it, knowing that there were many desperate characters abroad, but Mellor was in no mood to waste time in parleying with her, and so alarmed her with his oaths and threats that at last she supplied their wants. Not daring to unbar the door, she handed them some muffins and water through a broken pane, for which they paid her a few pence, and then once more resumed their journey.

The whole of the party appear to have reached their homes or places of hiding in safety; but Haigh suffered so much from his wounded shoulder that he found it necessary to seek surgical assistance, and applied next day to Mr. Richard Tattersall, who lived at an out of the way place about four miles from Huddersfield. The surgeon asked him how he came by the wound, and Haigh replied that he had received it by falling down a quarry. He went again on the Tuesday to the quiet surgery to have his wound dressed, but finding the day after that many arrests were being made in and around Huddersfield, he began to feel alarmed, and slipped away in the night with his master, a man of the name of Ardron, who was anxious to shield him if possible. Ardron took him to the house of a relative named Culpan, who lived at Penistone Green, fourteen miles from Huddersfield, in a lonely house. They reached there between twelve and one at night and roused Culpan and his wife, who were in bed. Haigh appeared to be much exhausted by his journey, and was allowed to rest in Culpan's bed. After resting there a few hours, they started before daylight for Ardron's mother's, who lived at Willow Bridge. Finding that the authorities were on his track, Haigh soon after removed to Wragby, and from Wragby to his brother-in-law's, at Methley, where he was apprehended on the 23rd of April.

In tracking the misguided Luddites and endeavouring to pierce the mystery that surrounded that strange organisation, the government made extensive use of hired spies, and there is no doubt that the contemptible miscreants who thus sold themselves to the authorities to hunt down their fellow creatures were often the instigators of the very crimes they afterwards laid to the charge of their poor deluded victims. Many of our readers will remember very well how this was shown to have been done by "the spy, Oliver," at Thornhill Lees, a few years later, and there is abundant evidence to prove that the government were simply doing then what they had done before in a more extensive way during the Luddite troubles. We may give one remarkable case which took place in this immediate locality as an instance in point. James Starkey, a honest, simple hearted carpet weaver, who resided at Millbridge, in one of the brick houses which a few years ago stood on the site of Messrs. Cook's handsome new mill, was accosted one day near his own house by a couple of these government spies. After some conversation, the two miscreants whispered in a very confidential manner that they were Luddites, their errand being to try to find out the best way of destroying Cartwright's mill, and artfully led Starkey to give his opinion on the subject.

"Well," replied the unsuspecting man, "I think it would be easy. The best way, I should say, would be to take a barrel of gunpowder up the goit, and firing it by means of a train, blow the whole concern up!"

The contemptible plotters no doubt rejoiced to hear the outspoken opinion. They had gained their point, and soon after left their victim, having taken care to ascertain his name and residence. To the amazement of Starkey, a troop of horse soldiers stopped at his door in the night and demanded admittance in the King's name. The poor man had been warned by a friend just before, that he had been conversing with spies who had betrayed him, and he had therefore some suspicions of the meaning of the appearance of the soldiers at his door, but instead of yielding himself prisoner quietly, Starkey unfortunately complicated matters by refusing to come out, and threatening what he would do to the first man that entered his house or touched his person. A volley fired in the air warned the bewildered man that it was useless to contend against fate, and he came out and was conveyed to prison to await his trial. Although we shall be anticipating, we may as well state here that Starkey had a very narrow escape of being hanged. Mr. Wadsworth, a solicitor, and the Rev. Hammond Roberson, who both knew him as a neighbour, and were well aware that he had had nothing to do with the Luddites in any way whatever, interested themselves strongly in his favour and got the trial postponed three times at great cost, until fortunately the judges were tired of hanging at the bloody assize that followed, and Starkey was liberated along with a great many others by the proclamation of the king, on bail to enter and try his traverse at the next assizes. He was summoned at the Lent assizes in 1813, but did not appear; one of his bail, however, came into court and said the defendant had been informed by Mr. Alison that it would be unnecessary for him to attend. Mr Parke said defendant had been ill-advised. It was his duty to appear personally in court to answer this indictment, as it was impossible that he could know what course might have been adopted respecting him; but it was not his intention to insist upon his appearance. If the defendant had been tried at the late assizes he (Mr. Parke) should have thought it his duty to have laid evidence before his lordship on the subject. But in consequence of the present tranquil state of the country—the result of those severe but necessary examples which were made on a late occasion—he had determined to lay no more evidence before the court, but to consent to the acquittal of the prisoner; and he hoped this would be considered as a further proof that the government's desire was to do nothing oppressive to any of his Majesty's subjects, and show that their only anxiety had been to restore tranquility and good order. Mr. Justice Le Blanc said there had probably been some mistake in this business. The defendant ought certainly to have appeared in court, but as the counsel for the crown had dispensed with his appearance, and had offered no evidence, they must find him "not guilty." The jury, of course, acquitted the defendant. James Starkey's narrow escape had, as might be expected, a great effect upon him, and he became a very serious character. Joining himself to the Wesleyans, he remained an active and esteemed member of the body at Heckmondwike to the end of his useful life.

Another man, a native of Huddersfield, who had almost as narrow an escape, was in the habit of calling to see James Starkey in after life, when the Luddite movement had been finally put down. This man, who was really a member of the Luddite fraternity, had enlisted in the militia and was ordered to be at York on a certain day. It had been arranged that some frames should be destroyed on the evening before the day in question, and the militia man took part in the business. He was seen and recognised while at the destructive work, and realising his danger he resolved to make a bold stroke to save his imperilled life. Having a friend in the neighbourhood who had a fleet horse, he borrowed it and

made for York at great speed. He had some relations on the way who also kept horses, and dismount-
ing from his tired steed at their door, he obtained a
fresh one and rode on. He arrived at York early in
the morning and walking at once to the quarters, he
represented himself as having arrived late on the
previous evening. The man who had seen him with
the Luddites gave information, and swore positively
to the fact of his having taken part in the frame
breaking, but the jury regarded it as impossible
that he could have been there at the time stated
and at York a few hours later, and consequently acquitted him.

Although the military were very industrious in
this neighbourhood, it does not appear that any great
number of apprehensions took place. The 10th
King's Bays, the 15th Hussars, and the Scots Greys
seem to have been alternately billeted in the town,
at quite inadequate rates, impoverishing the landlords, irritating the discontented and half-starved
portion of the population, and contaminating the
whole neighbourhood. After evening parade they
were told off into parties to patrol the main roads.
As their movements were well known and the
clank of their swords and the tramp of their horses'
feet were to be heard at considerable distance in the
stillness of night, it was easy for anyone to avoid
them, and the Luddites were doubtless often obliged
to them for the distinct manner in which they announced their approach. Practical jokes were, of
course, sometimes played off upon them, which
appeared greatly to have irritated them. Jonathan
Ovenden, a blanket weaver, who resided in one of
the houses on Cawley Hill, determined to play the
soldiers a prank, and with the aid of one or two
cronies loaded a cannon, such as boys have on Guy
Fawkes's day, and fired it in the evening when all
was quiet. The soldiers in the town below took the
alarm and were soon afterwards riding up the hill
at great speed with drawn swords, presenting such

a martial aspect that Jonathan, seriously alarmed by the result of his escapade, hid his cannon in an ash-pit and ensconced himself in a neighbouring hay mow. On arriving at the top of the hill the soldiers made a careful search in and around all the houses, but as they copld find nothing they were obliged to trot their horses down the hill again, chagrined and disappointed at their failure. It is also handed down amongst the traditions of this stirring period that Stephen Greenald, of Healey, then a youth sowing his wild oats, once caused serious perturbation of mind to Mr. Robert Dex, and consequences of a still more direful nature to a doughty soldier who was keeping watch with him over some cropping machines in the mill now occupied by Messrs. John Burnley and Sons (or rather in what existed then of the mill). Passing down the road a night or two after the attack on Cartwhight's mill, Greenald threw a stone through the window.

" The Philistines are upon us," cried Dex, and summoned his martial companion to the defence, but found, alas, that he had fainted with terror.

CHAPTER XIV.

ATTEMPT TO SHOOT CARTWRIGHT.

We cry for bread, your answer is cold steel;
God help the starving poor!—*Kendrew*.

His horse's clanging hoof spurning the solid ground,
As if 'ware of lurking danger.—*Willis*.

Although the check which the Luddites received
at Cartwright's mill seemed to depress the members
of the fraternity and check the practice of frame
breaking for a short time, there was no sign that
the movement was put down or that the men were
likely to return peaceably to their avocations and
accept their defeat quietly. Throughout the country
the half-starved populace rose time after time in rebellion and the military were greatly harassed in
attempting to control them. A tumult took place
at Sheffield on the Tuesday after the attack on Cartwright's mill. A great advance had taken place in
the price of potatoes, and an unreasoning multitude
assembled in the Market-place and attacked the potato
dealers. In the struggle which ensued bushels of
the article were scattered about the streets and large
quantities were carried away in carts, &c. Two or
three sacks of corn were also purloined, and large
quantities of butter and fish speedily disappeared
from the stalls. After two hours the magistrates prevailed upon the rioters to disperse, but unfortunately
in one division of them a cry was set up, " To the
volunteer depot for arms; " and thousands swarmed
in that direction, but luckily the arms were got
away; the disappointed rioters in their rage, however, broke the drums, &c., and did much damage
before they were dispersed by the hussars. On the

day following, a riot broke out at Barnsley, caused chiefly by the high price of provisions, especially potatoes and flour, and the royal volunteers and Wakefield yeoman cavalry had to be sent for to put down the tumult. At Stockport riots also took place, while at Middleton, a few miles from Manchester, four Luddites who were attacking a mill were killed by Mr. E. Burton and a guard of sixteen men, who, encouraged by the example of Cartwright, had determined to defend it.

Throughout the whole of this immediate locality, great alarm and uneasiness prevailed, and the military and magistrates were kept unceasingly at work. The Rev. Hammond Roberson, the martial parson referred to in a previous chapter, was very busy, but the result of his labours to discover lurking Luddites was on the whole of a very unsatisfactory character. The Huddersfield authorities were well aware that the great bulk of the men who had attacked the mill at Rawfolds came from their town, and they were busy all the week hunting supposed culprits. Very few, however, were convicted, as little or no evidence could be obtained, and matters generally wore a very unsatisfactory aspect. Numbers of croppers disappeared from the town; some enlisted for soldiers and were never seen again at their old haunts; while others who had gone away, returned after the disturbances were finally over. Wounded men who had received their injuries at the famous attack on the mill were kept carefully concealed until they had recovered from their hurts. Three were seen in the little plantation near Lower Blacup farm on the morning after the conflict, laid helpless on the ground, unable to proceed, but when the authorities reached the place they had been spirited away, and no one was able to trace them further. The inference is that some of their friends in the adjoining town of Cleckheaton had conveyed them away. As we have before said, the authorities found themselves baffled at every turn, owing to the unmistakable sympathy of the general body of the people with the desperate wretches, who in many cases were positively starving.

Anyone who has studied the history of his country will be well aware what great effects have been produced by ballads in which the uncultured minstrels of the time enshrined the records of the notable deeds of some great leader, or of some movement, and there are evidences that the Luddite rebellion was not destitute of poets who celebrated in rough but vigorous rhyme the progress of the triumphant croppers in their crusades against the machines that robbed their children of their food; or appealed solemnly to the God of Heaven to smite with swift vengeance the oppressors who despised the cries of the poor and needy and ground them down to the very dust. Most of these ballads are triumphant pœans on the glorious deeds of the " cropper lads," like that sung by Walker, at the Shears Inn, Hightown, but some are full of expressions of bitter hatred of Cartwright, who, under a thinly disguised cognomen, is likened to a bloodhound delighting in hunting to death those who opposed his arbitrary will. No doubt these rude home-spun songs, which are now remembered only in disjointed fragments by the few old people who have a personal knowledge of those unhappy days have often been chanted to the music of the sounding " shears," and have fired the heart and stirred the sluggish blood of many of the dreaded fraternity whose deeds at one time daunted the bravest. In collecting materials for this history, we were fortunate enough to fall in with an intelligent, bright-eyed old lady, who, though she was nerly four score, still retained all her faculties unimpaired. She was just one of those garrulous, sharp witted people, full of old world tales and folk-lore, which it delights the hearts of antiquaries to converse with

She knew a great deal about the Luddites, and gave us snatches of ballads which were universally sung amongst them in those troubled times. Here is a specimen verse of one composed after the destruction of the mill between Horbury and Ossett, referred to in a former chapter, in which many from Heckmondwike, Liversedge, Mirfield, Brighouse, and the district round took part: —

Come all ye croppers stout and bold,
  Let your faith grow stronger still,
Oh, the cropper lads in the county ofYork
  Broke the shears at Forster's mill.
    The wind it blew,
    The sparks they flew,
  Which alarmed the town full soon
And out of bed poor people did creep
And ran by the light of the moon;
Around and around they all did stand,
  And solemnly did swear,
Neither bucket, nor kit nor any such thing
  Should be of assistance there.

We will give a specimen verse of another, of a less jubilant character, composed after the failure of the attack on Cartwright's mill, and then introduce our readers once more to the head-quarters of the Yorkshire Luddites: —

How gloomy and dark is the day
  When men have to fight for their bread;
Some judgment will sure clear the way,
  And the poor shall to triumph be led.

Although the authorities were not quite satisfied about some of the croppers at John Wood's workshop, they had not been able to find any positive evidence of wrong doing on their part. Most of them had showed themselves openly in Huddersfield on the morning after the attack on Cartwright's mill, and done their utmost to ward off suspicion by attending strictly to their work on the week following.

We must now ask our readers to accompany us again to this famous finishing shop. Most of the

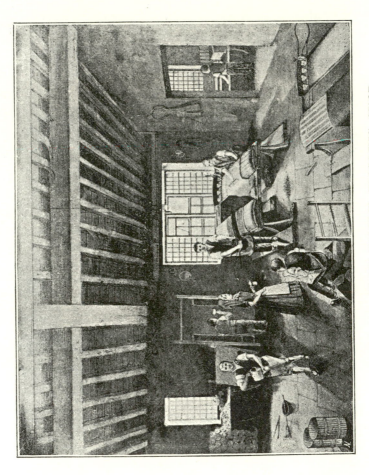

INTERIOR OF JOHN WOOD'S CROPPING SHOP.

men who were present at the initiation of poor John
Booth into the Luddite brotherhood, a few short
weeks before, are present now.   Instead, however,
of being dressed in the croppers' working garb, they
have all their best clothes on.   Some are attired
in black—rather rusty in most instances it is true—
and all have bands of crape round their hats.   They
have all been into the town to attend the funeral
of Booth, whose body, as we stated in a previous
chapter, it had been publicly announced would be
interred about noon.   When they entered the busy
main streets they encountered many who, like themselves, had come to join in the melancholy procession, and learned to their mortification that the
alarmed authorities had caused the body to be
interred some hours before.   If there existed in
George Mellor's dark, flinty heart a particle of
feeling, it had been entirely monopolised by his
dead friend, Booth, and when he ascertained that
he had been deprived of the melancholy satisfaction
of following Booth's dead body to the grave, his
whole frame quivered with passion, and his alarmed
comrades, afraid of what he might divulge in his
wild outburst, persuaded him to return with them
to the workshop.   Arrived there, his long suppressed emotion found vent and he raged about the room
like an imprisoned tiger.   His companions listened
for some time in gloomy silence to his wild curses,
but his fellow workman, Smith, at length attempted
to pacify him.

"Come, Mellor," said he, "if we cannot storm
and curse as heartily as thee, we all feel the loss
of poor Booth as well as thou does.   If cursing
could do any good I should say curse on and would
do my best to help thee, but it will not, and I think
it behoves us to consider the living as well as the
dead."

"Curse the villain, Cartwright! I will yet have
his heart's blood," yelled Mellor, ferociously, his

lurid eyes flashing fire. "Lads," said he, and his voice suddenly changed to a low tone, "have you heard he is coming here on Saturday?"

"Coming where?" asked Thorpe, in a startled some time back by the rapid movements of the tone.

"Coming to Huddersfield to be a witness at the trial of the soldier who is to be brought before a court martial on that day, because he would not fire at us out of the mill. I am told by one of my friends at the barracks that the trial will begin at two o'clock. Now Cartwright puts up at the "Plough," can't some of us go there, and poison, stab, or shoot the villain?"

"Poison him you can't," replied Thorpe. "Joe Drake who sweethearts the barmaid, says he neither tastes nor sups anything at the 'Plough.' The grim-looking old bloodhound pays for his dinner and his glass, but he finds someone else to eat and drink for him. Since the Ludds threatened his life he suspects everybody, and will neither bite nor sup anything at the inn. He seldom leaves the town now later than four o'clock in the afternoon, and then when in a lonely place tears away at the greatest speed of his horse."

"Well, now, look here," said Mellor, after a long pause, during which he stood with knitted brow and bent head, "let some of us go to Bradley Wood and wait his coming. If we plant ourselves on each side of the road we can surely hit him. Come, now, we'll draw lots who takes the job."

About a dozen men stood round and drew lots silently, but upon whom the lots fell is not positively known. Suffice it to say that when the day came "the avengers," as they were called, were at their posts.

On Saturday, April 18th, the day appointed for the trial of the disobedient soldier, Mr. Cartwright arrived at the Plough Inn, Huddersfield, a little before two o'clock, and leaving his horse in care of the ostler, walked to the building where the court martial was to be held. He was warmly welcomed by the officers, who had conceived a great admiration for him on account of his brilliant defence of his mill. The military had been much harassed for some time back by the rapid movements of the Luddites, and also by the cowardly conduct of the masters. The very name of Luddites seemed to strike terror into the hearts of the master cloth finishers, and instead of attempting a defence, their only plan seemed to be to summon the military.

As the Luddites had generally completed their work before the soldiers could get to the spot, the poor men had often to wince under the jeers and laughter which followed them as they trotted back to their quarters. Here at last, however, was a millowner who was resolved to hold his own, who had taught the rioters a lesson they were not likely to forget, and the officers naturally received him with great demonstrations of respect.

The trial of the soldier occupied but a very short time. His offence was so grave that no defence could be offered, and when Mr. Cartwright had given his evidence the case was complete, as the soldier neither denied nor attempted to defend his breach of dicipline. The officers had been put to great trouble and inconvenience by the persistent attempts of the Luddites to corrupt their men, and now they had at last caught an unmistakable traitor, and his punishment they determined should be heavy. Dead silence pervaded the court as the presiding officer rose and after enlarging on the enormity of the crime committed, concluded by announcing that the court adjudged the traitor 300 lashes. An involuntary exclamation burst from the lips of the man at the fearful sentence, and even Mr. Cartwright craved the merciful consideration of the court on behalf of the prisoner. The only

reply of the president to Mr. Cartwright was a
courteous bow, and the proceedings were closed.

Within two hours of his arrival at the "Plough
Inn," Mr. Cartwright was again on horseback, canter-
ing through the streets towards home. The horse
ambled gently along until the outskirts of the town
was reached and the houses grew fewer and fewer,
and then the gentle trot became a rapid gallop. He
had only proceeded about a mile from Huddersfield
when the clatter of the horse's heels were heard by the
two "avengers" who were lying in wait in a thick
coppice. On he came at a great speed, when suddenly a pistol was discharged and a ball went whizzing
over the horse's hind quarters. The dash of the
rider had spoiled the intended assassin's aim. Cartwright struck his spurs deep into his good horse,
which wheeled suddenly and again started at a
famous speed. Just as the horse swerved another
pistol was discharged from the opposite side of the
road but this too missed its aim, and the startled
horse bearing its rider madly onward was speedily
out of sight. The "avengers" were thwarted;
their prey had once more escaped, and hiding
their pistols among the tree roots, they ran off in
different directions towards Huddersfield. Cartwright's bravery was beyond all question, but he
felt sick at heart as he drew the rein at his own
door. If he were thus to be made a target in open
day, within a few miles of his own house, life would
not be worth living.

CHAPTER XV.

PUNISHMENT OF A TRAITOR.
MR. HORSFALL, OF MARSDEN.

A universal horror
Struck through my eyes and chilled my very heart.
—*Rowe*

I do defy him, and I spit at him ;
Call him a slanderous coward and villain ;
Which to maintain, I would allow him odds ;
And meet him were I ty'd to run on foot.
Even to the frozen ridges of the Alps.—*Shakespeare.*

On the Tuesday following the events recorded in
the last chapter, a procession of a striking character passed along the road which had been the
scene of the audacious attempt on the life of Cartwright. On the morning of that day a troop of
cavalry escorted to Rawfolds the miserable delinquent who had been condemned by the court martial
to receive his punishment at the scene of his crime.
The decision of the court with respect to the place
where the sentence was to be carried out was not
made known to Mr. Cartwright, and he was much
pained when he found out that the soldier was to
be whipped near his mill. The appearance of the
military with the prisoner in their midst attracted
hundreds of people, who formed in a ring when the
place was reached, and the trees around were black
with those who had climbed them to witness the
novel spectacle. As the man appointed to inflict
the punishment produced the instrument of torture,
and the soldier was bound and his back laid bare,
the onlookers watched the preparations with evident

concern. And now all is ready for the infliction
of the fearful chastisement. Stepping forward and
measuring the distance for an instant the man raises
the whip, it whistles swiftly through the air and
descends on the white back of the soldier on which
a broad red line appears, while underneath the
muscles quiver visibly. Again and again the whip
is raised and descends, and by and bye the onlookers
are shocked to observe that the skin is broken, the
blood begins to trickle slowly down, and the sight
soon becomes sickening. The women in the crowd,
for there are many present, turrn their eyes from the
sight, and even stout-hearted men cannot forbear
to express their pity for the poor wretch, who with
pale face and firmly compressed lips, suffers the
dreadful torture. There is a movement at the outskirts of the crowd and a lane is formed, down
which Mr. Cartwright passes, closely guarded
by soldiers, who clear the road for him. Many
make way sullenly, gazing upon the stern man with
dark and threatening brows and muttering fiercely.
Their thought plainly is that " the bloodhound,"
as they now almost invariably call him, has come
to gloat on the sufferings of the victim, but to their
astonishment, when he reaches the place where the
officer is standing, he asks that the bloody scourge
may now rest and that the remainder of the sentence
may not be carried out. The officer in command
listens to him respctfully and then, without answering, signals after a brief pause to the man who
wields the cat to go on. Again the whip descends,
and at every stroke the skin seems to be stripped
from the shoulders to the loins. Only twenty
lashes have been given as yet; two hundred and
eighty more are required to complete the sentence.
It is plain that the man will never live to receive
them. The cries of the women wax louder: the
ominous muttering of the man grows fiercer. The
doctor examines the sufferer and feels his pulse.
The surging crowd gather nearer to hear his report,
but the stolid fuctionary simply steps back to his

place saying nothing, and the signal to proceed
again is given. Five strokes more are inflicted
and the crowd surges wildly, angry exclamations
filling the air. Again Cartwright stands before
the officer and pleads, passionately this time, for
the remission of the remainder of the sentence. He
is listened to as before respectfully, and is this time
answered. He urges his request with greater
vehemence, and at last he prevails. The signal
to stay the punishment is given, and the sufferer,
who seems dazed and almost unconscious of what
is passing around him, is unbound.

Cartwright's successful pleading on behalf of the
soldier restored him a little to popular favour,
which he had almost wholly lost by his unnecessarily
harsh behaviour towards the two men who were
shot down at the recent attack on his mill, but
the current of feeling ran strongly against him,
and he was obliged to take great precautions to
shield himself from the vengeance of the Luddites.
Only a short time after this, thirteen pairs of
shears belonging to him which he had sent to Huddersfield to grind were, to his intense mortification,
broken to pieces, and he was given to see repeatedly that it would be dangerous to relax any of the
precautions he was taking. As we have repeatedly
shown there were many, amongst the middle and
trading classes even, who sympathised with the
class below them, knowing well their half-starved
condition. Although they did not defend the lawless proceedings of the mobs, they looked upon their
rash deeds as the acts of desperate men, who, finding themselves unable to obtain employment, or in
danger, if the introduction of machinery was not
stopped, of losing the little work they might have,
were ready to embark in any enterprise however
wild that promised an alleviation of their cheerless
lot. The feeling of the crowd in favour of the
soldier who would not fire on those he called " his
brothers " was unmistakable. Men driven mad by

starvation ought not, they thought, to be shot down like dogs, and it was no doubt a feeling of this kind that induced Mr. Abraham Jackson, of Hightown, a man remarkable for kind heartedness, to slip dexterously into the suffering soldier's hand a guinea as he stood near him when his punishment was over.

A little later in the day the feeling we have just referred to was again manifested as one of the soldiers who had formed the little garrison was fighting the battle over again, and telling to a little group how he had fired through the hole in the mill door and hit the swarming Luddites. So far from calling forth the admiration of his hearers the astonished boaster found himself looked upon with something akin to disgust by his listeners, who seemed to regard him almost as a murderer. The notable door was, of course, removed when the mill was restored, and lay in the mill yard a long time. Eventually it was taken to the graveyard of the old White Chapel at Cleckheaton, where it was used to protect the coffin of one of the Blakelock family from the desecrating hands of the "Resurrectionists," or "Body snatchers," who were then in the habit of robbing the graves to supply the doctors with subjects for dissection. The horror which was felt throughout the country at the practices of these men will be remembered by the elder portion of our readers, who will dobutless be familiar with many a frightful tale of their proceedings. The money made by these degraded men was fabulous. A leading Resurrectionist once received £144 for one evening's work, and at his death left £6,000 to his family. The door that had withstood the attacks of "Enoch" may, however, be trusted for the protection of the body which now lies beneath it.

Next to Mr. Cartwright the most hearty opponent of the Luddities was Mr. William Horsfall, of Marsden, brother to Mr. Abraham Horsfall, of the Wells, Huddersfield, a well known family of the period.

This Mr. Horsfall was an excitable, impetuous man, violent in manner, but kind and forgiving to his own workpeople, by whom he was respected and beloved. He was well known to be an implacable enemy to the Luddities, who, as may well be imagined, returned his hatred with interest. Mr. Horsfall never talked of the dreaded fraternity with bated breath, like most of his neighbours, but spoke defiantly about them at all times and in all places. He had been heard, indeed, in one of his fits of passion to express his desire to ride up to the saddle girths in Luddite blood! Exasperated by the successes of the rioters in demolishing frames, he grew so violent in his hatred of the Ludds that it culminated in a positive craze, and the children to teaze him would run out in front of his horse and cry "I'm General Ludd!" "I'm General Ludd!" on which he would immediately fall into a violent passion and pursue the frightened urchins hotly with the horsewhip. Such being the character of Mr. Horsfall it can scarcely be wondered at that his mill should be marked out for destruction at the meeting held at the Crispin Inn, Halifax, as narrated in a former chapter, indeed as we have said it was only decided to attack Cartwright's first by the tossing of a shilling. At Horsfall's mill at the upper end of the road and on an elevation about level with the present dam, cannon were planted behind a wall pierced with openings three feet ten inches wide. Through these apertures the cannon could be pointed so as to command the entire frontage of the mill and be fired upon an approaching enemy. This somewhat primitive battery still exists, but the artillery has been removed long since. The apertures just referred to have been walled up, but their outlines are still plainly to be traced. In addition to these means of defence the workmen employed at the mills were armed and kept watch and ward all through the night as at Cartwright's.

In the noble defence of Rawfolds mill Mr. Horsfall had taken the warmest interest. He congratulated his friend on his pluck and determination at their first meeting at Huddersfield after the event, and loudly expressed with great heat his own determination to defend to the utmost his machines, if it should prove necessary. Not content with this loud avowal of his resolution, Horsfall did his best to infuse some of his own daring spirit into the people with whom he came in contact. Mr. Woodcock, late of the Marsh Iron Works, near Cleckheaton, states that his grandfather, Mr. Jonathan Brook, of Longroyd, was a manufacturer of cropping machines, and that about this time he received a letter, signed "Captain Blunderbuss," stating that "if he made any more such machines, Ned Ludd would fire his premises and lay his works in ashes." On receipt of this Mr. Brook decided to abandon the trade and to issue hand-bills announcing it. On going to the printing office he was met by a cropper (the family always thought it was George Mellor) to whom Mr. Brook stated his errand, when the cropper said, " If you assure me this is true you need go no further." The resolution of Mr. Brook and the conversation related above became known in Huddersfield in a few days. Mr. Horsfall called at the foundry soon after, when Mr. Brook, on meeting him, held out his hand as usual. "No," said Mr. Horsfall, drawing back, " I understand you dare not make any more cloth-dressing machines. I won't shake hands with a coward."

From what we have stated our readers will be able to realise clearly the sort of man Mr. Horsfall was, and will easily comprehend how he came to be feared and hated by the Luddite fraternity. Up to the time of the attack on Cartwright's mill the star of the frame breakers appears to have been in the ascendant. Everywhere they were feared and dreaded, and by their rapid movements and daring actions they struck terror into every heart, but now the spell was broken. Cartwright, with his small garrison, had defeated them utterly, and now under the remonstrances and inspiriting advice of Mr. Horsfall the masters were beginning to talk of organised resistance to the rioters and were showing a bolder front to the enemy.

The Luddite leaders were fully alive to the fact that their movement had received a serious check, and that something must be done to restore its lost prestige and to teach the masters a salutary lesson. The mysterious messenger of the Luddites had been flitting about pretty frequently since the affray at Cartwright's mill, and a number of meetings had been held, but the activity of the authorities had frightened the timid, and the musters were not so large as formerly. Besides this, the perils from which so many were hardly sure they had escaped daunted their hearts, and their talk was of a more cautious sort than of old. Mellor was getting tired of all this doubt and uncertainty and resolved upon a blow which would strike terror into the hearts of his enemies. The failure of the attack on Cartwright's mill and the loss of his friend Booth had almost driven him frantic, and he raved at the Luddite meetings like one possessed. These violent outbursts had only the effect of scaring effectually the more timid, who knowing their movements were watched, were afraid lest Mellor's rash language and proceedings would place all their lives in jeopardy.

In our next chapter we must again introduce our readers into the councils of the Luddite leaders.

CHAPTER XVI.

A DEED OF BLOOD.

Is there a crime
Beneath the roof of heaven that stains the soul
With more infernal hue than foul
Assassination?—*Cibber*.

We have said that if there existed a particle of
feeling in the dark, flinty heart of George Mellor
it was certainly monopolised by his dead friend
Booth. After the decease of that poor misguided
young man he seemed altogether to lose his balance.
He grew perceptibly day by day more bitter against
the masters who had adopted the new machinery,
and his subtle brain was always planning and schem-
ing for their injury or destruction. Naturally gloomy
and reserved in disposition, and given to fits of
violent passion, he grew more gloomy and desperate
still. Booth had exercised a restraining and beneficent influence over him, and now he was dead,
Mellor's whole thoughts appeared to be engrossed
with what he deemed the wrongs of his class, and
the whole subject of his conversation with his fellow
workmen was how to avenge them. His outward
appearance was a true index of the fierce and tumultuous passions that reigned within his soul. He
had grown careless and slovenly of late, his cheeks
had become pale, his brow careworn, and his lurid,
bloodshot eyes were now habitually fixed upon the
ground. The man was sinking, gradually perhaps,
but surely; the hot insatiate craving for revenge
which filled his bosom seemed to shrivel him body
and soul.

THE RISINGS OF THE LUDDITES.

It is the afternoon of Tuesday, the 28th of April, 1812, seventeen days after the attack on Cartwright's mill, and the scene is John Wood's workshop. Mellor, who had been exceedingly violent in his language in talking to his fellow workmen during the dinner hour, had been continuing his invectives in conversation with his companion Smith during the labours in the afternoon, when so excited did he become that he eventually worked himself into a positive frenzy, and, as his manner was when strongly moved, paced backwards and forwards in the room with rapid and uneven strides, stopping now and then to give vent to his feelings in threats and curses. Some of the men have been repeating to him Mr. Horsfall's latest words of contempt and defiance of the Luddites. They are keen and biting like most utterances from that quarter, and, as might expected, their effect on Mellor is great. All his pent up evil passions are let loose, and he positively roars with fury. By and by he becomes quieter and gradually sinks into one of his moody fits. His busy brain is at work and he soon after propounds a dreadful scheme of revenge on the daring manufacturer, in which he allots his fellow workman a part. Smith stands aghast at first, but frightened by the vehemence of Mellor, consents in the end to stand by him and aid him in the execution of his foul plot. Having secured the adherence of Smith, Mellor next went into the adjoining room, where he found Benjamin Walker, William Hall, of Liversedge, William Walker, and Walker's father, all Wood's workmen, and William Thorpe, who worked at Fisher's shop across the way.

"Now lads," said Mellor, abruptly, "I've made up my mind. We must give up this frame breaking—it's no use. Since that cursed attack on Cartwright's place we've just been jeered and laughed at. Horsfall is crowing louder than ever, as you all know, and unless you're prepared to make an example of him we may just as well shut up. Now, lads, there's only one way. Smith and I have settled it. We're going to shoot Horsfall to-day, and we want thee, Thorpe, and thee, Walker," (nodding his head towards the two men) "to help us. Two could not hit Cartwright the other day, let's see if four can down Horsfall."

For a moment there was no reply to this atrocious proposal; the harsh voice of Thorpe, however, soon broke the silence.

"I'll make one, George," he said, in his usual low, sullen tone; "it's true, as thou says, we are jeered and laughed at now. It's about time we let some of them see that the Ludds are not a pack of scared old women."

"Now, then," said Mellor, turning to Walker, "thou must make up thy mind, Ben, whilst I am away at my 'drinking.' It's hard if poor Booth and Hartley are to be shot down like wild animals and we are never to have our revenge for the murder of our brethren.

Then raising his voice and striking his clenched fist on the frame over which Walker was bending with a half scared look on his face, he added in a vehement shout, "I'm determined to do for Horsfall this day!" Then turning on his heel, he left the building.

Benjamin Walker ,went to his "drinking" also soon after, and was absent about half-an-hour. When he returned he found Mellor in his room and with him Varley, Hall, Smith, and Thorpe. Mellor was loading a large pistol of peculiar construction, and William Hall was watching him. The pistol had an iron handle, was curiously ornamented with screws at the sides, and had a formidable-looking barrel nearly half a yard long. It was of foreign manufacture, and had been brought from Russia by Mellor who had been in that country. Hall seemed to be watching the loading operation with much interest.

Mellor put a considerable quantity of fine powder into it, and afterwards two others flattened and cut partly into slugs. The charge appeared to be a heavy one, but to the astonishment of Hall, Mellor then put in a fourth ball and rammed the whole well down.

"You surely don't mean to fire that, George," exclaimed the astonished Hall, "why, man, it will burst."

"I do mean to fire it," replied Mellor, emphatically, "I mean to give Horsfall this! Will you go with us?"

"No," stammered Hall, "I don't like to go."

Mellor turned from him in disgust. "Here, Walker," said he, handing him a pistol, "that is yours. It is loaded with double ball like mine. It will be strange if we can't some of us hit the sneering villain!"

Walker hesitated on instant and then took the pistol, but with evident unwillingness. Examining the weapon he found it was primed and loaded nearly to the top.

While this was going on in one part of the room, the grimly, taciturn Thorpe was standing at a window, chopping a bullet in pices for slugs. Having accomplished his purpose, he too loaded his pistol, and then stood ready for action.

"Now you, Walker and Smith, can start, and Thorpe and I will follow by another road," said Mellor. "If we were to all go together we should attract attention may be. You go up the road, and we will meet at Radcliffe's plantation. When you get there climb over the wall and wait; you will most likely be there first."

Walker and Smith, in obedience to the order, immediately left the shop and proceeded up the highway to the appointed rendezvous; and Mellor, putting on a bottle-green top coat, concealed the pistol beneath it, and signalling to Thorpe, left the building in his company.

As Smith and Walker proceeded up the highway past the Warren House Inn, Walker, who had gone thus far in absolute silence, suddenly stopped when above the houses, and leaning against the wall, said, " I will not do this deed, Smith."

"Well," replied Smith, "I don't much like the job myself, but it will never do to turn back now Let us go on and try to persuade Mellor and Thorpe to give it up."

Walker hesitated a few minutes before deciding and thought the matter carefully over. To return and have to answer to the impetuous, headstrong Mellor for deserting him would never do. Walker knew well the man with whom he had to deal, and shrank from the contest. There was the chance that he might be persuaded to give up his mad scheme when they met in the wood, as suggested by Smith, and he therefore decided to go on to the appointed place of meeting. If the reader supposes from the hesitancy displayed by Walker that he was any better than the rest of the villains leagued to carry out this foul plot, he is woefully mistaken. Mellor, with all his faults, had a good share of brute courage, but Walker was not only a great coward but a contemptible sneak.

Smith and Walker had been in Radcliffe's plantation about ten minutes when Mellor and Thorpe leapt the wall a short distance from where they were standing. Walker seeing them urged Smith to go to them at once and try and persuade them to give up the scheme; Smith accordingly went. Both Mellor and Thorpe treated the suggestion with utter contempt. Mellor stormed in his usual fashion.

"Now look here, Smith," said he, "if either of you attempt to leave the plantation before the deed is done, I will shoot him whichever it is. Stand where Walker is, and Thorpe and I will be at the corner. If we miss Horsfall then you two be ready to fire. I will whistle when we see him coming."

Smith left them and went to the spot where Walker was waiting, about twenty yards away, and Mellor removing a stone out of the wall at the corner, so as to be able to command a view of the road without being seen, got his pistol in readiness and stood on the look-out for his victim. Anyone viewing the little plantation now would scarcely think there was sufficient covering to screen anyone, but it would undoubtedly be much thicker wooded at that time. It stands in a corner where four roads meet, and any one taking up the position occupied by Mellor and Thorpe will see that it commands the highway up which the doomed horseman was to come. At present there are some houses close at hand, but these are evidently modern erections, and the same may be said of the houses below, down to the old buildings just above the Warren House Inn. The road at the point where Mr. Ratcliffe's plantation is would doubtless be rather lonely at the time of the Luddite disturbances, but after all it was a thoroughfare much frequented, and there was always on market days an intermittent stream of people coming towards the town or returning homewards—farmers in gigs, labourers with carts, little clothiers with their samples on their shoulders, or cottagers with their market baskets and bundles.

At about half-past five o'clock on this evening Mr. Horsfall had mounted at the door of the George Hotel, Huddersfield, rash and defiant as usual, and ridden off on his homeward journey. A few minutes after he was out of sight, his friend, a Mr. Eastwood, of Slaithwaite, who had often remonstrated with him on the imprudence of his foolish and defiant talk respecting the Luddites, called at the George to propose for protection and companionship to ride home with him. On hearing he had gone Eastwood cantered quickly after him, hoping to be able to overtake him. About a quarter to six o'clock Mr. Horsfall pulled up his horse at the Warren House Inn, at Crosland Moor, kept by Joseph Armitage.

Finding there were two of his old workpeople there,
John Sykes and Joseph Sykes, who had taken up
the trade of cloth hawkers, he treated each of them
with a glass of liquor in a friendly way. He did
not alight from his horse, but drank a glass of rum
and water on the saddle, and then rode on. At
the time he left the Warren House Inn door, a man
named Parr was riding about a hundred and fifty
yards behind him, and had him in full view on
rising ground up which they were going. Mr. Horsfall, who very seldom rode fast, is proceeding
steadily on his journey. He nears the little plantation where the assassins are waiting for him, and
when he comes nearly abreast of it Mr. Parr sees
four men in dark coloured clothes walking
under the boughs. All at once—there comes
a crack as of a gun and a puff of smoke—
Mr. Horsfall's horse jibs round and Mr. Parr sees
him fall with his face on its neck. Two other shots
are then fired. Parr spurs his horse and rides swiftly to the spot. By a great effort the wounded man
raises himself painfully up by the horse's mane
and calls out "Murder!" As the cry reaches his
ear Mr. Parr sees a man in a bottle green topcoat
spring on to the top of the wall with one hand and
both feet as if intending to attack Horsfall. Parr is
now quite near and calls out to the murderer "What!
are you not contented yet?" and rode up to the
wounded man, who was already dripping with blood,
upon which the assassin, who it would appear had
not seen Parr before, dropped back over the wall
and disappeared. Horsfall said to the farmer, for
such he was, who came so providentially to his
assistance,

"Good man, you are a stranger to me, but pray
ride to Mr. Horsfall's house and get assistance. I
am shot!"

Parr, supporting him in his arms—for he grew
sick and faint and was falling—said, "Are you Mr.
Horsfall, of Marsden?"

"I am," he groaned, and the blood spurted from his side as he fell off his horse.

Parr then drew him to the side of the road, and a clothier, named Bannister, who had come up directly after Mr. Parr, supported him in his arms until two boys, who came up with a cart, removed the dying man to the Warren House Inn.

The murder was also witnessed by a labourer in a field near the spot, but he was seized with terror and fled. As poor Horsfall was carried down the road he bled profusely from the wound. Two children who were gathering dung on the road had run past the Warren House Inn, calling out " Mr. Horsfall is shot," and the landlord and the two hawkers ran to the spot and reached it in time to assist in his removal. An old cropper, who has lived close to the inn all his life, told us that he well remembered the wounded man being brought to the door in the cart, and saw the blood run down his clothes to the ground as they carried him in. The old hostelry exists no longer as a separate building: a co-operative store has been built in front of it, and the room into which Mr. Horsfall was borne now forms a portion of the stores. The old cropper went with us into the building and showed us the room into which he remembered Mr. Horsfall being taken, but it is of course much altered, nothing but the outer walls remaining as they were at that time.

CHAPTER XVII.

DEATH OF HORSFALL : FLIGHT OF THE ASSASSINS.

It is hard
To feel the hand of death arrest one's steps ;
Throw a chill blight o'er all one's budding hopes
And hurl one's soul untimely to the shades —*Kirk White.*

From the body of one guilty deed
A thousand ghostly fears and haunting thoughts proceed.
Wordsworth

Poor Horsfall was laid upon a bed in the best room of the Warren House Inn and a messenger despatched for medical assistance. In compliance with the request he made as he fell wounded from his horse, Mr. Parr had ridden rapidly off to acquaint the brother of the unfortunate man with the tragic event that had happened. Dr. Houghton did not arrive till between eight and nine o'clock and found that another medical practitioner had been summoned and had done his best for the doomed man. The patient was lying on the bed with his clothes off. He was pale, sick and much exhausted from the great loss of blood ; his pulse being so weak and tremulous that it could scarcely be felt. On examining him Mr. Houghton found that he had two serious wounds on the upper portion of his left thigh, and five others on different parts of his person. Two balls were extricated and some restoratives administered, after which the patient seemed to rally, but no well founded hope was held of his recovery. It was almost certain that the femoral artery was seriosly injured, a ball having passed from his left to his right side from whence it was abstracted. About four o'clock on Wednesday he appeared to be better and was more cheerful. Turning to Mr. Houghton, he said,

"What is your opinion, doctor?"

The doctor had just heard the fervent wishes of Mr. Horsfall's brother for his recovery, but he could not encourage any hope.

"Indeed, Mr. Horsfall," he replied, "I consider you in a dangerous state."

"These are awful times, doctor," sighed the poor victim.

Mr. Scott, a magistrate, was summoned, to whom Mr. Horsfall made a declaration, after which his strength gradually failed him, and he died about thirty-six hours from the time of being shot.

The crowd who had surrounded the building, discussing all kinds of wild rumours of the aims and intentions of the desperate Luddites, heard of Mr. Horsfall's death with dismay, and hastened home with pale faces to spread the news that the man who had so often defied the Ludds lay cold and still at the Warren House. The lost prestige of the Luddites was for the moment restored. Their deeds were again the theme of every tongue.

Turn we now to the four assassins. The shots were no sooner fired and the result seen than they all fled in terror from the spot. As Mellor reached the place where Smith and Walker were standing, he cried

"Curse you for chicken-hearted cowards that you are! You should have fired however it had been."

Then after a pause, he cried with exultant voice as they ran across the wood, "The villain, Horsfall, is done for however. I am pleased our plot has succeeded this time."

His companions, however, did not share in his brutal joy; terror and remorse seemed to have laid fast hold of them already as they fled across the intervening fields towards a dense wood at hand. Thorpe handed his pistol to Walker, probably wishing to be relieved of it. The latter took it mechanically, noticed that the barrel was still warm and the pan

open, proving that it had been fired; then in a fit
of terror he threw it from him. Mellor, who was
the most collected of the four, knew that if the
weapon was left there it would be likely to lead to
their being traced and apprehended, he therefore
stopped to pick it up, grumbling fiercely at Walker
for his recklessness. A labourer in the field they
were crossing saw them running. He was ignorant
of the tragic event that had transpired in the
highway beyond, but the speed of the runners
attracted his attention. As they climbed over the
wall into Dungeon Wood, Mellor's overcoat flew
back and the huge pistol he carried became visible.

The ploughman caught sight of the formidable
weapon, and said to himself, "There go the Ludds;
we shall have mischief to-night."

On arriving at Dungeon Wood, Smith and Walker
hid their pistols in some ant-hills and the four
separated. Before parting, Mellor gave Walker two
shillings, as the latter had no money, and ordered
him and Smith to go towards Honley and they would
take another direction. Walker and Smith went as
requested to Honley, and entering a public-house
at the lower end of the town called for beer.
Opposite where they were sitting was a drunken
collier, who had evidently been carousing pretty
deeply. Soon after some pale, frightened men came
in from Huddersfield market and brought word that
Mr. Horsfall had been shot and was lying half dead
at the Warren House. Upon that being said, Smith,
who excelled in whistling, began to whistle a merry
tune, and the tipsy collier, pleased with the perform-
ance, got up and tried to dance. This circumstance,
so trivial in itself, was the means of fixing the events
of the evening in the memories of all who witnessed
the scene in the public-house After drinking some
eight or nine pints of ale at the inn, Walker and
Smith left and made their way home, which they
did not reach till near ten o'clock.

After the four confederates had separated in
Dungeon Wood, Mellor and Thorpe made for the
house of Joseph Mellor, a cloth dresser, who was a
cousin of George's. Entering the workshop, Mellor
took off his topcoat and then asked Thomas Durrance,
one of his cousin's apprentices, to go with him upstairs. Durrance accompanied as requested, and
when the upper room was reached Mellor produced
two pistols, and they hid them beneath some flocks.
Mellor told Durrance that he need not say anything
about them, but the latter did not like to comply
with this request, and as soon as Mellor had left
the house he showed the weapons to his fellow
apprentices, Joseph Holdham and Francis Vickerman. After Mellor had disposed of the pistols he
came down into the workshop again and passed into
the house, accompanied by Thorpe, where he found
his cousin's wife, whom he asked if her husband was
within. She replied that he was not. He had gone
to Huddersfield market, but she expected him back
soon. Mellor then asked her if they wanted a workman, if so his friend wanted work, but she replied
they had no occasion for one. He then requested
her to lend him a handkerchief. He next wished
her to allow the gentleman who was with him to
wash himself, and she accordingly allowed Thorpe to
do so. After stopping talking about a quarter of an
hour, Mellor rose to go, but before leaving asked
her to lend him an overcoat. She told him her
husband's overcoat was in the shop, and he might
take it. They then went into the shop, saying that
if they did not meet her husband they might probably
call again that night about ten o'clock, and after
Mellor had changed his bottle-green overcoat for his
cousin Joseph's drab one, both men left the house
and proceeded towards Huddersfield.

When the news of the assassination of Mr. Horsfall
reached Marsden there was a great deal of excitement, but the authorities, undismayed, prepared for
all emergencies and redoubled their precautions.

The head-quarters of the cavalry were at the house of Mr. Robert Taylor. It was at that time the principal inn in the village and known as the Red Lion, the landlord's name being John Race. The large room, which still extends over the entire building and which is now applied to a far different purpose, was converted into barracks for the cavalry, their horses being kept in the adjoining stables. At Ottiwells, where a portion of the infantry was constantly on guard, prompt measures against a probable attack was made. Watch and ward was maintained by the soldiers and the local constabulary, a surveillance was kept over all suspected individuals, and no lights were permitted in any dwelling after nine o'clock in the evening. It was naturally anticipated Woodbottom mill and its proprietors would be the next objects of vengeance, and preparations were made to meet the danger. For months past Enoch and James Taylor, who first made the obnoxious machines as narrated in a former chapter, had slept in the mill in consequence of their lives being threatened and their own dwellings being unsafe, and they formed part of the mill garrison at night. Their future partner, Arthur Hirst, was the woollen engineer at the mill, and he laboured vigorously to convert the factory into a fortified place, becoming for the time quite a military engineer. The windows of the first story were barricaded, and the doors coated inside with sheet iron. All communication between the first and upper stories could be cut off, and the defenders inside were able, as at Cartwright's mill, to fire upon an attacking force, from the upper stories while sheltered themselves. A trap door on a floor over the water wheel was so ingeniously planned by Arthur Hirst that if the rioters had gained an entrance, they would, on touching the flooring, have dropped through it into the wheel race below.

The murder of Mr. Horsfall produced, as might be expected, great sensation and alarm, and the im-

mediate effect of that dastardly crime was to rouse
in the spirits of most a determined resolution to
put down the disgraceful outbreaks of the Luddites.
Foremost in these exertions was Mr. Radcliffe, the
owner of the plantation from which the fatal shot
was fired, who was afterwards made a baronet for
his bold and fearless conduct at this critical period.
Under his supervision and arrangement a vigorous
body of police was formed, and the Luddites soon
began to discover that they could not carry on their
destructive plans with impunity. So closely were
they watched indeed that they found it dangerous to
meet as before, and their meetings being thus interfered with, their organisation, once so dreaded and
so formidable, seemed to lose all its power of co-
hesion, and the members found themselves as it
were scattered and unable to act together as formerly.
The cold blooded murder of Mr. Horsfall appeared
in fact to destroy all the public sympathy which
existed for them at the beginning of the movement,
and everybody seemed anxious now to root out the
society which had planned and executed the foul
crime. The public admiration of Mr. Cartwright
now rapidly revived and extended, and a subscrip-
tion was entered into for him amounting to three
thousand pounds, which was presented to him and
his family. The committee of the associated masters and manufacturers also passed a cordial vote
of thanks to Mr. Cartwright for his intrepid defence,
and presented fifty guineas to the men who had so
nobly assisted him.

The members of the firm of Messrs. Abraham and
John Horsfall took the death of their son and
nephew greatly to heart, and they appeared from that
time to imbibe a dislike to Marsden. Singularly
enough, though Luddism, as we have pointed out,
fell rapidly after that sad event into disrepute the
use of the obnoxious machinery was discontinued at
Ottiwells, and cropping by hand resumed. In a
few years afterwards their mill property in Marsden

was disposed of, Bankbottom mills passing into the
hands of Messrs. Norris, Sykes, and Priestley, and
Ottiwells to Messrs. Abraham and William Kinder.
It is related that after his son's death Mr. Abraham
Horsfall never again entered the mill at Ottiwells,
and when riding past on his way to Bankbottom he
invariably averted his face from the mill as if the
very sight was hateful or painful to him.

CHAPTER XVIII.

THE ASSASSINS ALARMED.

Sworn on every slight pretence
Till perjuries are common as bad pence;
While thousands, careless of the damning sin,
Kiss the book's outside who ne'er look within.—*owper*

I'll make assurance doubly sure
And take a bond of Fate.—*Shakespeare.*

In perusing the account of the assassination of
Mr. Horsfall the reader will doubtless be impressed
by the singular daring and the disregard of the
commonest precautions which characterised throughout the proceedings of the four murderers. That the
foul deed should be discussed in the open shop might
be deemed sufficiently dangerous even if all the men
had been sworn members of the brotherhood, but it
is well known that some of those who were present
when the hot-blooded Mellor avowed his determination to shoot Horsfall had not joined the Luddites,
though there is no doubt they sympathised strongly
with the movement. When George Mellor came
into the room where Benjamin Walker was working,
and after bluntly avowing his murderous intention,
asked him to accompany them, Walker's father was
present, and yet, strange to say, he does not appear
to have offered a single word of objection to the
proposal that his son should participate in the
murder. Doubtless the knowledge they all possessed
of the desperate character of the Luddite leaders
would make Walker and the others afraid of calling
down upon their heads the swift vengeance they
were well aware would await the traitor who should
obstruct the movement, but even this is scarcely

sufficient to account for the strange silence on the part of Walker. One would have thought that, seeing he was afraid to imperil his own safety by joining the lawless band, he would have felt sufficient solicitude respecting his son's welfare to have taken advantage of the time when the latter was absent from the workshop at his "drinking" to warn him of the tremendous danger which must attend the execution of the foul plot laid before him by Mellor. The father does not, however, appear to have given a word of warning to his son, and though he was present afterwards when the latter consented to take the heavily loaded pistol from the impetuous leader's hands, he is not reported to have offered a single word of remonstrance. The fact seems to be that the chief characteristic of the elder Walker was great cowardice, which was also indeed, as we have already stated, the leading point in his son's character. They were both quite capable of doing villainous deeds, but were afraid to put themselves into positions of danger. We have shown how this craven fear for the safety of his own neck was overpowered in the case of the younger Walker by a dread of the vengeance of the desperate villain, Mellor, in the plantation from which the deadly shot was fired, but if the strangely callous father had only risked consequences and advised his son to reject the foul proposal, Mellor, disgusted with his want of spirit, might have passed him by contemptuously, as he did William Hall.

When Walker returned home from Honley on that fatal night he told his mother what had traspired at the little plantation on Crosland Moor a few hours previously, and though she would be somewhat comforted to learn that her son had not actually committed the deed of blood, her feelings, we are sure, would be sufficiently distressing.

The news of the murder reached John Wood's workshop about an hour after it had been committed,

Mrs. Hartley, a widow who lived near, running in with the startling intelligence. Mellor and Smith appear to have returned to their work that evening, though not at the time stated by John Bower, one of Wood's apprentices. It was a very busy day, and George Mellor and Thomas Smith, Benjamin Walker, and others, he states, were working till late. This lad Bower, Thomas Smith, George Mellor, and William Hall slept in Mr. Wood's house; Mellor and Hall sleeping in one bed, and Bower and Smith in the other. Mellor told Hall as they were going to bed that the heavily loaded pistol had jumped as the latter warned him it would and had hurt his finger. The conversation was carried on in whispers, the presence of the youth who shared Smith's bed preventing them from speaking out.

The great theme of conversation next morning both within and without the workshop was the tragic deed of the previous evening. The Warren House Inn was only a short distance above, and a constant succession of callers kept Wood's men informed respecting the condition of Horsfall until, to the scarcely disguised joy of the croppers, word came at last that he was dead. The authorities, spurred on to renewed exertions by this startling atrocity, were everywhere making enquiries and causing suspicious persons to be apprehended. It was rumoured too that a large reward was offered to any one not actually the perpetrator of the deed who would give such information as would lead to the conviction of the assassins. When Thorpe heard this talked of at Fisher's, he grew very uneasy, and went to the neighbouring workshop to consult with his friend Mellor.

"George," said he, "hast thou heard the news?"

"I have heard more news lately than I have wanted to hear," replied Mellor, gloomily, "what is there fresh now?"

"They say that a heavy reward is offered— thousands of pounds our chaps report—for the conviction of the man that shot Horsfall. Now I've just been wondering this morning if all the men in your shop that know or suspect anything are to be trusted.

Mellor's brow darkened and his face grew livid with passion.

"If I thought there was one man who would whisper a single word he either knows or suspects, this day would be his last," he thundered out.

"Come, George," said the phlegmatic Thorpe, looking upon his companion with an expression of disgust on his stolid face, "I didn't come to hear thy ravings and threats; I came to make sure there were no traitors to fear. What does young Bower know?"

"Nothing, I think," answered Mellor, sullenly.

"He might overhear something, however, if the men are not cautious. What about Ben Walker?"

"Walker's a sneak," replied Mellor, "but he's in at it, so we're safe there. I hardly like his wanting to creep out of the job at the last moment, but he'd never much pluck. It was a mistake to ask him?"

"But he did not fire, thou sees, so he might save his neck by splitting on us perhaps."

"The first word of that sort from him would be the last he would ever utter in this world," replied Mellor in loud tones, his feeling again getting the mastery of him. Checking himself he enquired anxiously—"But what makes thee talk like this, Bill? Thou'rt the last man I should ever expect to show the white feather."

"I'm no white feather chap, George," replied Thorpe, "but I've thought since the affair happened that we might have gone a better way about it. If we two had just quietly laid our heads together we could have done for Horsfall, and then all the shop would not have known about it. When thou came storming into the room on the day the job was done

I was taken unawares; but then thou blabbed out all the business before anybody could speak."

"Well, I had been stung beyond endurance by Horsfall's taunts, which were told me by the men, and I am not such a cold blooded animal as thee," retorted Mellor.

Thorpe's dark brow grew darker, his heavy jaws were clenched savagely, and his eyes flashed with fury, when fortunately Mellor's fellow workman Smith, who was returning from his morning meal entered the room. He had heard the taunt of the fiery Mellor as he entered and seeing the effect it had upon Thorpe he realised the fact at once that the two confederates in many a dark deed were quarelling seriously. As Smith like the rest was always afraid of what Mellor might do or say when he was carried away by his fearful outbursts of temper, he hastened to throw oil upon the troubled waters.

"Come, Thorpe," he said quietly, "I thought thou had more sense. Let us hear what it is all about."

Thorpe recognised instantly the folly of quarrelling, and calming himself, told Smith the ground of his disquietude. Smith glanced round the room uneasily when he heard what had given rise to the dispute, and when Thorpe had concluded, asked pointedly,

"Does thou suspect anybody, Will?"

"No," replied Thorpe, "but it is as well to take proper precautions I think."

"And I agree with thee," said Smith, "I think we might insist on all the men taking an oath not to divulge what they know."

"Well," put in Mellor, who, having had a little time for reflection, began to see the folly of neglecting precautions, "I agree with that. We'll make every man in the place who knows anything about the matter take an oath of secrecy. Thee go into

the new shop, Thorpe, and start with Sowden ; bring
him into the press room, and I will see about the
rest."

Thorpe left the room as requested, and went into
the new shop where Sowden worked.

" Here, Sowden," he said, standing in the door
way, " I want thee."

The man addressed left his work and went into
the adjoining room. Thorpe closed the door and
then turned towards the astonished workman.

" Sowden," he commenced, " thou knows all about
Horsfall's affair."

" I know what thee and the rest have told me,"
replied Sowden.

" Well, I must have thee swear to keep Horsfall's
murder in all its circumstances a strict secret," continued Thorpe.

" I can keep the secret without being sworn," said
Sowden.

" Well, maybe thou can, but I intend thee to be
sworn," answered Thorpe, firmly.

" Now look here, Thorpe," replied Sowden, dogged-
ly, " I do not belong to the Ludds because I do not
agree with them in all things, but you need not be
afraid I shall peach. I never took an oath in my
life and I don't mean to begin now. Besides the
oath you would administer is an illegal one, and you
are well aware I should be liable to seven years'
transportation if I took it."

" Oh yes ! its all very nice," sneered Thorpe, " for
such chaps as thee to stand on one side and say you
don't agree with the Ludds, leaving others to do
all the work and risk their lives. I have already
said thou shall take this oath and thou shall, or I will
shoot thee dead where thou stands ?"

Thorpe produced a loaded pistol, which he always
carried, and planted himself in front of Sowden.
Lifting the trigger he fixed his eye on his prisoner,
and raising his voice said,

" Now, will you take the oath?"

" I will," responded Sowden, who saw it was vain
to contend further with the desperate man before
him.

" Repeat after me then," cried Thorpe, and Sowden
repeated after him the following oath :—" I, Joseph
Sowden, do hereby declare and solemnly swear I
never will divulge to any person or persons under
the canopy of heaven the names of the persons concerned in shooting Horsfall, nor do anything nor
cause anything to be done which might lead to the
discovery of the same, either by word, deed, or sign,
on penalty of being sent out of the world. So help
me God to keep this my oath inviolable."

" Now kiss this book," added Thorpe, holding a
Bible to Sowden's lips.

Sowden placed the book to his face as if kissing
it, but did not actually do so.

" Now I have not done with you yet," said Thorpe,
still presenting the pistol. " As you have given
me some trouble I will make you administer the
oath yourself to every man that is brought into the
press shop ! "

Sowden had nothing wherewith to defend himself. He knew he was in the hands of a desperate,
unscrupulous man, who would not hesitate to carry
out his threats. He saw therefore that it was useless to resist.

" Now, sit here," commanded Thorpe, " on the
press table ; take this book and read the oath
written on the paper at the back to all who are
brought before you; say nothing to any but what
I said when I administered the oath just now, and
remember that I stand beside you and that my
pistol is handy in my pocket here."

Having thus spoken, Thorpe drew the bolt back
in the door, and Mellor entered, accompanied by
Benjamin Walker. The latter looked astonished

to see Sowden there taking the leading part in the
proceedings, but he took the oath with a cool and
indifferent air, offering no observation, and then
gave place to his fellow workmen who were brought
one by one into the room by Mellor.

CHAPTER XIX.

MURDER OF THE PRIME MINISTER.

For murder though it have no tongue
Will speak with most miraculous organ.

Shakespeare

The daring assassination of Mr. Horsfall in open day spurred on the Huddersfield authorities to make still greater efforts to discover the Luddites who, they were well aware, were very numerous in the town and neighbourhood; but they found their task more difficult than ever, as the old fear of the vengeance of the dreaded fraternity had resumed its sway over the minds of the people since the murder, and many who might put the officers of the law on the scent were fain to bury their information or suspicions deep in their own hearts.

On the evening of Monday, the 27th of April, the military authorities received an anonymous letter informing them of the hiding places of three wounded men who, it was thought, had been concerned in the attack on Cartwright's mill. Steps, which eventually proved successful, were made to effect their apprehension after nightfall, and the prisoners were conveyed to Huddersfield barracks for safety. The captures were cleverly and quietly effected, but the news soon spread amongst the Luddites, and in the dead of the night the stables adjoining the room where the prisoners were confined were found to be on fire. It was thought the object of the incendiaries was to distract the attention of the guard, and if this ruse had proved successful an attack on the temporary prison was to have been made. The sentries, however, had been too well trained to leave their posts, and the men within the building having been roused from their slumbers the fire was speedily extinguished and the purposes of the Luddites defeated. When morning dawned the prisoners were escorted under a strong guard to the Court-house, where in due time they were brought up for trial. The constables had been doing their best in the meantime to ferret out some evidence against them, but, as usual, they failed, and the prisoners were eventually discharged.

Notwithstanding the military were harassed by night watches, and patrols were continually march-ing through the suspected districts, great robberies of arms took place during the month at Almondbury, Wooldale, Melton, Netherthong, Marsden, Elland and Honley. The Ludds mustered in gangs of twenty or more and stripped those localities of guns, pistols, swords, and all other weapons, little or no resistance being offered. Major Gordon and his troop, finding they could not hinder the raids, per-ambulated through the places which had been thus visited and seized all the arms they could possibly find to prevent the rioters from getting them also. While on one of those expeditions, William Sykes, a Melton shopkeeper, who, thirsting probably for notoriety, represented himself as one of General Ludd's men, and said he had been engaged in seizing arms for the fraternity, was taken into custody and committed to York.

At Nottingham the disturbances continued much the same as before, the Luddites showing no signs of discontinuing their lawless movements. On the 12th of May the rioters were thrown into a delirium of joy by the arrival of the startling intelligence that Spencer Percival, the hated Prime Minister, who had forced through the House of Commons the sanguinary measure making it death to destroy a frame, had been shot the day before as he entered St. Stephen's. Immediately on the news becoming known a tumultuous crowd assembled in the market-place and paraded the town with drums beating and flags flying in triumph.

The account of the Luddite excesses would be incomplete were we not to introduce into the narrative the particulars of this assassination, an event which produced in the two Houses (assembled at the time) the utmost consternation and also throughout the country at large, as the news spread abroad according to the means available in those days of not over-rapid communication. The bloody deed was perpetrated on the afternoon of the 11th of May, 1812, and as the fight at Rawfolds Mill had taken place on the 11th of the preceding month and the murder of Mr. Horsfall on the 16th, and as up to the time of the shooting of Mr. Percival no clue had been obtained to lead to the discovery of the actors in either the Rawfolds mill fight, or the assassination on Crosland Moor, it was but natural to conclude. at the first, that the shooting in the lobby of the House of Commons was part and parcel of the tactics of the Luddite conspirators; and almost universal was the alarm and dread as to what would happen next, or whose turn it might be to fall by the hands of the assassins. This fear pervaded the minds of both Ministers and Parliament, as is evidenced by the speech of the Lord Chancellor (Eldon) in the House of Lords on the day following the murder of Mr. Percival; a speech indicative of the utmost alarm, as to what might follow in the then "state of the country." This alarm, however, gradually gave way as it became more and more apparent that John Bellingham, the man who shot Mr. Perceval, had acted in the matter entirely on his own account, and had no accomplices whatever. The Luddites were thus cleared of all participation in the shocking deed, which had at first been attributed to them; and one result was that some further coercive legislation, intended to put down the Luddite disturbances, was abandoned.

THE RISINGS OF THE LUDDITES.

The account we subjoin, which is the most complete we have met with, was written by the famous " master of the English language," the late William Cobbett. He was, at the period in question, serving out a sentence of two years' imprisonment in New-gate (with the additional punishment of having to pay a fine of £100 to the king), for having expressed indignation at the flogging of English militiamen under a guard of Hanoverian bayonets—a sentence of extreme judicial savagery, and for a cause which now would be hailed as an act of patriotism. The account was, as the reader will see, in the form of a letter, which we now proceed to give.

" My Dear Friend,—In your last letter received by me in this place, you requested me to write an account of myself and family, and also to give you a true description of the situation of " Old England, the beloved and venerated country of our forefathers. First, then, I have the pleasure to tell you that, though I have been in jail upwards of twenty-one months, I have never been ill a single moment ; that I never had even a headache, and that I feel myself as strong as at any period of my life. What my wife has suffered, I shall leave you and the kind families at Bursledon and Bibery, who know her, to guess. This much for my private concerns, which may, I hope, also suffice as an answer to our old and kind friend, B. Story, from whom, to my indescribable satisfaction, I received a letter no longer ago than Saturday last. With respect to public matters, I shall begin by telling you, the Prime Minister of the Prince Regent, Spencer Perceval, the man during whose administrations I was sent (for you know what) to this jail, was shot dead by the hand of an English-man, named John Bellingham. The affair I should not have written much about, because in spite of all the falsehoods which the hired newspapers of London have and will publish upon the subject, the people will get at the truth ; but I am anxious that the truth should be known all the world over, and particularly in the American States, whence, even from the banks of the Mississippi, my own writings, issuing from this jail, have returned to me through the channel of the American press. This fact, by making it obvious to me that I am writing for the use of America as well as for that of England, points out to me that it is my duty to give only a true account of the trial and execution of John Bellingham, but also that I should give it in such a way as may make the whole affair plain to persons who were never in London, and to whom many circumstances must, without explanation, remain wholly incomprehensible. My intention, therefore, is to present to you, in the first place, with a regular narrative of the facts from the time of the pistol being fired to the moment of the death of the man, who fired it, uninterrupted by any commentary of my own, and shall inform you of what has been done by Parliament in consequence of that event. By way of introduction you should be told that, owing to a scarcity of work for our manufacturers (arising from laws of France and America), added to a dearth of provisions, there have for many months existed great disturbances in the counties of York, Lancaster, Chester, Leicester, Stafford and Nottingham. A considerable regular army is assembled in that part of England for the purpose of opposing and putting down the people who have risen; and a law has been passed inflicting the punishment of death in certain cases, where the punishment before was transportation. To give you some idea of the sufferings of the poor people, it will be quite sufficient for me to state these facts; that the weekly wages of a working man does not, upon an average throughout England, exceed 15s.; that the price of a bushel of wheat is, upon an average, 18s.; that the price of a bushel of potatoes has been for some time past, upon an average, 8s. 6d. To you, who know what food a man and his wife and three or four children require; to you, who have a heart to feel for every fellow

creature : to you, at whose home the traveller, be
he who or what he might, never needed even to ask
for victuals and drink ; to you I need say no more in
order to show you the extent of the distress of the
labouring people in general; but, I ought to add,
that in the manufacturing countries a want of work
has co-operated with scarcity of the late harvest,
and that both together have rendered the situation
of the people truly deplorable. There is another
great cause of national poverty and misery, namely,
the taxes, caused by the fearful war, which are now
become enormous ; but this is a cause which is always
operating. The extraordinary causes are those that
I have just mentioned. In consequence of these
distresses, numerous petitions have been presented
to Parliament, but as I said before, the only law
passed respecting the disturbances, or the cause of
them, is a law to punish with death the crime of
frame breaking, which was formerly punished with
transportation. Another law is brought into the
House of Commons for making it death to take or
administer unlawful oaths, upon the alleged ground
that the disturbers of the peace are combined together by an oath. The Act had been introduced,
read a first time, and was, I believe, to have been
read a second time on the evening of the day when
the Prime Minister was killed. Such was the state
of the country, when on Monday the 11th of this
present month of May, 1812, and at five o'clock in
the afternoon, Spencer Perceval, who had formerly
been Attorney General, and who was now become
First Lord of the Treasury, Chancellor of the Ex-
chequer, and Prime Minister of the Regent, and who
held besides two sinecure offices, was shot just as he
was about to enter that House of Commons where he
long carried everything before him, and where all
opposition to him appeared in vain. The place and
manner of his death were as follows :—There is to
the house where the members meet (which was
formerly a chapel dedicated to St. Stephen) a sort

of ante-chamber or outer-room, which for what
reason I know not, is called the Lobby. During the
time the House is sitting there are always a great
number of persons in this lobby. Attendants of one
sort or other; persons who have petitions or private
Bills before the House; in short, any body of toler-
ably decent appearance, whom business or curiosity
may bring there, and for whose accommodation there
are a fire-place and some benches. Amongst those
thus met on the day before mentioned was John
Bellingham, who, upon the Minister entering at the
Lobby door, went up to him with a pistol and shot
him in the heart, in consequence of which he stumbled forward towards the door of the House, fell and
expired in a few minutes, with a faint exclamation
of 'Oh, I'm murdered! I'm murdered!' Bellingham, the moment he had shot off his pistol, went
and sat down very calmly upon one of the benches.
Such was the surprise, the confusion, and consternation amongst all present, that he might easily have
gone out at the lobby door and escaped for a time
at least; but, as afterwards appeared, this was not at
all his design; therefore, when the consternation
was enough abated for some one to ask, who and
where was the murderer, he answered, 'I am the
man that killed Mr. Perceval,' whereupon he was
seized and searched, and another pistol, loaded, was
found in his pocket. When the knowledge of the
event was communicated to them, great indeed was
the alarm and confusion. Bellingham was dragged
into the House of Commons, whither he was followed
by the people in the lobby; so that the House was
filled with strangers, reporters, messengers, and
persons of all discriptions, mingled pell mell with
the members, and it was some time before anything
like order was restored. The alarm in the House of
Lords appears to have been greater. All forms were
cast aside, and confusion seemed to reign in their
stead. The Lord Chancellor himself made a motion
for instantly shutting the doors, in order to prevent

further mischief being perpetrated. In the meantime the Duke of Cumberland had been and seen the dead body, and he now declared the fact. The chief Judge (Lord Ellenborough), who had been sitting in the Court of King's Bench, and who, upon hearing what had happened, had quitted the court (all under the same roof) and hurried into the House or Chamber of the Lords, rose and moved that some evidence might be taken at the bar, whereon to ground a regular proceeding of some sort. This was at last agreed to, and after evidence had been produced and taken down in great haste proving that Mr. Perceval had been killed in the lobby of the Commons, the Lords, upon the motion of the Earl of Radnor, passed hastily a resolution for addressing the Regent upon the subject, requesting him to issue a Proclamation for the speedy prosecution of the offender or offenders in the case. This motion being passed, the House immediately adjourned.

Bellingham was brought to trial at the Old Bailey and convicted of the murder, and before nine o'clock in the morning of the Monday following was hanged and his body in the hands of the surgeons for dissection. When the operation was performed the doctors found his heart still faintly beating. The whole of this dismal tragedy was enacted within one short week."

CHAPTER XX.

THE APPREHENSION OF BAINES, THE HALIFAX LUDDITE LEADER.

But far too numerous is the herd of such
Who think too little and who talk too much.—*Dryden.*

A prison is a house of care—
  A place where none can thrive;
A touchstone true to try a friend;
  A grave for one alive.
Sometimes a place of right,
  Sometimes a place of wrong;
Sometimes a place for rogues and thieves,
  And honest men among.
Inscription on Edinburgh Tolbooth.

The magistrates and military were more successful in Nottingham, Cheshire, and Lancashire, in arresting Luddites than were the authorities in this locality. Special commissions for the trial of the rioters were opened at Lancaster on the 23rd of May, and at Chester on the 25th. Great excitement prevailed throughout both counties and an organised attack to rescue the prisoners was talked of in Cheshire. In consequence of these rumours the alarmed authorities concentrated upwards of a thousand picked troops in Cheshire Castle yard, by whom the approaches to the court were carefully guarded during the whole of the sittings. Many of the rioters were imprisoned for long periods; a number were transported beyond the seas; two were hanged at Chester, and eight at Lancaster.

The talk about a general rising still continued, and during the whole of June raids for arms took place almost nightly throughout parts of the West Riding, especially in the neighbourhood of Huddersfield, Halifax, Brighouse, Elland and Dewsbury, and large

bodies of men were seen almost nightly in the Yorkshire clothing districts, performing military exercises
in secluded places. Soothill was a favourite rendezvous, and Cawley Wood, at Heckmondwike, was
also frequently visited by the disaffected in that
immediate locality. The whole of the towns and
villages around those centres were denuded of arms
of every kind by the men, the robberies often taking
place as they returned from the drills, which were
generally held after midnight on Saturdays. Great
numbers of leaden vessels, also sheet lead, lead
pipes, &c., were likewise stolen to melt down for
bullets.

On the 23rd of June, James Oldroyd, of Dewsbury,
was denounced as a Luddite, one who had been at
the attack on Cartwright's mill, and he was apprehended the same day by a troop of the King's Bays.
He was conveyed to Huddersfield for examination
and committed for trial at the assizes, which were
opened at York on the 18th of July. Although the
Government spy swore positively against him he
was fortunately able to prove an alibi to the satisfaction of the Jury, and was consequently liberated.
In this respect Oldroyd fared much better than old
John Baines, of Halifax, president of the Democratic
Club, to whose case we must now refer.

From what we have already said about Baines,
and from the address he gave at the meeting when
the attack on Cartwright's mill was resolved upon,
our readers will be well aware that although he was
a member of the Luddite fraternity he had very
different ideas respecting the aims and objects of the
organisation than were entertained by such men as
Mellor and Thorpe. Assassination found no advocate
or defender in the old democrat Baines. His aim
was not to shoot the masters, but to rouse the people
en masse to assert their rights as citizens to a share
in the Government; to overthrow what he called
the "bloody rule of kings and aristocrats," and

establish democracy in its place. Like the great
bulk of ...is class he was not sufficiently enlightened
to appreciate the value of machinery, in fact he regarded it as wholly a curse, and rejoiced to hear of
the destruction of that which he thought was calculated to still further diminish the scanty earnings
of the poor; but in joining the men who had done
so much to prevent its general introduction he had
no idea that their aim was to confine themselves to
merely local conflicts. As we have already seen,
he had strongly supported the scheme of a general
rising as advocated by the Nottingham delegate,
Weightman, and had regarded the breaking of
machinery and the attacks on the mills simply as
preliminaries to the general movement which was
to result in what he called "the enfranchisement of
the long-suffering, trodden-down people." He had
always urged on the raids for arms that were at
this time more prevalent than ever, in order that
when the signal was given the people might be ready
for the struggle. Conceiving the time to be very
near, he had also endeavoured to extend the organilsa-
tion, but in enrolling new members he had not
exercised sufficient care in administering the oath.
So imprudent had he become of late, indeed, that
the suspicions of the local magistrates were directed
towards the St. Crispin Democratic Club and its
president, but they had not been able to obtain any
positive information. The failure of the local magistrates being reported to the Government, which,
since the attack on Cartwright's mill, and especially
since the assassination of Horsfall, had been spurring
on the authorities in the disaffected districts and requiring frequent reports, it was decided at head-
quarters that other steps should be taken to break
up the mysterious organisation which was evidently
taking such deep root and extending so rapidly. For
this purpose two spies were sent to Halifax from
Manchester by the famous detective Nadin to endeavour to entrap the leaders. One of these spies

was an Irishman named M'Donald, who, before he
took up the disreputable profession, was a weaver.
It need hardly be said that he was a low fellow who
had lost all self-respect; for none but such would
consent to make a living by hunting down their
fellow creatures for blood money. M'Donald appears to have been worse than the average of his
abominable class, for when the time came for him
to give evidence against his victim, he was found
to be in prison himself, and had actually to be
brought up by habeas corpus to give evidence, and
yet the statements of a vile wretch like that, supported partly by that of another spy, a man of the name
of Gossling, a broken down fustian cutter, were ac-
cepted as trustworthy, and the evidence of respectable tradesmen, in defence, was entirely passed over
and ignored.

The two spies, having received their instructions,
left Manchester early on the morning of the 8th of
July, 1812, and arrived at Halifax about noon.
They were dressed in their ordinary working clothes
and passed themselves off as men in search of employment. They made direct to the St. Crispin
Inn, where they partook of some refreshments, and
then went out to seek lodgings. On returning to
the public house in the evening, they found a man
whose name they afterwards discovered to be Charles
Milnes, and they immediately led him into conversation. This Milnes, who was a cardmaker, was
very intimate with John Baines, and was in fact a
Luddite, though he does not appear to have taken
any part in frame breaking. He was an off-hand,
careless talker, and M'Donald soon saw that he
was just the man he wanted. The two spies were
extremely frank and friendly, and Milnes soon became quite confidential. They said that work in
Manchester was very bad and they thought they
would come and try if they could get a job at Halifax, where, they had been told, work was more
plentiful and provisions cheaper.

"Whoever has told you that," replied Milnes, "has told you more than they can prove, I think. Trade is bad enough at Halifax, and as for cheap provisions I and a good many more would like to know where they are. In all the towns round here the rich subscribe pretty liberally to help the poor to get flour and potatoes or they would starve."

"You seem to have plenty of soldiers in the town, however. I and my mate have been out seeking lodgings and we were both struck with the number we saw idling about the streets."

"Yes," said the unsuspecting Milnes, "we are not short of them whatever we are short of besides. I suppose they are looking after the Luddites, but they connot find them. Since Cartwright's mill was attacked and Horsfall shot they look as sharp as weasels, but it is no use."

"We have heard something about those affairs at Manchester, but we are told the Ludds lead them some wild goose chases. Fun of that sort would just suit me and my mate here."

Milnes chuckled merrily. He liked to pass himself off as a cute fellow and he could not resist the temptation of telling M'Donald how cleverly he had once outwitted the soldiers by stealing some cartridges from them. The two spies were vastly tickled by Milnes's story and loudly applauded his cleverness.

"But didn't they try to catch you?" enquired Gossling.

"Why, yes," said Milnes, puffing his pipe tranquilly, "they tried and they were on the scent too, but finding it was getting rather warm I just disguised myself a little, levanted to Dean Common and acted as assistant shepherd to a friend of mine three or four weeks. When I returned the affair had blown nicely over."

The spies laughed once more at Milnes's tale and M'Donald said he was glad he was not taken.

"As for the machines that were broken," said Gossling, "I don't pity the masters a bit. The people are starving and the country seems going to the dogs. But were not the Ludds licked at Cartwright's?"

"Well, they couldn't get in," said Milnes, "but the worst of that affair was that many were hurt, and you may have heard that two were shot and died."

The two spies thought they had heard something of the sort.

"Yes," resumed Milnes, shaking his head, "I knew them both very well. Poor fellows, it was a sad affair."

"You knew them, did you?" enquired M'Donald, "Were they Halifax men?"

"One was," replied Milnes, "and a fine fellow he was too."

"Then you know this General Ludd, perhaps," queried M'Donald, speaking in a careless tone.

"General Ludd! exclaimed Milnes, laughing heartily, "nay I know no generals."

"But didn't he command at Cartwright's affair?" enquired Gossling. "We were told at Manchester that they had a commander who was called General Ludd."

"Well they might call him so," said foolish Milnes, "but that was not the real name. I happen to know that much."

The conversation continued, and Milnes, as he imbibed glass after glass of the potent compounds, grew more and more communicative, and at last M'Donald hinted that he and his mate should like to enter the fraternity, and they would be as active as anyone if they were "twisted in."

"Well, now, look here," said Milnes, in low tones, "if you really mean that, I think I know an old man not very far from here who will perhaps do it if I introduce you."

"Well, I am willing," said M'Donald, what say you, mate?"

"Well," replied the person addressed, in a hesitating voice, "I don't know as much about them as you seem to do, but I will join if you do."

"We must wait till dark," said Milnes. "The magistrates are on the look out, and it would not do to be seen entering Baines's house, as he told us at our last meeting that he is certain it is carefully watched."

"If that's the case," said Gossling, with well-feigned alarm, "I don't think I'll join to-night. There's no hurry, let us consider about it a bit.

"I shall consider no more," said M'Donald, "I will go with you, friend," and leaving Gossling as if in disgust he seated himself beside Milnes, who shook him heartily by the hand.

"All right, brother," cried Milnes, "I think it's dark enough ; we'll go now."

"Well, I'll just take a turn round, perhaps call at the lodgings, and will come back here," said Gossling, rising and walking out of the inn.

Milnes paid for another glass for his new friend they then left the St. Crispin arm in arm and proceeded to the house of John Baines.

There is no information respecting what transpired at Baines's house, except what was afterwards given in evidence by M'Donald. He stated that it was nearly ten o'clock when they got there, and that he found seated round the fire the old man, two of his sons, one—Zachariah—being a lad of fifteen, also William Blakeborough and George Duckworth, shoemakers, both members of the St. Crispin club. Charles Milnes introduced M'Donald, saying that although he was a stranger, he was a good fellow and wishful to be a brother. The old man, who seemed a little flurried, said they must be very handy, for the watch and ward might call at any moment. He then got a paper and a book about the size of a New Testament and which probably was one. Handing the book to M'Donald, he said, "Now, what is your name?"

"My name is John Smith," replied M'Donald.

Baines looked at the paper which he had in his hand, and appeared to be reading from it, telling M'Donald to repeat after him the oath which he then administered. The ceremony being concluded, Baines bade him kiss the book and he did so. The company, he states, were all sitting when he went in, but during the time the oath was being administered they all stood up, and that the lad, Zachariah Baines, stood with his back against the door to prevent any one from entering suddenly. M'Donald himself was afraid the watch and ward would come in and he was glad when the ceremony was over. Before leaving, he offered to pay for something to drink, but the old man at once declined the offer, and they then all left the house except the elder Baines and the lad who held the door. John Baines, the younger, Charles Milnes, Blakeborough, and Duckworth, walked with M'Donald to the door of the St. Crispin, where he stated Duckworth left them. Gossling, the other spy, soon after joined them, and they sat drinking for some time. Calling Gossling by his assumed name, which does not appear to have been handed down. M'Donald told him he had got "twisted in," and the remainder confirmed it, Charles Milnes adding that he had introduced him. They continued drinking till between twelve and one, when they all accompanied M'Donald and Gossling to the door of their lodgings.

M'Donald and his brother spy were naturally well pleased with their speedy success, but they did not think it advisable to rouse suspicion by leaving Halifax suddenly, besides they were hopeful that others might be drawn into their net. With this view M'Donald called several times at Baines's workshop and engaged him in conversation, observing care fully who came and went. He does not appear to have had any further success. The old man tried to discuss political questions with him, but as M'Donald was so ignorant that he did not know the difference in the meaning of the two words "aristocrat" and "democrat," he would doubtless find that he had not got a very promising pupil. Observing that M'Donald often referred to his being "twisted in," Baines warned him against talking about it, and said it was rumoured that there were two Bow Street spies in the town.

"Two Bow Street officers in the town!" exclaimed M'Donald. "Have they been seen by any of the brethren?"

"Not yet, but they are on the look out for the rascals," replied Baines.

M'Donald looked hard at the speaker, and Baines afterwards remembered the look. It puzzled him then, but he soon after began to understand it.

The spies had heard a great deal about the sure vengeance that followed traitors in the Luddite ranks. It was evident, M'Donald thought, that they suspected that spies were in the town. Perhaps they suspected them! That night the two rascals disappeared.

A few days after, the shop of old Baines was surrounded by soldiers and he was committed to prison to await his trial. His two sons, Charles Milnes, William Blakeborough, and George Duckworth, shared his fate.

CHAPTER XXI.

THE ARREST OF HARTLEY AND THE MURDERERS OF HORSFALL.

Canst thou not minister to a mind diseased?
Pluck from the memory a rooted sorrow ;
Rase out the written troubles of the brain ;
And with some sweet oblivious antidote,
Cleanse the stuffed bosom of that perilous stuff,
Which weighs upon the heart?—*Shakespeare.*

Pity—it is a pity to recall to feeling
The wretch too happy to escape to death
By the compassionate trance, poor nature's last
Resource against the tyranny of pain.—*Byron.*

We must now introduce our readers once more into
the poverty-stricken home of William Hartley, who,
as we stated in a former chapter, had joined the Luddites in a fit of desperation, hoping it might lead to
some good.   That his condition could not be made
worse he was well assured, for his wife and young
family were, at the time he made the rash venture
which he afterwards bitterly regretted, actually starving in the miserable house they called home. After
the Luddites in this district had adopted the Nottingham system of levying subscriptions for the support
of their poorest members, Hartley was relieved by
an occasional donation, but the doles were but small
and were given out at long intervals.   The fact was
that Hartley was not in favour with the dispensers
of these gratuities.   He exhibited very little enthusiasm in the cause in which he had so rashly
embarked ; he did not attend the meetings with
any degree of regularity, and was therefore naturally
regarded with suspicion by the reckless leaders of
the band, who would fain have made an example of
him had they not been deterred by some of the more
feeling members who knew and pitied the offending
brother.   The excuse set up for Hartley had al-

ways been his poor health, and the plea was a true
one.   Naturally he was not hardy, and hunger and
privation had reduced his strength and rendered
him incapable of almost any exertion.   Work he
had little or none, and as he seldom went abroad he
was accustomed to sit brooding all day long over his
melancholy lot.   His wife, too, naturally delicate,
had been weak and ailing for some time, and was now
confined altogether to bed.   Hartley knew well that
what she chiefly required was plenty of nourishing
food, but he could hardly procure for her a dry crust,
and he was daily tortured by witnessing her and her
little ones slowly pining away before his eyes.
During the early summer months he had secured
occasionally a few days' field work from the farmers
around, and now that golden August had come and
the grain was ripe for the sickle he hoped again to
be able to add a little to the scanty earnings of the
family.

The day had been hot and sultry, and a heavy
thunderstorm had passed over the hills.   As darkness
came on the rain had gradually abated, but the
thunder rolled in grand and majestic peals, and ever
and anon the rugged scenery around the poor little
homestead of the Hartleys was vividly lighted up.
The clock of the distant church had boomed out the
midnight hour in slow and solemn strokes, but a
light proceeding from an oil lamp still glimmered
faintly through the holes of a print quilt which had
been stretched across the window of Hartley's house.
Hours before the watch and ward had passed, and a
soldier had struck the door with the flat side of his
sword, and cried "Why burns the light within?"
Hartley had explained the reason, and extinguished
the lamp, but he was obliged to relight it to procure
something for his suffering wife, and it still remained
burning.   The interior of the cottage presented much
the same picture of wretchedness as when we described
it before.   The plaster had dropped from the walls
in perhaps still larger patches, and notwithstanding

it was summer the floor seemed black and wet with damp. The poor, tattered, shut-up bed was let down, and in it was Hartley's wife. She had had a bad day and looked emaciated and sickly. On the other side of the fireplace sat Hartley, gazing steadfastly into the grate, speaking but seldom and then very briefly in reply to some question or observation of his wife, who seemed to make efforts from time to time to rouse him from his stupor. She had urged him a few minutes before to put out the light and retire to bed, but he had made no attempt to comply with the request. There had been a meeting of Ludds on the moors, a mile or so away, and he had not been there. He had not named the gathering to his poor, sick wife, for fear of agitating her, and he had been hoping all the evening that she might drop asleep, and then he could steal out unobserved, and be spared the sight of her agonised looks and of the big tears rolling down her wasted cheeks. His frequent absence from the drills had been strongly commented upon by the commander, and when his number was called out and there was as usual no response, his loyalty to the cause was called in question, and the fearful enquiry was solemnly made,

" Is it safe that he should remain alive?"

A general cry in the affirmative went up from the ranks, and silence then prevailed for a brief period.

" Number seventeen to the front," called out the leader, and Hey stepped forward and stood before him.

" You command a party told off to collect arms to-night?" said the leader.

" I do," he replied.

" See that Hartley goes with you. If he is not there report."

Hey, after saluting his commander, resumed his place in the ranks, and the drill commenced. The men are formed into columns; they march and retreat, break rank and re-gather, until the chief,

satisfied with their movements, calls them once more
to form in a compact mass in front of him, and then
proceeds to address them in a wild harangue which
stirs the blood of the men. In response to his
rousing appeal they lift up their guns and pikes, and
the air is filled with murmurs of approbation. When
it is concluded they grasp their arms firmly, separate
in silence, and wend their way with scowling brows
to their homes.

About a quarter of an hour after the drill was over,
Hartley was startled out of his stupor by a stealthy
knock at his door. His sick wife, who had heard
the sound too often not to know its meaning, was
strongly agitated and a faint cry which betokened
agony and terror escaped her lips as some half-dozen
men filed into the little room. Job Hey, the first
that entered, appeared not to see the occupant of
the bed. His eyes were fixed upon Hartley, who,
pale and impassive as usual, had not raised his
stony gaze from the fireless grate. Hey walked
rapidly across the floor and putting his hand firmly
upon the shoulder of the strangely silent man, hissed
in his ear,

"The roll has been called to-night and another
black cross stands opposite thy name. Beware! or
thy doom is certain."

Then unfolding a paper on which was a rough
representation of a death's head resting on cross bones,
he held it suspended before Hartley, who gazed at it
fixedly, but his lips uttered no sound. Suddenly the
silence was broken by a piercing cry and every eye
was attracted by a painful spectacle. The sick
woman had raised herself on her elbow and was
gazing wildly at the dreadful symbols, the perspira-
tion standing like great beads on her forehead.
Hartley started to his feet and the lawless gang
involuntarily gathered round the bed. Suddenly a
pale frightened girl appeared on the scene crying
piteously, "Mother! Mother!" and kissing her

wildly, bathed her temples in cold water.
The rough men, feeling this was no place for them,
silently made toward the door, and Hartley, after
satisfying himself that the feeble pulse did beat,
followed them.

"Bring thy arms with thee," whispered Hey in his
ear, "we have work to do to-night."

Hartley seemed as though he did not hear him and
walked moodily on speaking to no one.

Proceeding to a lonely house they demanded admittance. There being no response, John Hill, who
was armed with a gun, proceeded to strike the door
savagely with the butt end, crying at the same
time:

"Your arms, your arms! My master, General
Ludd, has sent me for your arms."

The alarmed master of the house sent an apprentice down stairs to give them up. The lad seems to
have had some suspicions respecting the identity of
some of the men who were in the kitchen, and may
possibly have caught sight of Hartley, who, as we
have said before, was unarmed and took no active
part in the outrage. Joseph Carter of Greetland, a
worthless fellow, was also present, and finding afterwards that he was suspected and in danger of apprehension, turned king's evidence and basely betrayed
his comrades. When the officers of justice came to
arrest Hartley his wife was violently agitated at the
sight of the poor man surrounded by his weeping
children, and with a tremulous cry she fell back in
what was supposed to be a swoon. Restoratives were
administered but it was found that the weary troubled
heart had ceased to beat and had laid down its heavy
burden for ever. While the misguided father was
carried to a felon's cell the stricken mother lay cold
and still in the wretched hovel they had called their
home.

* * * *

Several other minor offenders were captured about this time, but the murderers of Mr. Horsfall were still at large. Although the secret was well known to many of the Luddite confederates it was securely kept for several months. In this particular no secret regarding the assassination of an Irish landlord could have been kept, notwithstanding the large reward offered, and the great and increasing efforts made by constables, military, and magistrates, to worm it out. Many had come to the conclusion that the assassins would never be discovered, when a paragraph appeared in the "Leeds Mercury" of October 24th, 1812, which caused great excitement throughout the country. It ran as follows:—"A man has been taken up and examined by that indefatigable magistrate, Joseph Radcliffe, Esq., and has given the most complete and satisfactory evidence of the murder of Mr. Horsfall. The villains accused have been frequently examined before but have always been discharged for want of sufficient evidence. The man charged behaved with the greatest effrontery till he saw the informer, when he changed colour and grasped for breath. When he came out of the room after hearing the informer's evidence, he exclaimed, 'Damn that fellow, he has done me.' It appears that this man and another have been the chief in all the disgraceful transactions that have occurred in this part of the country, especially at Rawfolds. This will lead to many more apprehensions."

The informer was Benjamin Walker, one of the four engaged in the murder. He had been taken into custody along with Mellor a short time before, but no evidence could be brought against them of a serious character, and they were both discharged. Soon after Walker heard Sowden read in the newspaper that a reward of £2,000 would be paid to anyone not actually the murderer who would give such information as would lead to the conviction of the guilty parties, and resolving to secure the money and save his neck by confessing and turning informer against his old companions, he sent his mother to Mr. Radcliffe, the magistrate, to make the offer. Upon the information given, George Mellor, William Thorpe, and Thomas Smith were apprehended. The reader will have no difficulty in discovering that Mellor was the person referred to in the paragraph just quoted from the " Mercury," and it was he and Thorpe that were discovered to be the ringleaders of the Luddites in this district. William Hall, of Parkin Hoyle, Liversedge, also turned informer, but he had to leave the village soon after the trials, as he did not consider his life to be safe. Of course, the informers, by turning King's evidence,· saved their own lives and secured the reward. Walker returned to Longroyd Bridge, and worked in the district for many years afterwards, but was generally disliked and avoided ; the finger of scorn was pointed at him daily, and he was by many regarded with much the same feelings of detestation as the Irish regard one of their countrymen who turns informer.

A fortnight after the apprehension of Mellor, Thorpe and Smith, William Hall gave information to the authorities that led to the capture of Mark Hill, John Brook, Charles Cockroft, George Brooke, James Brook, John Walker, Joshua Schofield, John Hirst, and Charles Thornton. These were charged with having been concerned in the attack on Cartwright's mill at Rawfolds. Other arrests followed in rapid succession, and before the close of the year sixty-four persons charged with offences connected with disturbances in the West-Riding were apprehended and lodged in York Castle.

The capture of the leaders cowed the Luddites, but acts of violence were still perpetrated at intervals, On the last day of the year, Joseph Mellor, an important witness in Horsfall's case, was fired at as he was crossing his own yard, but the contents of the pistol lodged in the wall. It was well-known that he was subpœned to give evidence at the trial which took place on the 6th January, 1813—six days afterwards—and the intended assassins were no doubt anxious to remove one of the most important witnesses out of the way.

CHAPTER XXII.

A NARROW ESCAPE.

" Escape for thy life; look not behind thee, neither stay thou on all the plain."—Gen., c xix, v. 17.

The traitors in the Luddite ranks had by their revelations put the constables once more on the scent, and the magistrates having secured the assistance of several sharp London detectives during the closing month of the year, a very large number of suspected persons were soon hauled up before the local tribunals. In very many cases the charges were trivial and could not be substantiated, but still many were committed on the evidence adduced, and before the year closed about a hundred prisoners were lodged in York Castle. As almost every village and town in the clothing district furnished its contingent the excitement grew more and more intense and large crowds gathered almost every day before the coaching houses to watch the constables bring their prisoners to take their seats on the outside of the vehicles. When Mellor was brought heavily handcuffed to be conveyed to York to take his trial, a very large crowd assembled and the constables and military assembled in great force to prevent a rescue; but the old sympathy with the Luddites had largely died out since Horsfall's murder, and when the daring leader of the once dreaded band raised his menacled hands as the coach started and called for a cheer, there was hardly a response. As Mellor noted this evidence of the great change which had taken place in the public feeling, his heart sank within him and the air of bravado faded away from his face.

One of the most active of all the local magistrates was Mr. Radcliffe, of Huddersfield, whose whole time was taken up at the close of the year in trying to lay bare the threads of the great conspiracy which had struck so much dismay into the hearts of the West Riding manufacturers. Amongst those who were brought up before this active and intelligent magistrate, was the young man, Rayner, whose race for life from the Luddite gathering at Cooper Bridge we have recorded in a previous chapter. During the examination of poor Hartley, it transpired that he and young Rayner had joined the Luddite ranks together, both being drawn in by a designing man of the name of Joseph Carter, who, when the hour of danger came, turned informer. At the time when the two neighbours became the prey of this glib, designing villain, they were both on the brink of starvation, owing to the dearness of provisions and the bad state of trade. Hartley and Rayner had taken the oath together, and both bitterly regretted it. In happier days Rayner had been a constant visitor at the house of Hartley, whose cottage was only about ten minutes' walk over the fields, and a strong attachment had sprung up between him and the beautiful daughter of the poverty stricken tailor. Burdened, however, as Rayner was with the maintenance of his aged grandmother, and scarcely able by means of the little work he could get to keep the wolf from the door of his humble cottage, he could only worship Mary at a distance, and regard her as a bright constellation which was altogether out of his reach. After his escape from the gathering at Cooper Bridge, Rayner resolved that come what would he would sever his connection with the Luddite party finally, and acting up to his resolution he refused to hold any communication with the men who would fain have drawn him once more into their toils. Had Luddism held the position it did previous to the attack on Cartwright's mill this course would have been perilous,

but after that time the discipline of the organisation grew more lax, many of the leaders winking
at irregularities they dared not punish. This became more especially the case after the murder of
Horsfall, which tragic event deprived the movement
of almost all popular sympathy. After that time the
fraternity found themselves obliged to act with extreme
caution for fear that they should excite the suspicion
of the many emissaries of justice that seemed to en-
compass them on evrey side. Such being the case
both Rayner and Hartley, who took a similar
course, escaped the dagger and bullet of the avengers. When, however, Carter turned informer,
Hartley was at once arrested, and Rayner, as we have
said, soon after shared his fate.

On being brought before Mr. Radcliffe, the informer swore that Rayner had gone in his company
to the meeting place, and that he lost sight of him
just before they left the field to attack the mill;
whereupon Rayner questioned the traitor as to the
time he last saw him at the meeting at Cooper Bridge.
Carter, who gave his evidence truthfully enough, was
enabled to answer the question with accuracy, as
Mellor, in his closing address had announced the
exact time when saying that they ought at once to
start. Mr. Radcliffe was quite satisfied that this
answer was correct after enquiring into all the circumstances, and making a note of it he waited for the
further development of the prisoner's defence.
Rayner, who knew that upon the incident of his race
for life rested his only chance of safety, had secured
the attendance of the village sexton, to whom it will
be remembered he spoke on that eventful night, and
when the old man was placed in the witness box he
stated how he had seen Rayner come sauntering
slowly past the church, and how he had held a brief
conversation with him as he stood at the gate.

" Can you tell me exactly what time it was when
you spoke to this young man as you have just stated?"
asked Mr. Radcliffe.

"I can," answered the sexton, "because the clock struck as we were speaking,"

"Well," said the magistrate, "supposing it did, that would be a common occurrence enough."

"Certainly," answered the sexton, but something happened then that was very uncommon, for the clock struck thirteen!"

Mr. Radcliffe looked keenly at the prisoner, as he exclaimed,

"Struck thirteen! Be careful, my man, and remember your oath. Are you prepared to prove that your church clock ever struck thirteen, and if it did that it was on this particular time?"

"That can be proved," firmly responded the witness "by testimony of at least four person who are present in the court, to two of whom I spoke the same night respecting it, and by two others living near the church who afterwards unasked named the curious incident to me."

"You do right to call it a curious incident," replied Mr. Radcliffe, with a half sneer, "clocks do not often strike thirteen."

"They do not," firmly answered the sexton, "but our clock had been out of order—the striking part at any rate—and Skelton, of Brighouse, had been trying to put it right so long as he could see to work. I went the last thing as I always do when anyone had been in the church to see that all was right before I retired to bed. It was near midnight when I left my house, and when I was looking the gates Rayner came sauntering slowly up the street. We exchanged a few words as neighbours, and as we were speaking the clock began to strike."

"And how came you to count the strokes?" enquired the magistrate, in a somewhat softened tone as the belief that the old man was speaking the truth grew upon him."

"Because, as I told you, the clock had been out
of order, and had struck irregularly for some days,
and I counted the strokes to see if Skelton had left
it right."

"Humph!" exclaimed Mr. Radcliffe, as he fell
back in his chair, "call the clock mender."

Skelton came forward into the box, and proved
from his books that the sexton was right as to the
date on which the clock was first seen. He added
that he had not been able to complete the work satisfactorily on the Saturday, and that he went again on
the Monday to finish. The witnesses who had noticed
that the clock had struck thirteen added their testimony, and then the magistrate after studying his
notes, and reflecting for a time adjourned the case.

The defence was undoubtedly strong, but what
they had proved seemed to Mr. Radcliffe almost incredible. Carter, the informer, had stated that when
he first missed Rayner, Mellor announced the time
as twenty minutes to twelve, and several others of
the Luddite leaders had looked at their watches and
confirmed that, the reason being that they had agreed
to meet the Leeds contingent to join them in the
attack on the mill, and they saw it was time to start.
He took it, therefore, for a settled fact that it was
that time when Rayner must have left the field, if he
was ever there as the informer asserted. Mr. Radcliffe knew the district well, and supposing Rayner
had run home he would have to cover at least four
miles in about eighteen or nineteen minutes at the
most. That the sexton and other witnesses spoke
the truth was beyond question in his mind, and on
the other side, there was the unsupported testimony
of the informer Carter. To credit Carter, he would
also have to believe that a man could run four miles
in twenty minutes at the outside. He regarded the
feat as utterly impossible, and on that ground Rayner
was next day set at liberty. Had Mr. Radcliffe enquired a little into Rayner's antecedents, he might
perhaps have hesitated a little longer. He was, as

we have already said, a trained runner, and the champion in the village races for miles around. From statements made afterwards it seems that the times given and the distance were correct. Rayner had covered the four miles in nineteen minutes.

When Rayner arrived once more at his native village, he could not rest many hours without longing to visit the abode of his friend Hartley, who, he knew had also been taken into custody. He had also been told how Hartley's poor delicate wife had succumbed beneath her load of trouble, and he wondered much what had become of the doubly bereaved family. As he journeyed through the quiet fields sounds of music were borne on the wind from all points of the compass, and he was reminded that it was Christmas day, and as he plodded on through the yielding snow his heart was the seat of many tumultuous emotions. Although he could not help feeling thankful that he himself had escaped the toils of the informers, all the joy died out of his heart as he thought of his poor friend Hartley in his prison cell, and of sorrow that would be felt by his much loved Mary, who he knew almost idolized her unfortunate father.

The shades of evening were drawing in when he walked quickly down the narrow lane which opened out from the fields, and he soon stood in front of the little cottage which had contained his greatest treasure in life. All without seemed silent and deserted, and when he knocked at the door no one responded. Peering through the sorely patched window he saw that there was no one within, and his heart ached as he gazed at the bare walls, the damp floor, and the shabby dilapidated furniture which remained in what had been a pleasant and a happy home. By and bye, a labourer passed the top of the lane, and from him Rayner ascertained that the sorely stricken family had been taken into their houses by the kind hearted neighbours, whose hearts ached to witness the sorrow of the seven children as their poor mother's remains were placed in a pauper's grave a day or two after Hartley's apprehension.

Though Mary rejoiced for an instant to see her lover once more at liberty, her satisfaction was short lived, and she wept bitterly as she told how her poor father, stunned and bewildered by his misfortunes, had been dragged from the bedside of his dead wife and lodged in a felon's cell. His examination before the local magistrates was very brief, the evidence was so overwhelming, and he was in less than an hour committed to take his trial at York along with Mellor, Thorpe, and others. The great wish of Mary's heart now was to see her father once more, and she eagerly discussed with her lover the feasibility of a journey to York for that purpose. Rayner thought sadly of his own deep poverty, but determined that the yearning wish of the poor girl should if possible be gratified. All the way home the lover pondered how to carry out his project. There were no railways in those days, but coaches ran pretty frequently to the city. Rayner, however, never thought of these. Mary had said that she would gladly walk the whole distance, and to Rayner such a task would be a very light one. At last an idea struck him. He would call and see his old friend the sexton, and see if he could help him. Old John received the troubled young man with a warm greeting. Since he had been fortunate enough by his evidence to save Rayner from a prison cell he had looked upon him almost in the light of a son, and when he heard his tale he at once proceeded to an old oak chest, and opening one of the tiny drawers brought forth two gold coins, his whole store, and Rayner received them with tears of thankfulness in his eyes.

He had gathered from the newspapers that the court would open at York on Wednesday, the sixth of January, and he determined to start on the Monday morning, and take two days journey so that Mary might not be too much fatigued. He re-

membered that he had an uncle who lived on the
road, and stopping there for the night, they next day,
by the aid of a few friendly lifts into passing vehicles
arrived in sight of their destination on the evening
of the second day, and Mary gazed with wonder at
the great walls that enclosed the city, and at the
grey old minster, whose massive towers excited her
awe and admiration.   After lodgings had been
secured, Rayner sought out the castle, and making
known who he was and his errand he was promised
admittance to the court if he presented himself early
in the morning.

CHAPTER XXIII.

TRIAL OF HORSFALL'S MURDERERS.

" Man's crimes are his worst enemies, following
Like shadows till they drive his steps into
The pit he dug."—*Cimon.*

Although Rayner and his companion were at the
Castle door before daylight on the morning after they
arrived at York they found a considerable number
waiting, and when the great doors were at last swung
back nearly one-half of the available space in the
Court was at once occupied. The trials naturally
excited immense interest both in the city and
throughout Yorkshire, and hours before the Judges
arrived the Court was so densely packed that the
counsel and officers, though they arrived in good
time, found it difficult to reach their seats. The
governor, who recognised Rayner and his companion
in the dim light, conducted them to one of the seats
set apart where they could have a good view of all
the proceedings. There was something in the aspect
of the court in the dim, uncertain light from the
swinging lamps which was calculated to chill the soul
of the bravest, and poor Mary's teeth chattered with
fear as she glanced timidly at her surroundings.
There on the right hand were the great chairs where
the Judges who held her father's life in their hands
would shortly take their places, and on the left was
the dock where he would stand to be gazed at by
the pitiless crowd of sightseers. As the day broke the
slanting rays of the cold wintry sun struggled in at
the high windows, lighting up for an instant the
gorgeous blazonry of the Royal coat of arms above
the judgment seat and then faded slowly away to be
followed by heavy flakes of snow. Rayner felt the
thin figure quivering beside him, and noticing her

awe struck face he tried to divert her attention by
pointing out the counsel who were to prosecute on
behalf of the Crown, and calling her special attention to the barrister who was to defend the Luddites
—Henry (afterwards Lord) Brougham—of whose
eloquence he had heard great things. As he spoke
the echoes of the clear blast of a trumpet swept
through the court and instantly all voices were
hushed. The Judges had arrived and soon after
they took their seats on the bench and the business
of the day began.

At nine o'clock the court was duly opened by the
cryer, and George Mellor, of Longroyd Bridge, and
William Thorpe and Thomas Smith, Huddersfield,
were placed at the bar, the judges being Mr. Baron
Thompson and Mr. Justice Le Blanc. The youth of
the three prisoners excited attention at once, and
their appearance was the next theme of comment.
Mellor was pale, but his iron will was plainly manifested by his calm and almost defiant demeanour.
Smith looked the most affected by his position.
Thorpe was, as usual, stolid and impassive. They
were all pretty well dressed and presented a very
respectable appearance. The counsel for the Crown
were Messrs. Park, Topping, Holdroyd and Richardson; attorneys, Messrs. Hobhouse, London; Alison,
Huddersfield, and Lloyd, Stockport. The leading
counsellors for the prisoners were Henry (afterwards
Lord) Brougham and Messrs. Hullock and Williams.
Attorney, Mr. Blackburn.

Mr. Richardson opened the proceedings, and Mr.
Park gave the address to the jury. After stating in
detail the evidence he was prepared to place before
the court, he concluded by saying, "It seems that
nothing can be clearer than the mass of evidence
I have gone through, and when it is laid before you
it will be impossible for you to arrive at any but one
conclusion, that the prisoners at the bar are guilty
of the crime laid to their charge. One cannot but
lament that three young men, the eldest of which

is not more than twenty-three years of age, should
have brought themselves into this situation. But
there is also pity due to the country, to those individuals who have suffered in their persons or their
properties from the attacks of lawless violence. You
have a most important duty to perform. If, after
hearing the evidence, you have any reasonable doubt
upon the case, for God's sake acquit the prisoners.
But if from the chain of evidence I shall lay before
you, and by which the finger of Providence has
pointed out these men, and furnished as strong
proofs of their guilt as if you had seen them commit
the murder with your own bodily eyes, you will
discharge your duty to God, to your country, and to
your own conscience, by finding the prisoners guilty,
and guilt must speedily be followed by punishment
against the crime of murder, on which the Almighty
has himself pronounced the penalty of death. He
who sheddeth man's blood, by man shall his blood
be shed, and God has declared that the land can be
purged of the guilt of blood only by the death of him
who shed it."

The first witness called was Joseph Armitage, of
Crossland Moor, publican, who was examined by Mr.
Topping and deposed as follows:—" I keep the
Warren public-house, and have known for many years
the late Mr. Horsfall, who lived at Marsden, and
was a merchant and manufacturer; I saw him on
Tuesday, the 28th of April, in the morning, on his
way to Huddersfield, which market he was in the
habit of attending. I saw him in the afternoon about
a quarter before six; he stopped at my house and
took a glass of rum and water. John Sykes and
Joseph Sykes, hawkers of cloth, were there and he
treated each of them with a glass; he stopped about
twenty minutes and then went away. There is a
plantation on the way to Marsden, about a quarter
of a mile distant on the Marsden road. About
half-past six some children came down the road and
said, "Mr. Horsfall is shot;' both the Sykeses and

myself went to the place, and found him sat upon
the road about thirty yards below the plantation
nearer my house. Joseph Bannister was with him.
Mr. Horsfall was brought down to my house, and
stayed there till the day but one following.

Cross-examined by Mr. Hullock: said he looked
at the clock, and said he knew it was a quarter to
six when Mr. Horsfall came, he did not alight, cannot exactly say how long he continued at his door;
the ground to the plantation is rising; Mr. Horsfall
seldom rode fast.

Henry Parr, examined by Mr. Holdroyd, said,
" I was going home from Huddersfield to Marsden,
on Tuesday, the 28th of April; I cannot say what
time it was when I left Huddersfield; when I came
near the Warren House, I heard the report of fire
arms, it was a very large crack, and seemed to come
from the nearest corner of Mr. Radcliffe's plantation; I saw the smoke, and saw four persons in the
plantation, from which I was about 150 yards. I
did not know the persons, but they were all dressed
in dark coloured clothes. After the report, the
horse of a person riding before me turned round,
and the rider, whom I afterwards found to be Mr.
Horsfall, fell with his face upon the horse's chine;
he raised himself up by the mane and called out
" Murder, and as soon as he called out murder,
one of the four men got upon the wall with one
hand and both feet, and I called out to him and said,
' What art thou not content yet?' I then rode up
to Mr. Horsfall at a gallop as hard as I could, and
the men ran out at the back side of the plantation
the furthest from the road; when I came up to Mr.
Horsfall he was sat upright on his horse, and said,
" Good man, I am shot." There was a mark of
blood on the upper part of his breeches; he fell sick
and was going to fall off, I took hold of his arm and
held him up; the blood gushed out of his side several
inches; he said Good man, you are a stranger to

me and I to you—go to Mr. Horsfall's;' he then
fell on the horse, both his feet were fast in the stirrups
and I loosed them out and lifted him to the ground;
two boys, both sons of Abraham Willie, were
gathering dung on the road, and I called them and
then galloped down to Mr. Horsfall's brother's
house."

Cross-examined by Mr. Williams: He has lived
in the neighbourhood of Huddersfield five years; he
does not know the young men at the bar; his attention was drawn to the place where he heard the
report; he saw four men together at the coroner of
the plantation nearest Huddersfield; the plantation
is only about thirty yards over·

Re-examined: Before Mr. Horsfall got opposite
the plantation, the four men were walking about
the plantation; he saw them before he heard the
crack; when he got up to the plantation one of them
stooped under a bough and fired a piece, the other
three were standing behind him.

Joseph Bannister, of Holdroyd, clother, said, " I
was riding from Huddersfield at nearly half-past six
in the evening of the 28th of April, and another
person on the same horse with me; saw Henry Parr
returning from Huddersfield; we rode up and saw
Mr. Horsfall lying on the road very bloody and took
him to the Warren House."

Rowland Houghton, of Huddersfield, surgeon, said,
" I was called in about seven o'clock, and went to
the Warren House as soon as possible. I got to
the Warren House between eight and nine, and found
Mr. Horsfall lying on a bed with his clothes off; he
was sick, pale, and much exhausted, and his pulse
could scarcely be felt, it was so weak and tremulous.
I found two wounds on the upper part of the left
thigh, about three inches asunder: another on the
lower part of the belly on the left side; another on
the lower part of the scrotum, and two more on the
right thigh, and a slight bruise, not a wound, on the
lower part of the belly; the ball had been extracted

from the right thigh; and I extracted one musket ball from the outside of the right thigh, near the hip joint, gave the ball to Mr. Horsfall's brother, the Rev. Abraham Horsfall. On Wednesday afternoon from four to five o'clock, Mr. Horsfall appeared in a more cheerful state, but I had never any well-founded hopes of his recovery—I had little hopes, as I apprehended the temporal artery was wounded, but his continuing so long gave me some hope.

The Rev. Abraham Horsfall produced one bullet which he received from Mr. Houghton, who on being re-called, said he believed that to be the bullet that he gave to Mr. Horsfall. Had no doubt that the wound which he described was the cause of Mr. Horsfall's death; not the smallest. He was present with the magistrate, Mr. Scott, when Mr. Horsfall made some declaration on the subject. Witness then conceived him to be a dying man. Mr. William Horsfall said, What is your opinion, Doctor?' and he replied, "Indeed, Mr. Horsfall, I consider you in a very dangerous state." The deceased answered, "These are awful times, Doctor."

Mr. John Horsfall produced a bullet which he saw extracted from the thigh of his brother.

Mr. Houghton, cross-examined by Mr. Brougham, said, this slug was extracted by two persons; his own assistant and a surgeon. Mr. Houghton corrected himself, and said it was the femoral artery, not the temporal that he supposed to be injured.

"Benjamin Walker" rang clearly through the court, and there was a rustle and a murmur as every one bent forward to look at the Luddite informer as he stumbled awkwardly into the witness box. He was trying desperately to put on an air of unconcern as he at last stood confronting the prisoners, but he trembled visibly as Mellor's lurid glance fell upon him. In reply to questions, he said, "I have worked at John Wood's near two years, at Longroyd Bridge, about a quarter of a mile from Huddersfield;

Mellor and Smith worked also at Wood's in April
last. Thorpe worked at Mr. Fisher's, a shop about
three hundred yards from Mr. Wood's—I was not
acquainted with Thorpe; I remember the report
respecting the attack on Mr. Cartwright s mill; it
happened before the shooting of Mr. Horsfall, and
was conversed about in the works of Wood; when
they conversed about it, Thorpe was one of the party,
and the men killed at Cartwright's were talked
about by them. They said it was a hard matter.
Mellor saiu the method of breaking the shears must
be given up, and instead of it, the masters must be
shot at. That was most I heard said; they said they
had lost two men, and they must kill the masters.
I do not remember what day Mr. Horsfall was shot,
but I was that day at Wood's; Smith and Mellor
worked in one room, and I worked in another; I remember being with Mellor between four and five in
the afternoon, and there was William Hall and my
father and William Walker. He asked me if I would
go with him to shoot Mr. Horsfall. After that he
went to his drinking, and was absent about half-an-
hour; on my return, I found Mellor in the shop, and
there was my father, \ arley, and Hall. He gave me
a loaded pistol, and said I must go with him and
shoot Mr. Horsfall; he told me it was loaded with
double ball; and it was primed and loaded nearly up
to the top; he ordered me to go to Mr. Radcliffe s
plantation; I think both Smith and Thorpe were
present; Smith and I went together; Mellor was
dressed in a drab coloured jacket when he was in
the shop, but when he came to the plantation, he
wore a bottle green top coat; Thorpe had a dark
top coat; Smith and I wore close-bodied bottle green
coats; Smith and I went up the highway past the
Warren House; Smith had a pistol with him, which
he told me he had bought of a person of the name
of Mills, at Throw; it was without a cock when he
bought it, but on the way to the plantation I saw it
had got a cock; he told me it was loaded.   We

had been at the plantation about ten minutes when
Mellor and Thorpe came, and they came past Daniel
Batty's on the footroad; Smith went to Mellor and
Thorpe, but I did not go. I told Smith as I was
going I would not do this deed; but Smith said let
us go forward, and counsel them to turn back, it was
a pity to go. On Smith's return from Mellor and
Thorpe, he said they told him if we offered to leave
them they would shoot us. I saw Mellor's pistol in
the wood after the job had happened; we were about
twenty yards from Mellor and Thorpe when Smith
went to him. I had not seen Mellor's pistol the day
we went to the plantation, but I had seen it before;
the barrel of it was nearly half-a-yard long; he said
he brought it from Russia, and that he had sold it
to Richard Hartley; Smith and I received orders
from Mellor and Thorpe to stand twenty yards from
them; Mellor and Thorpe stood in the corner of
the plantation nearest the Warren House; Smith
and I were ordered to fire if Mellor and Thorpe missed
him; they were to whistle when Mr. Horsfall was
coming. One of them (I think Mellor), on the
approach of Horsfall, said—"He is coming." The
plantation is surrounded by a wall a yard and a
quarter high; Smith and I got up when we
heard he was coming. I do not know what
Mellor and Thorpe did, I could not see
them for the wood; we heard pistols go off,
and Smith and I fled back into the wood, and
were joined directly by Mellor and Thorpe; I then
saw Mellor's pistol, and Thorpe gave me his, saying
he would not carry it any further. Mellor damned
Smith and myself, and said he should have shot however it had been. On receiving Thorpe's pistol, I
observed that the cock was gone down, and the barrel
was warm. I never saw Mr. Horsfall. We all went
over the fields to Dungeon Wood; I saw three or
four men coming up, as we crossed the road from
Huddersfield; we went off as fast as we could run,
we were so flaid over th' job.' I threw down
Thorpe's pistol, and Mellor took it up. Both Smith

and myself hid our pistols in a mole-hill. On separating, Mellor gave me two shillings, because I had no money on me. They ordered us to go towards Honley, which is two miles from the Dungeon Wood, and we went thither. Mellor gave me some powder in a horn, which horn I hid near the Dungeon Wood, after I had hid the pistol. The public-house we went to is at the bottom of Honley; we found a collier drinking, nearly drunk, and making a deal of game. A man came in from the market and said Mr. Horsfall had got shot; on that, Smith struck up whistling, and the collier danced to it. We left the public-house in Honley between eight and nine o'clock. Smith and I had seven or eight pints of ale, and when we got home it was nearly ten at night. We were all four together on the following day. Mellor sent for me into the shop on the following day, by a person of the name of Sowden, about nine o'clock in the morning, and I was ordered to be sworn to keep the counsel. Thorpe produced a Bible, and Mellor ordered him to take the book, and swear, and told me my father, my brother William, and Varley had been sworn. I took hold of it, and an oath had been read to me from the Bible, but I do not know what chapter it was; I do not recollect a word he used; Thorpe ordered me to kiss the book, which I did, and returned the book to Thorpe. I had no conversation with them about the wall; Mellor's finger was tied up, and he told me he had hurt it with firing; Thorpe's face was bloody when he was in the Dungeon Wood, and he said he had hurt it in the plantation. Mellor told me next morning that they had been at Joe Mellor's near the bottom of Dungeon Wood.

Cross-examined by Mr. Hullock: Does not recollect the words used when the oath was administered, but does recollect that he has sworn to-day to speak the truth. Witness is twenty-four years of age; he came from Manchester on Saturday, and had been at the castle at Chester ten weeks. Was at Little-

wood's, the adjutant, at Huddersfield. It was about
six o'clock when the misfortune happened, and he
returned from his drinking about five; Hall, Varley,
his father, and his brother were in the shop when
Mellor came in, and the first thing that Mellor asked
him, was to go with him to shoot Mr. Horsfall; and,
after taking time while he cut two boards of cloth, to
consider it, he said he would. This was before he
went to his drinking; on his return Mellor had a
pistol for him, which he delivered to him in the
presence of all the persons mentioned above. They
all heard the conversation, and Thorpe was in the
shop at the same time. He ordered Smith and me
to go off together. This was Huddersfield market-
day, a deal of people passed them on the road. It
was a distance of twenty yards or more, when Smith
left him to go to Mellor and Thorpe, but he could
not see them, because they were higher up in the
wood. A person coming up the road from Warren
House, he thinks, could not see him and Smith, because they were laid down near the wall. The
height of the wall might be a yard-and-a-half. They
were never all four together in the nook (corner) of
the plantation. Mellor and Thorpe complained of
their not shooting, because they were not as ill as
they were; Mellor told him after that he would not
have minded if he, like Smith and witness, had not
shot. Smith and witness were at Honely about
two hours. He first told this story to his mother
that night when he went home; told both his father
and mother how they had gone on. His mother
went to Mr. Radcliffe about a week before he went
to Chester, which is about ten weeks ago. It will
be either eleven or twelve weeks on Wednesday
since they first went to Mr. Radcliffe. The witness
had been taken up before he turned informer. Mellor
and he were taken together. Had never before opened his mouth to any person, except his own family;
his mother went to tell Mr. Radcliffe, by his direction. He could not read. He heard a reward of

£2,000 was offered for giving the information. Never heard of any reward but from Sowden, who said it was in the newspaper. He heard of this reward before he went to Mr. Radcliffe,. Saw Maria Dransfield, and requested her to go to desire Mrs. Hartley to go to Mr. Radcliffe, and to swear that she was the first to come into the yard to tell him, because he thought she would be a safeness to him. as he had told the Justice so, but in truth, he never saw Mrs. Hartley at all on the evening Mr. Horsfall was shot. Had some conversation with a person the evening Mr. Horsfall was shot, and told him he knew nothing of it, but that was not true. He thought Mrs. Hartley would come up and say they were all at Wood's.

Re-examined by Mr. Topping—said he had never ridden from the Warren House to the plantation. Mellor was at work on the night of the murder, and employed in pressing. Before he was taken up Sowden had read the newspaper in the works that mentioned the reward.

The informer seemed glad to get down when told to do so, and to slink back into the back seat again. And now there was another murmur and rustling as the cryer called for William Hall, also one of John Wood's workmen, who had turned traitor.

William Hall said " I worked at the time of the murder at John Wood's; I was applied to by Mellor on that day, between four and five o'clock in the afternoon, for the Russian pistol which I had bought of a man on Mirfield Moor, near Thomas Sheard's, the Star Inn; the pistol had an iron end, with screws at the side, and a barrel about a foot long; I had heard from Mellor that he had brought the pistol out of Russia, and sold it to Richard Hartley. Mellor is the son-in-law of John Wood; I lent him it. Saw George Mellor load it; he put nearly two pipe-heads full of fine powder into it and then a ball and some slugs which he beat out with a hammer from balls; and put two or three in, and then put in

a ball at the top, and rammed them all down. I
asked him if he meant to fire that, as I knew the
pistol would jump when he fired it. He said he
meant to give Mr. Horsfall that. He asked me to
go with him, but I said I did not like to go; he
had a bottle green top coat, under which he put the
pistol. He saw Thorpe that afternoon, with a
pistol in John Wood's shop, and saw Thorpe braying
some slugs in the shop window, to put in his pistol;
both Thorpe and Mellor said they meant to shoot
Horsfall that day. Smith and Walker were present,
and when Mellor asked witness to go with them,
Walker said they would go. The morning following
a Bible was produced in Wood's shop; witness went
in, and saw Thorpe and Sowden sit at the press-
table, and Mellor and some other persons were present, but cannot recollect exactly who they were.
The Bible was on the press-table; when he went in,
a paper was on the table, which said, if ever we re-
vealed any thing concerning that thing, we were to
be shot by the first brother. Sowden gave him the
Bible into his hand, and he kissed it. Mellor complained on the Tuesday night, when they were going
to bed, and said he had hurt his finger by the firing
of the pistol, and did not know whether it would be
right again or not. Witness slept with Mellor, and
Smith was in the same room. They heard of the
murder about seven o'clock in the shop where Mellor
works; the information was given by old Widow
Hartley. Mellor told him that he and Thorpe had
called at his cousin's, at Dungeon-end, and left the
pistols in some flocks, and said Joseph Mellor's
apprentices were in the shop, and he told them they
must give them to their master when he came home.
He said they came through Lockwood to Huddersfield, and there parted. Smith came home at ten
o'clock or after; he said he and Walker had been at
Honley. Saw Mellor give Smith a guinea or a
pound note on the Monday after the murder. It was

three weeks before witness got his pistol again, and it was then delivered to him by Varley. Mellor told him there were some men come from Leeds that wanted arms, and asked witness if he would let his go, and after some hesitation he consented. Mellor asked him, one Saturday night after the murder, which was two or three days before he was taken up, and when he was expecting being apprehended, Mellor. wanted him to take the coat Thorpe wore when Horsfall was shot, as he was likest Thorpe, to go before Mr. Radcliffe, the magistrate, when they were called on; he was to go in Thorpe's place, and say he was going with Mellor to his cousin's, and it was he for whom he wanted work; he consented that night, but bethought himself after that the witness might swear to him instead of Thorpe. He had heard Mellor talk of going to America. He went with Smith the Sunday morning after Mr. Horsfall was shot, to seek the pistol. They hunted all up and down amongst the ant-hills, but did not then find it; Smith showed him the pistol two or three weeks after, and told him he had found it.

Cross-examined by Mr. Williams: Mellor had lived for a long time with his step father, Mr. John Wood, who is in an extensive line of business. Witness knew what was to be done with the pistol when it was borrowed. He was Mellor's bed-fellow. Knew the last witness was taken before Mr. Radcliffe; witness had been examined on a charge of shear breaking, but was not examined for Walker. Does not recollect meeting either James Harper or Joseph Rushworth, and saying to . them, he had cleared Walker by showing that he was not at the place when the murder happened. Did not see Benjamin Walker sworn, he met him coming in as he was going out of the place where the oath was administered. When he was sworn what was read was not out of the Bible, but from a paper.

At the conclusion of this evidence the court adjourned for a short time for refreshments, and Rayner and Mary, who had listened spellbound to the evidence, discussed the probabilities of the prisoners being condemned. Although Rayner had not been intimately connected with the Luddite leaders he had of course seen them at the few meetings he attended, and though he had no sympathy with them in their crimes, he felt a feeling of disgust and loathing as Benjamin Walker and William Hall entered the witness box to swear away the lives of men who were at any rate no worse than themselves.

CHAPTER XXIV.

CONTINUATION OF THE TRIAL OF HORSFALL'S MURDERERS.

> Crime
> Has in the moment of its perpetration
> Its own avenging angel—dark misgiving,
> An ominous sinking of the inmost heart.
> *Coleridge.*

On the court resuming, the next witness called for the prosecution was

Joseph Sowden, a cloth dresser, who was examined by Mr. Richardson, and deposed as follows :—I lived at the Yews on the 28th of April; between half-past four and five I saw Mellor and Thorpe come into the new shop at John Wood's, with each a pistol in his hand. All the shopmates were in, but one who was at Huddersfield. There were Benjamin Walker, John Walker, and his son William, Varley and William Hall. I heard George Mellor order Benjamin Walker to go home, and fetch top coats and a pistol. He went out, but I was not in when he returned. I do not recollect seeing Smith that day, and did not learn whether the pistols were loaded or not; they were of the horse pistol kind, and one of them was a brass mounted and brass guard pistol, three inches longer than Smith's. I did not see any of the prisoners till after Mr. Horsfall's death. I saw nothing in their dress but what was common. I saw Mellor on the evening of the murder about half-past seven. I had then heard what had happened to Mr. Horsfall. The following day, the three prisoners and Benjamin Walker, jointly and separately represented to me the circumstances of the murder, substantially the same as you have heard to-day. Either next morning or the morning following, Thorpe came into the new shop and said "Sowden I want thee, and must have thee sworn to keep Horsfall's murder in all its circumstances a secret." I objected, and said I never took an oath in my life, much more an illegal oath, and the consequences would be seven years' transportation. He said, if I did not he would shoot me dead; I knew that he would carry out his threat, as he never went without loaded pistols about him. I submitted, and he administered the oath the substance of which was to keep the murder of Horsfall a secret in all its circumstances, on pain of death, and being finally put out of existence by the first brother I should meet. After that he made use of the same threatening language, and swore by his Maker, "Now thou shall administer it to the others, or I'll shoot thee dead." I did under the same influence of the same terror, administer it to Thomas Smith, Benjamin Walker, John and William Walker, W. Varley, and Joseph Hall. Mellor brought the men into the shop to receive the oath.

Cross-examined by Mr. Brougham: One of the two pistols had a brass end as well as brass mountings. He heard Benjamin Walker sent to fetch great coats and a pistol, but witness did not know for what purpose they were intended; saw none of them that night after the murder but Mellor, and he never spoke to him that night. He heard it the following day, when they came to him and told him all the circumstances. He next swore him to keep it a secret. Told them taking the illegal oath was punishable with seven years' transportation. He received the oath, but did not call it taking it, because it was not voluntary; he did not kiss the Bible, he only put it to his face. He read the paper to Walker amongst others. He was not secretary to any association whatever, nor did he ever make a tour to see other societies. John Walker, worked in the shop of Wood; his son William Walker had always lived at home.

Martha Mellor, the wife of Joseph Mellor, a cloth dresser, cousin to George Mellor, one of the prisoners at the bar, said, " We live at Dungeon Bottom, about two hundred yards from Dungeon Wood. I heard first of the firing at Mr. Horsfall that night between eight and nine o'clock; our family consisted then of only one child and four apprentice boys, and a servant girl. One of the apprentices, Joseph Hold-ham, left our employment on account of misbehaviour, about a week after George Mellor was committed to York. I saw Mellor in the afternoon of the day of the murder, about a quarter past six o'clock; there was a gentleman with him, whom I have not seen since. They came from the workshop into the house. George asked if my husband was in. I told him he was at the market. He then asked me if we wanted a man to work. I told him we had no occasion. He asked me to lend him a handkerchief, and I lent him a black silk one. He asked me if I would allow that gentleman to wash himself. He had not then a great coat on, he had put it off. The other person had a great coat—George asked to borrow a coat, and I told him my master's coat was in the shop. They stopped about a quarter-of-an-hour.

Cross-examined by Mr. Hullock: Did not know where the apprentice was that ran away; he stopped with his father a few days. Fixed the time by the return of her husband, which was near seven o'clock. Mellor has always borne a good character since she knew him, which was about two years.

Thomas Durrance, apprentice of Joseph Mellor: Is about 17 years old, was with Mellor in April last. Does not know George Mellor, but thinks he saw him at his master's house, in the shop, on the night of the murder. There was a man with him; thinks Thorpe was with him. They had dark coloured coats when they came into the shop, he thinks top-coats. George Mellor took off his topcoat, and had then an under-coat, the topcoat he put on the brush-ing stone. Witness went upstairs with George, the

other man did not go; when he got upstairs he gave
him two pistols, about a foot long, they both put
them under the flocks, which are refuse of the cloth;
this was a room where they work, there was not many
flocks but sufficient to hide the pistols. Did not
observe in what state the pistols were; did not know
whether the trigger was up. Mellor said he need
not say anything about them, but witness told his
master when he came home. Soon after they had
hid the pistols, the persons left off work. Kinder,
Joseph Holdham and Francis Vickerman were his
fellow apprentices, he did not observe whether the
pistols were discharged or not. His master and he
hid them in the barn, and put straw upon them.
He saw Mellor before Justice Radcliffe, and saw him
afterwards, when Mellor told him to mind and speak
the truth about what he said and what he had seen.
Mellor gave him five shillings and told him to give
half to his fellow apprentice, Kinder, and not to say
anything about the pistols.

Cross-examined by Mr. Williams: Had never seen
Mellor before that afternoon, and he was with him
only a short time.

Judge: " What time did you and your master
take the pistols into the barn?"

Durrance: " In about two hours after they were
put in the flocks."

Judge: " What time did your master return
home after those people were in your shop?"

Durrance: " In an hour-and-a-half."

John Kinder, apprentice to Joseph Mellor, upwards of 18 years of age, says:—He had not known
Mellor a year, and did not know him right when Mr.
Horsfall was shot; told Durrance he thought it was
George Mellor; met him coming down from the
flocks room that evening; he went into the room and
Durrance showed him two pistols which he took from
under the flocks. Does not know whether they were
loaded, but thinks he blew through one of the touch

holes and found it empty, he observed that it was not primed. He had half-a-crown from Durrance.

Mr. Joseph Mellor, cloth dresser, cousin to George Mellor:—Remembers the time when Mr. Horsfall was shot; witness left Huddersfield that evening at six and got home about seven o'clock. Durrance showed him two pistols that night; had not then heard that Horsfall was shot, but had seen a bustle among the military. Durrance and he went to hide the pistols in the laith under some straw. They did this for fear they should be found on his premises : one of the pistols had a larger bore than the other He had heard Mellor say he had brought a pistol from Russia. One of them was without ramrod He found on his return home a dark topcoat on the brushing stone with two cartridge balls in the pockets, he also found another dark green topcoat next morning; neither of these coats belonged to him. James Varley came on the Sunday after and he told him where the pistols were."

Judge: "Was there any coat of yours missing which you had left at home?"

Mellor: "Yes, a light drab topcoat."

Mr. Staveley, the gaoler at the Castle produced a dark bottle green coat, which he said he took from Mellor soon after he came into the castle; and Joseph Mellor, being again called and asked to look at that coat, said it was like the coat he found on the brushing stone, but he could not swear to it.

Abraham Willie, a workman to Mr. Radcliffe, was in a building attending his horses that evening in the first close beyond the plantation. He did not see any man in the wood, but saw four persons run down the plantation towards Dungeon Wood. They were within fifty yards of him. They all wore dark coloured clothes. They were out of sight when they got a field length off. He heard that Mr. Horsfall was shot about three or four minutes after from two of his boys who were getting dung on the road.

Edward Hartley was coming from Lockwood the evening Horfall was shot ; was near the spot and heard a report of a gun, and he saw soon after four men run out of Mr. Radcliffe's field, and jump over a wall in the direction of Dungeon Wood, they were all dressed in dark clothes ; he saw the brass end of a pistol from under the coat of one of them ; witness made an observation about seeing the pistol to a person who was with him, which he supposes must have been heard, as the man who held it immediately covered it with his top-coat.

Mary, the wife of Robert Robinson, publican, at Honley, heard of Mr. Horsfall's murder the day it happened. Two young men came to their house that night and had something to drink. She remembers a collier was present, and one of the young men whistled very much and well, and the collier danced. The news of the murder was brought in soon after the young men entered, and she thought they looked down when they heard of it. They came between seven and eight and went away about nine. Her husband asked them where they came from, and they said from Longroyd Bridge.

The case for the prosecution being now finished, Mr. Justice Le Blanc looked at the prisoners an instant in silence ,and then said

" This is the time, prisoners, to make your defence. Would you George Mellor, William Thorpe and Thomas Smith, wish to say anything for yourselves?"

Prisoners: We leave it to our Counsel.

THE DEFENCE.

William Hanson, the first witness called on behalf of the prisoners, said that he was at Huddersfield on the 28th of April, saw Mellor about a quarter of a mile from Huddersfield, going to Longroyd Bridge, about a quarter before seven.

John Womersley is a clock and watch maker, saw Mellor the evening Mr. Horsfall was shot, at a quarter after six in Huddersfield, at the corner of

Cloth Hall-street, had a note in his pocket for him he owing him seven shillings for work done; went with him to Mr. Tavenor's, the White Hart, near the Cloth Hall, and stopped in the house about twenty minutes, where he drank with the prisoner, Mellor, and left him there with one William Battersby. Witness then went to the Brown Cow, another public-house, and he had no sooner got in than the news arrived that Mr. Horsfall was shot, and the soldiers were going.

Cross-examined by Mr. Park: Had just time to go to the Brown Cow after he had left the prisoner at Tavenor's, it was about twenty minutes to seven o'clock, the prisoner paid him the seven shillings and he could produce the note; had no particular acquaintance with him, but had done work for his father for many years. From Longroyd Bridge to Huddersfield is about a quarter of a mile.

Re-examined: Crosland Moor is more than twice as far from Huddersfield as Longroyd Bridge.

William Battersby, the next witness, lived then at Taylor Hill; and recollects that evening by being at Tavenor's, saw George Mellor and Jonathan Womersley, and drank with them; they had two pints of ale, and Jonathan Womersley left him in company with George Mellor, they were at this inn half-an-hour. At the end of that time they heard of Mr. Horsfall being shot for the first time. They came out and he parted with Mellor at the door.

John Thorpe, lives at Castle Street, Huddersfield; has known Mellor sixteen or seventeen years; saw Mellor in Huddersfield, near the George Inn, on the evening Horsfall was shot, at ten minutes before six, witness had a watch he wanted to sell him, and stopped with him two or three minutes; he asked him if he would buy his watch, and produced it, when it appeared to be the time mentioned.

Cross-examined by Mr. Topping: Does not know what street in Huddersfield the George Inn is in; says it wanted just ten minutes to six by his watch;

Mellor examined the inside, and asked him the price of the watch; witness valued it at £3 13s., but he did not buy it.

Jonathan Battersby, a shoemaker, remembers the evening Mr. Horsfall was shot; he saw Mr. Horsfall that evening in his father's yard; he was on horse-back, and went in the direction homeward; it was between five and six o'clock; he went into his own house, stopped till he got his tea, and then put on his coat and went up the street, this was about twenty minutes after he had seen Mr. Horsfall ride up. He saw Mellor in the New Street, and con-versed with him a minute or two. It was not quite six o'clock when he parted with the prisoner at the bar, he then went home, and heard of the shooting of Mr. Horsfall as soon as he got home.

George Armitage, blacksmith, living at Lockwood, knows where Joseph Mellor lives, his house is be-tween the Dungeon and Huddersfield, saw George Mellor come past between five and six o'clock, they go to their drinking sometimes at five, and some-times at half-past. That evening he had been de-tained by a job till after five o'clock; had conversa-tion with the prisoner; observed that he was coming from the bar, and going towards Huddersfield. He said he was coming from Joseph Mellor's.

Cross-examined by Mr. Park: Mellor said he had been at Joseph Mellor's, with a man that wanted work.

Joseph Armitage, saw Mr. Horsfall at his shop door, going towards Huddersfield from Lockwood Bar, saw his brother talking with George Mellor at drinking time, between five and six o'clock.

Charles Ratcliffe, cloth dresser, of Huddersfield, was at Mr. Fisher's, of Longroyd Bridge, on the afternoon of the day of Mr. Horsfall's murder, seek-ing work; was in the raising shop at half-past five; knows Thorpe, and saw him raising a blue coat piece in that room; he conversed with him for a quarter-

of-an-hour or upwards; left him there, and there
was a young woman fetching water in a can, out of
the raising shop. He returned to Huddersfield,
where he arrived twenty minutes after six, by the
Cloth Hall clock; about half-an-hour after he heard
of Mr . Horsfall being shot at.

Cross-examined by Mr. Topping: He was in
search of work, did not see Mr. Fisher; Thorpe was
the only man he saw or conversed with there.

Frances Midwood, of Longroyd Bridge, keeps her
father's house, and says that on the 23th of April,
as their usual practice is, they drank tea about half-
past four o'clock. The next day was their washing
day, and they got water from Mr. Fisher's shop.
About five o'clock, just after tea, she went with a
can to fetch water from that shop. The first time
she went there was nobody in the shop; it requires
about ten minutes to go, and she returned immediately, and then saw William Thorpe. He asked
her if she was fetching water, and she said " Yes."
Went the third time, some other person was with
him. She continued fetching water for some time.
Saw W. Thorpe every time she went for water except
the first. One of the times she saw Abraham
Pilling, a shoemaker, who was bringing her a pair
of new shoes. He followed her into the shop and
she left him with Thorpe.

Cross-examined by Mr. Park: She does not know
how long it takes to go from Joseph Mellor's to
Fisher's, nor does she recollect when she was first
asked at what hour they drank tea on the 29th of
April; it was not within these few days. When
she was asked it was in the presence of Mr Blackburn, the prisoner's attorney. A person fetched
her to Mr. Blackburn's, but that person did not put
the question to her; she first told them soon after
the prisoners came to York, but she cannot recollect
the exact time.

Abraham Pilling, shoemaker, made the last wit-

ness's shoes and delivered them on the night the
murder was committed; he took them from Huddersfield to her father's and he saw her crossing the road
with a can in her hand. He followed her to the
door which goes into the raising house; found Fanny
Midwood and William Thorpe there, she was lading
water out of a cistern with a can. He waited till
she had done. It was a quarter to six when he
set off home, and his house is a mile from Longroyd
Bridge. She asked the price of the shoes, and
went and fetched a guinea note belonging to Ingham's bank. He continued in the place and had
some discourse with Thorpe. He stopped in the
place about half-an-hour, when he set out for the
Marsh, which is nearly another mile on the Lindley
Road, but when he came out of the raising shop and
had just got into the lane, he was told that Mr.
Horsfall was shot.

John Bower, a boy, about seventeen, apprentice
to Mr. Wood, of Longroyd Bridge, examined by
Mr. Williams said,—Mellor superintends the work
for Mr. Wood; recollects the day Mr. Horsfall was
shot at; saw Mellor that day in the afternoon;
they were pressing. The press was to harden, and
Mellor assisted at hardening the press; there
were Thomas Smith, Benjamin Walker, James
Varley, and John Walker; it was near seven o'clock;
is quite sure Benjamin Walker and Smith were
present at the hardening of the press; Smith, the
prisoner, was an apprentice. William Hall and he
slept in the same room.

William Hall says: Widow Hartley brought the
news about seven o'clock, it was a particularly busy
day, and they did not go to drinking till six o'clock,
and soon after they heard that Mr. Horsfall was
shot.

William Hirst, of Longroyd Bridge, has lodged
at Mr. Wood's some years. Remembers Benjamin
Walker; remembers the time when Mr. Horsfall was

shot, there was noise enough about that; when he first heard of it, he said to Benjamin Walker, "Horsfall is shot!" and Walker replied, "That is too good news to be true."

It was objected by the Counsel of the Crown, that what Walker said was not evidence and ought not to be received, and in that objection his Lordship concurred. William Hirst, in continuation, said he had been at Huddersfield that day, and left it about twenty minutes before seven o'clock.

Cross-examined by Mr. Topping: He was no relation to any of the prisoners; his son is a merchant in Huddersfield, and employs Mr. Wood as well as many other people. On being asked what he meant by saying that there was noise enough about the murder of Horsfall, he said all he meant was, that it was a very bad thing, and produced a great outcry.

Joseph Rushworth, the last witness called, said he lived at the bottom of Cowcliffe, that he knows William Hall, who has been examined here to-day, remembers being before Mr. Radcliffe on the 12th of October; Hall was coming to Mr. Radcliffe's when he saw him, but had no conversation with him after he had been before the Magistrate.

CHAPTER XXV.

EXECUTION OF MELLOR, THORPE, AND SMITH.

" Let no one trust the first false step
Of guilt, it hangs upon a precipice
Whose steep descent in sure perdition ends."—*Young.*

The witnesses now having all been examined
Mr. Justice Le Blanc proceeded to sum up, and in
doing so recapitulated the whole of the evidence.
He went through that for the defence with special
minuteness and pointed out the conflicting statements made with respect to the time the various
witnesses asserted they saw prisoners, concluding
his long address as follows :—" This, gentlemen
is the evidence produced on the part of the prisoners; evidence of different persons coming in at different times, for the purpose of shewing that, at points
of time on that evening which they fix, they saw
either all the prisoners, or some of them, in situations not consistent with the time allotted by the
account given by the other witnesses for this transaction. When you see the point of time at which
it took place, and the nearness of all the different
spots where they were to the place in question,
perhaps it is not so surprising that there should, at
such a distance of time, be so much variance in the
account given by different witnesses as to the periods
of the day, as there appears to be upon the occasion.
Even supposing the witnesses to come under no im-
proper bias or influence in what they are saying,
they are speaking of a transaction which not only
took place a long time ago, but was not imputed
to the prisoners at the bar till a considerable time
after it had taken place. For this happened in

the month of April, and it does not appear that enquiry was made before a magistrate, or any of these persons committed, till the month of October. Nothing happened immediately after the transaction, to lead these persons particularly to watch, so as to be accurate in the hour or time on the particular evening, when they saw these persons at a particular place; and then we know how persons are apt to be mistaken, even when care is taken in point of time. However, gentlemen, it is for you to compare the evidence. The evidence on the part of the prosecution rests, not on the testimony of Benjamin Walker only, but of several other workmen in this manufactory, who are not accomplices in this transaction, though they appear to have had a knowledge of it, which I cannot say is not to a certain degree guilty. For I cannot hold them innocent in knowing of such a transaction going on, and treating it so lightly as to give no information respecting it, and to keep it concealed longer than while there was an immediate impression of fear of personal danger to themselves. But, independently of this, you have evidence of that which appears to me to be the strongest part of the case, and requires the most explanation, but which has not been explained, and which applies particularly to the prisoner Mellor, and to Thorpe, if you are satisfied he was with Mellor; I mean the transaction which took place at Joseph Mellor's house at Dungeon Wood, and which goes to contradict, in point of time, the evidence given by the different witnesses on the part of the defendants. The enquiry is a serious one, not only as regards the prisoners themselves, but as regards the public peace and security. You, who have heard the evidence, which lay the facts together in your minds, will do justice between the country and the prisoners."

The jury retired at half-past seven, and returned five minutes before eight, finding,—

GEORGE MELLOR, GUILTY.
WILLIAM THORPE, GUILTY.
THOMAS SMITH, GUILTY.

The prisoners being severally asked in the usual manner, by the Clerk of Arraigns, if they had anything to say, why sentence of death should not be pronounced upon them, answered:

Mellor.—"I have nothing to say, only that I am not guilty."

Thorpe.—"I am not guilty, sir; evidence has been given false against me: That I declare."

Smith.—"Not guilty, sir."

THE SENTENCE.

Mr. Justice Le Blanc immediately passed sentence of death upon them in the following words:

"You, the several prisoners at the bar, have been tried and convicted of wilful and deliberate murder —under all circumstances an offence of the deepest malignity, but under the circumstances which have appeared in this case in particular, as far as one crime of the same denomination can be distinguished from another, this may be pronounced a crime of the blackest dye. In other cases, the court has been able to discover something which might work upon the passions of mankind, and induce them to commit an act, at whch in their cooler moments their minds would have revolted, but, in the present case, the crime was committed against a man who appears to have given no offence to any one of you, except that he was suspected of having expressed himself with a manly feeling against those who had set up a right to violate all property, and to take away the life of any man who had been supposed to encourage others to do, (what I trust there still are men sufficient in the country to do,) to stand manfully forward in defence of their property. For that reason, he was marked out by you as an object of the most cowardly revenge. You, attempting to associate with yourselves such men as you could prevail upon

to join in your wicked purposes, waylay him at the
moment when he is returining home, almost in midday with a boldness which one had scarcely ever
witnessed in trying offences of this description. But
in the course of your trial, proceedings have come
before the court, at which human nature shudders.
That the national character should be so debased ;
that men, who ought to boast of their character as
Britons should have dared to hold forth, in the
language which you have held forth, and with so
little discretion, assassination and destruction of property were instruments in your hands, to be exercised
at your pleasure, and against any person who had
happened to offend you—independently of this, that
you should have dared to take into your hands the
Holy Scriptures, and to administer an impious oath
to those who were cognisant of your offence, calling
the Almighty as a witness, (that Being whom you
were conscious you had offended in the highest
degree ;) calling upon Him for vengeance upon the
heads of those who should discover your crimes ;
these are circumstances which have appeared in the
course of this trial, and which have scarcely ever
appeared in the course of any trial which has been
brought before a court of justice.

"It is not upon the testimony of one, or two, or
of three witnesses, that your guilt depends ; and let
me advise you not to lay that balm to your souls,
that you have been deprived by false accusation,
and by false oaths, of your lives.   A chain of circumstances has been discovered in the course of this
trial, which does not depend upon the oath of any
one, or two, or three men, whom you may denomi-
nate even as bad as yourselves.   But even from the
testimony of those, who, if they had not been honest
to a certain degree, would have' given a different
evidence, it is clear that two at least of you were
guilty ; and as little doubt remains, from other
evidence, upon the guilt of the third of you.

' In the shop where you have worked, some of
you appear to have gained such an ascendency over

the minds and over the consciences of the workmen, who were in some degree under your control, that you could mould and fashion them to any wicked purpose you yourselves might imagine. Their eyes, I hope, will be opened by the fate which awaits you; they will see, that though for a short time the career of the wicked may continue, yet the law is sure at length to overtake them.

" To you, the unfortunate persons who stand at the bar, (for every man who has disgraced his character as you have must be deemed unfortunate,) to you the only kindness I can offer, is in the advice to prepare, as speedily as you can, for that execution of this sentence, which must shortly await you; to make the best you can of the period still allotted to you in this world—longer far than was allowed to the unfortunate person who was the object of your revenge; that you will take the opportunity of making your peace with the Almighty Being whom you have offended; that by the sincerity of your repentance, the fulness of your offences, you may endeavour to obtain forgiveness in the world to come which I connot hold out to you any hopes of obtaining in his world.

" It remains only for me to pass upon you the sentence of the law. That sentence is—That you, the three prisoners at the bar, be taken from hence to the place from whence you came, and from thence, on Friday next, to the place of execution; that you be there hanged by the neck till you are dead, your bodies afterwards to be delivered to the surgeons to be dissected and anatomized, according to the directions of the statue. And may God have mercy upon your souls."

The prisoners, who still retained their self-possession, were then removed from the bar, where they had stood from nine o'clock in the morning to nine o'clock at night. During the whole length of the trial, and even while the solemn sentence of the law was passed, not one of them shed a tear, but their behaviour was perfectly free from any indecent boldness or unbecoming levity. The proceedings of the court were conducted with unusual solemnities, and the behaviour of the spectators was strictly decorous and becoming. From amongst the numerous relatives and friends of the unfortunate malefactors, an expression of anguish frequently reached the ear, but it was deep, not loud; and in that part of the auditory that was connected with them, only by a common nature, abhorrence at their enormous crime was not unmixed with commiseration, at the premature fate of three victims of a lawless confederacy.

So engrossed had Raynor and Mary been in the trials that they did not know how time flew; and when as they left the crowded court the great bell overhead struck nine, they were greatly astonished. They made their way swiftly to their lodgings full of excitement at the events they had witnessed.

At the opening of the court on Thursday morning, the jury recommended Thos. Smith to mercy, and an application was made to the Judges to have the sentence of the law, on such of the murderers as they might think proper to order for execution carried into effect not at the usual place of execution, but on the spot where the murder was perpetrated: but it was not thought expedient to comply with these applications.

THE EXECUTION.

In the interval between the trial and the execution, the prisoners behaved very penitently, though they refused to make any confession either in the prison, or the place of execution. Thorpe, on being asked if he did not acknowledge the justice of the sentence said—"Do not ask me any questions." Mellor declared—"That he would rather be in the situation he was then placed, dreadful as it was, than have to answer for the crime of their accuser, and that he would not change situations with him, even for his

liberty and two thousand pounds;" but with all his
resolution, he could not conceal the agonies of his
mind, for on the night before the execution he fell
on the ground in a state of insensibility, and it was
thought he would have died in his cell; but he slowly
recovered, and in the morning his health seemed to
be restored.

The execution of these unhappy men took place on
Friday, January 8th, 1813, at nine o'clock, at the
usual place behind the Castle, at York. · Every precaution had been taken to render every idea of a
rescue impracticable. Two troops of cavalry were
drawn up in front of the drop, and the avenues to
the castle were guarded by infantry. Five minutes
before nine o'clock the prisoners came upon the fatal
platform. After the ordinary had read the accustomed forms of prayer on these occasions, George
Mellor prayed for about ten minutes; he spoke with
great fervency and devotion, confessing in general
the greatness of his sins, but without making any
confession of the crime for which he suffered. He
prayed earnestly for mercy, and with a pathos that
was affecting. William Thorpe also prayed, but his
voice was not so well heard. Smith said little, but
seemed to join in the devotion with great seriousness.
The prisoners were then moved to the front of the
platform, and Mellor said—"Some of my enemies
may be here, if there be, I freely forgive them, and
all the world, and I hope the world will forgive me."
William Thorpe said—"I hope none of those who
are now before me will ever come to this place."
The executioner then proceeded to perform his fatal
office, and the drop fell. Some alteration had been
made in the drop, so that the whole of the bodies
were visible when they were suspended; in former
executions only the feet and head could be seen by
the spectators. They were executed in their irons.
They appeared slightly convulsed for a few moments.

The number of people assembled was much greater
than is usual on these melancholy occasions, but not

the slightest indication of tumult prevailed, and the greatest silence reigned during the whole of this solemn and painful scene. Such was the issue of that fatal system, which, after having produced in its progress great terror and alarm, and much mischief to the community, at length terminated in the death of those who were its most active partizans. And thus perished in the very bloom of life, three young men, who, had they directed their talents to lawful pursuits, might have lived happy and respected. They were young men on whose countenances nature had not imprinted the features of assassins.

CHAPTER XXVI.

TRIALS OF THE HALIFAX LUDDITES,
ALSO OF WILLIAM HARTLEY
AND OTHERS.

" Quick with the tale and ready with the ie,
The genial confederate and general spy.—*Byron.*

" A hopeless darkness settles o'er my fate,
My life is closed."—*Basil.*

The excitement of the eventful day proved too much for Mary Hartley. So long as her mind was occupied by watching the tragic proceedings she was not conscious of her weakness, but when her lodgings were reached she fell down in a dead faint, and had to be carried to bed, where she passed the night in a state of fever, and when the morning dawned was utterly unable to rise.

Leaving her in the care of the kind landlady, Rayner next day again made his way to the Castle. Again he was placed in a good seat by the custodian, and after several weary hours of waiting the court was opened in due form, and the Halifax Luddites were placed in the dock.

These were old John Baines (66), Charles Milnes (22), John Baines, the younger (34), William Blakeborough (22), Geo. Duckworth (23), and Zachary Baines (15).

The prisoners were charged with administering an unlawful oath to John McDonald, on July 8th, 1812.

The prosecuting counsel said that it appeared that in July last, John McDonald and another spy were sent from Manchester (by Mr. Nadin, a very active police officer there) to Halifax, to discover offenders of the description charged in the indictment, and

they arrived there on the 8th of July. They went
to a publichouse called the Crispin; there they
dined, and afterwards went to look for lodgings and
then returned. The circumstances of the attack on
Cartwright's mill were talked about at the Crispin.
The prisoner Milnes was there, and M'Donald entered
into conversation with him about the hardness of the
times. In the course of the conversation about the
mill, Milnes said he knew the two men who were
killed there very well, and spoke of the activity of
the person who commanded as an officer. M'Donald
said he would be as active as any of them if they
would twist him in, or swear him in. Milnes said
he had got many blank cartridges from a soldier,
that he had been searched for, but he got away and
stayed away three weeks. Milnes told M'Donald he
could get him sworn in by an old man who lived near.
M'Donald said he was willing. They sat together
till it was dark, and then went together to Baines's
house about ten at night; all the prisoners were
there. Milnes told them that he (M'Donald)
was a stranger, but a good fellow, and wished to
be a brother. Old Baines then said, he must be
handy about it, because he expected the watch and
ward in before eleven o'clock. He said nothing
more, but got a paper and a book about the size of
a Testament; put it into M'Donald's hands, and
desired him to say after him. M'Donald said his
name was John Smith, and repeated after Baines,
who appeared to read from a paper.

M'Donald does not recollect many words, but it
was that he should never reveal any brother's secrets,
either by signs or words; and if any traitors rose up
against them, they were to be put to death: and repeated much more than he could recollect, and kissed the book. Prisoners were all sitting down until
the oath was administered, when they all stood up.
Zachary Baines, the boy, stood with his back against
the door, to keep it shut. M'Donald himself was
afraid, lest the watch and ward should come; he

however sat down, and said he would pay for something to drink for them. Old Baines said he expected the watch and ward, and they had better go; that one of the neighbours had reported to the magistrates, and he was afraid of the watch and ward All the prisoners, except old Baines and the boy, went with M'Donald to the Crispin; Duckworth left them at the door; the said three went in. Gossling (the said police assistant) came in immediately after, and they sat drinking together. M'Donald told Gossling in the presence of the three prisoners then in the house, that he had been '' twisted in," and they said, " Yes he had:" and Milnes said he had introduced him. A day or two afterwards they met again, when M'Donald told Gossling, "That is the old man that '.twisted' me in." Baines said he had, and put his hand up and said they must be cautious where they said that; hush! his eyes had been opened a matter of three-and-twenty years. This was confirmed by Gossling.

Mr. Joseph Nadin, a police officer at Manchester, stated that the two witnesses who had been examined on the part of the prosecution, had been employed by him to go to Halifax and other places, for the purpose of detecting persons in the habit of administering illegal oaths.

On the part of the prisoners, separate alibi were set forth for each of them, supported by witnesses apparently unconnected with each other.

John Thomas, a master shoemaker, and Thomas Cockroft, his apprentice, deposed that John Baines, the younger, was working at his shop at Luddenden, on the 8th of July, the day sworn to by John McDonald, and that he remained all night at their house. Luddenden is about four miles from Halifax.

William Longbottom, who lives at Outlane, six miles from Halifax, had occasion to come to Halifax on some business, and remained there over the night of the 8th of July, where he slept at the prisoner's (George Duckworth's) father's. On the night of the 8th of July was with the prisoner, George Duckworth, the whole of the evening, and could undertake to swear that he was not at the house of John Baines the elder, that night.

William Duckworth spoke to the fact of the last witness being at his house on the 8th of July, and remaining there all night.

Thomas Elwall is son-in-law of John Baines, the elder; is a private in the 33rd regiment; was at his house on the 8th of July last; went about eight o'clock and remained until twelve at night, and during that period no person came into the house except Zachary Baines, his brother; being asked how he could amuse the old man so long, he said he had been in the East Indies, and though he had often told the story before, the old man liked to hear it again and again.

Hannah Crowther, of Halifax, stated that she saw Blakeborough on the 5th of July last, and it was proposed to go to Saddleworth on the 8th of July, to his brother's; that they went on the day appointed, in the morning, and remained there ten days. Witness paid ninepence a day during the time she was there; paid between eleven and twelve shillings when she came away, to the prisoner's brother. Witness is generally employed in burling cloth.

John Blakeborough stated the facts as deposed to by the last witness, as to his brother coming to his house on the 8th of July; that he remained there ten days. The last witness, Hannah Crowther, was there; she had money to pay for her board, but she did not pay him any.

After a charge from the Judge, the Jury retired for some time and then returned into court, and found a verdict of Guilty against all the prisoners, except Zachary Baines, who was acquitted.

A smile lighted up for an instant the wrinkled face of old John Baines as he heard that his son Zachary was acquitted, and then he turned with a defiant air towards the Bench to hear his own sentence. The Judge cast an almost sympathetic glance at the stern old democrat, who had all his life suffered for the people's cause, and who now faced him with unblanched cheek to hear what he knew would be his final doom. There was a moment's dead silence in the court, and then the Judge slightly waved his hand as a signal for the removal of the prisoners. He would consider his sentence.

Scarcely was the dock clear, when the voice of the cryer of the court was heard, and one of the names was that which Rayner longed, yet feared to hear, " Job Hey, John Hill, Wm. Hartley," rang through the court, and soon the three prisoners stood in front of the dock—the two first pale even to the lips, but the third wore his usual air of serious abstraction, which never for an instant left his face during the proceedings. Rayner gazed upon the face of his old friend with intense pity, and felt thankful that his daughter was not able to be present. Though only just turned forty, he looked as bowed and withered as one who had reached the full term allotted to man by the psalmist.

Mr. Park stated that the offence with which the three prisoners was charged, was connected with the disturbances in the West Riding. The obtaining of arms was one of the most prominent and alarming features attending that system of terror and outrage which had been carried to so great an extent. The crime of burglary was a capital one ,and to constitute this offence there must be a breaking into the house in the night-time, with an intent to steal; but as he had occasion to state to a jury on a former occasion, it would be the same thing in point of law, if the occupier of the house was by threats and intimidation compelled to open it; nor was it material whether the property was taken by the persons so entering the house, or delivered to them through fear.

George Haigh lives at Copley Gate, in Skircoat ;
in August last, he had a person lived with him of the
name of Tillotson. On the night of the last Saturday
in August he heard a loud rapping at the door ; on
hearing the noise he got up, and went to the landing
place at the top of the stairs ; heard a loud rapping
at the door, as if with the butt end of a gun. Witness
then heard the voices of several persons at the door.
The first thing he heard, was, " Your arms ! your
arms !" Witness then cried, " Holla, holla ! what
do you want ?" and was answered by one of the party
" General Ludd, my master, has sent me for the
arms you have." Witness said to this demand, " I
have nothing of the kind, for God's sake go home."
They then began firing: there was a continual noise,
occasioned, as he supposed, by beating against the
door in the porch, which reverberated the sound.
Witness proceeded to state, that after some alterca-
tion with them, in which they insisted that he had
two guns and four pistols, his apprentice said to
him, " Master, you had better give them up, or
they will shoot us," on which he consented that he
followed him into the house ; they had guns with
them, having again threatened to shoot him, if he
did not give them the pistol.   When the pistol was
delivered to them, they told him if his master did
should give them the gun. Tillotson took it to the
door to them.   Witness never saw anything of the
party ; heard them say, " Your arms, your arms ! be
quick or we will shoot you ; " the voice then seemed
to proceed from the kitchen.

John Tillotson lived with the last witness in
August last ; remembers some persons coming to
their house in the night, but does not remember the
day of the month ; heard a great knocking at the
door ; witness then declared the circumstances stated
by the last witness, as to the terms in which the
demand was made for arms, but further stated that
the people on the outside of the door said, if the door
was not immediately opened, they would break into

the house. His master told him he must get up, open the door, and give them the gun. When witness opened the door, some persons ran away from it to the corner of the house, where they were joined by some other persons; when they returned, they asked for guns and pistols; witness gave them the gun before they came into the house; witness remained within the door. They enquired if the gun was fireable, witness said it was; the ramrod being wanting, they told him if he did not find it immediately, they would shoot him; witness said he could not find it, on which they said there was another pistol, which they must have, and they not sell his milk among his neighbours, they would visit him again, with instant death. They took away with them a top-coat which belonged to him, but the coat was left at a farmhouse for him, and was returned next morning. Found the butt-end of a gun next morning near the door. The time of the attack was a little after twelve o'clock at night.

Cross-examined by Mr. Williams: They were not more than two or three minutes in the house, it was dark at the time. Neither of the two last witnesses spoke to the persons of any of the prisoners.

Joseph Carter (the informer) lives at North Green, in Greetland; knows the three prisoners; was in their company the latter end of August. Witness knows George Haigh; himself and the three prisoners went to various places, and among others to George Haigh's; the three prisoners at the bar were there; some of the party went to the kitchen door, and others to the front door; they knocked very hard, and demanded arms. Witness then stated the circumstances related to by former witnesses, previous to their entry into the house. When Tillotson delivered them the pistol, they then told him if his master did not sell his milk to his neighbours at twopence a quart they would visit him again. One of the party took a topcoat, and threw it on Job Hey's arm, and he carried it from the house; after some time he enquired which of the party it belonged to, and finding that it did not belong to any of them, he said he would not have anything to do with it, and he left it at a farmhouse to be returned to Haigh's. Job Hey took the gun into his possession, and another of the prisoners took the pistol. The gun was carried into North Dale. Job Hey had a gun when they went to Haigh's house, with which he knocked at the kitchen door, and broke it, a part of the stock was left behind; there were no firearms discharged; he struck the door very hard. The gun that was broken had been got that night.

Cross-examined by Mr. Williams: He is a cotton spinner and came to York from the House of Correction at Wakefield; got home between one and two in the morning; did not get drunk that night, it was another night, had been regularly employed in stealing arms for six weeks or a month; was taken up on a Saturday night in December. Witness afterwards corrected himself, and said, that enquiries having been made after him, he surrendered himself up.

Thomas Clark is a serjeant in the Suffolk Militia; there is a party stationed at Elland; apprehended Job Hey at his house in North Dean. On searching his house he found 3¼lbs. of gunpowder. Job Hey told him he had had it sixteen years, but the gunpowder was fresh, and could not have been kept so long. In consequence of directions from Job Hey, he found a pistol concealed between the chimney and the roof.

The examination taken before Mr. Radcliffe was then proved and read. Job Hey says, " I was there, at George Haigh's;" and John Hill says, " I was there, but there was never any gun fired." William Hartley, being charged with a felony, says, " I was there, but I had no arms, nor did I make any demand for any." The examination contained an admission of other depredations, but only those parts were read which applied to the present charge.

Two witnesses were called to speak to the character of the prisoners, who represented them as honest, industrious men.

Mr. Justice Le Blanc, after commenting upon the evidence, and stating the law to the jury, as laid down by the counsel for the crown, said, that character, which could not weigh much except in case of doubt, had less weight than usual in the present temper and discontent which had mani-fested itself in those districts, and where men, who would have shrunk back from the proposal of an ordinary robbery, engaged with alacrity in those depredations.

The Jury, without retiring, found the prisoners— Guilty.

The prisoners received sentence of death on the following day, and were among the unhappy prisoners left for execution.

230

CHAPTER XXVII.

TRIAL OF THE RAWFOLDS RIOTERS.

" Too late we find
Nor faith, nor gratitude, nor friendly trust ;
No force of obligations can subsist
Between the guilty."—*Brooke.*

On Saturday, January 19th, 1813, James Haigh, of Dalton, aged 21 ; Jonathan Dean, of Huddersfield, aged 30 ; John Ogden, of Huddersfield, aged 28 ; James Brook, of Lockwood, aged 26 ; John Brook, of the same place, aged 22 ; Thomas Brooke, of the same place, aged 32 ; John Walker, of Longroyd Bridge, aged 31 ; and John Hirst, of Liversedge, aged 28 ; were indicted for having, in company with George Mellor, William Thorpe, and Thomas Smith, and one hundred persons and upwards, to the jurors unknown, riotously assembled on the night of the 11th of April, and having begun to demolish a certain water mill, occupied by Mr. Wm. Cartwright, situate at Rawfolds, in the parish of Liversedge.

The three last persons mentioned in the indict- ment were executed for the murder of Mr. Horsfall, the preceding day.

The prisoners pleaded—not guilty.

The following gentlemen composing the jury were then sworn :—Isaac Newton, John Micklethwaite, Godfrey Park, Wm. Parker, Henry Popplewell, Gervas Seaton, Christopher Smith, Robert Stubbing, Richard Tottie, Thos. Tootal, Richard Waddington, Henry Wilkinson.

Counsel for the Crown, Mr. Park, Mr. Topping, Mr. Holroyd, and Mr. Richardson.

Counsel for the Prisoners : Mr. Brougham, Mr. Hullock, and Mr. Williams.

The jury desired to have a list of the prisoners, which was delivered to them.

All the witnesses, both on the part of the crown and of the prisoners, were directed to withdraw.

Mr. Park said he should be under the necessity of frequently mentioning the names of the unfortunate men now no more, though he did not wish to say anything harsh of them, but because it was unavoidable.

Mr. Richardson opened the indictment, and Mr. Park stated the case on the part of the prosecution, and called the following witnesses : —

Mr. William Cartwright, examined by Mr. Topping. He stated, that on the 11th of April last, he was in possession of a mill at Rawfolds, in the township of Liversedge, in the West-Riding. Had been in possession of it nearly three years. It was a water mill, erected for the express purpose of finishing cloth by machinery. Previous to the 11th of April he had been apprehensive, or rather expected an attack being made upon it, and in consequence of this expectation he had taken such measures for its security and protection as he thought best adapted to the purpose. He had slept in the mill for six weeks previous to the attack, and had procured musketry and ammunition, and several of his workmen slept in the mill for the week immediately preceding the attack. Witness had beds in the mill, and himself slept in the counting house.

On the 11th of April last, which was Saturday, he had in the mill five soldiers and four of his own people besides himself. Witness retired to bed at twenty-five minutes past twelve o'clock; in a quarter of an hour he heard the dog bark furiously; it was on the ground floor, and had been placed there for the purpose of giving the alarm on the approach of any person in the night-time. He got out of bed supposing the dog had given a false alarm, because he expected the first alarm to proceed from the watch at the outside of the building. As soon

as he opened the counting-house door he was astonished by a heavy fire of musketry, accompanied by
a violent breaking of windows on the ground floor;
the crash was considerable; a violent hammering
was at the same moment commenced at the door,
and a part of the assailants went round to the other
door at the end of the building. One side of the
building was protected by a pond of water, and on
that side there was only a narrow footpath. Mr.
Cartwright proceeded to state that they flew to
their arms instantly, which had been piled the night
before; they had not time to put on any of their
clothes, nor did he think of it, but commenced a
brisk firing.

A bell had been put upon the roof for the purpose
of giving alarm to a small detachment of cavalary
stationed in the neighbourhood. This bell was immediately rung, but unfortunately the rope broke.
They fired through loop holes which were in an
oblique direction with respect to the interior of the
building, but which commanded the front of the
mill. The firing was kept up regularly by the
people out of doors for a considerable time. He
continued to hear the most violent crashing and
hammering against the doors, and occasionally heard
loud cries of "Bang up, lads," "In with you,"
"Are you in?" "Keep close," "D— the bell, get
to it and silence it." The bell rope broke almost
immediately on the first ringing of it, but so important did he consider it that it should continue to
give the alarm, that he ordered two men to get upon
the roof to ring it. Mr. Cartwright said he distinctly heard the expressions, "In with you, lads,"
"D— them, kill them every one." The number
of people appeared considerable. A constant firing
on both sides continued for some time, but from the
number of shots fired by them he supposed it must
have occupied as much as twenty minutes. After
the firing without had slackened, they abated theirs
within, with a view to save the effusion of blood.
He then heard a confused alarm on one side as if

an attempt was making to carry off the wounded men. The people in going off appeared to divide and take different roads, but both of them leading ultimately towards Huddersfield. Witnesses would not for a moment have delayed giving assistance to the wounded after their companions had left the ground, had he not considered it imprudent to open the doors before the arrival of some person who could witness the situation in which the building and doors were; this he thought a necessary precaution, in the state of mind in which many persons were towards him. The first person that came was Mr. Cookhill, and the doors were then opened. They found two men wounded of whom as much care was taken as the bustle and confusion would allow. Mr. Cartwright then proceeded to describe the situation of the mill after the attack; the windows on the ground were entirely broken with the exception of nine squares of glass, out of three hundred, and the woodwork of the windows was damaged so much as to be entirely useless, and all the frames were obliged to be taken out. One of the doors was almost literally chopped to pieces, and holes made in it that a man might put his hand through; in striking at the door they sometimes appeared to have struck the stone work about the door. The other door had suffered no injury. The windows in the upper storey had also suffered considerable damage. The building, which was of stone, had received a number of shots, the marks of which were still visible. A number of implements used in the attack were found by himself and workpeople the next morning. Mr. Hullock merely asked some questions to ascertain whether Mr. Cartwright was the sole occupier of the mill, which he answered in the affirmative. Mr. Cartwright said he was not able to speak to the person of any individual concerned in the attack. In answer to a question from the bench, he stated that all the frames of the windows on the ground floor were so

much damaged as to be obliged to be taken out.
Mr. Cartwright produced a large bag filled with
hatchets, mauls, hammers, masks, and other implements used in the work of destruction, also the butt
end of a musket, and a man's hat, which was found
in the mill dam.

James Sands was next called, who proved the
finding of most of the articles contained in the bag
produced by Mr. Cartwright, on the morning after
the attack.

James Wilkinson found a bag in the mill dam, on
the morning of the attack about five o'clock, witness
picked up some of the instruments produced by Mr.
Cartwright, near the mill, some of them were found
in the inside of the mill.

William Hall (informer) stated that he was a
cropper, remembered the Saturday on which Mr.
Cartwright's mill was attacked; witness worked at
John Woods at Longroyd Bridge, near Huddersfield, none of the prisoners worked there; he knew
Joshua Dickenson, who was a cropper, saw him
about the middle of the day at John Wood's shop;
Sowden was there at the time, he came to bring
powder and ball; none of the prisoners were there;
he brought a good deal of powder, about a pint, and
a good deal of ball; the powder was in paper, and
the ball in a little bag; he also brought two or three
cartridges; gave him directions what to do, and in
consequence of these directions he went to a field
belonging to Sir George Armytage; he went with
Smith and George Dyson, and overtook George
Brook, of Lockwood; got to Sir George's field about
ten o'clock, found two or three score people collected
when he got there; remained there a good part of
an hour, and during that time a number of other
persons joined them; could not state the number,
but there was a good deal more than a hundred.
Witness stated that before they left the field they
called over the people, not by name but by numbers,
each person answering when his number was called;

DUMB STEEPLE.

witness was number 7 ; there was a man to put them
in order.   They were formed into companies ; witness
was in the pistol company.   Mellor and Thorpe
were the men who formed them into line ; there were
two companies of pistol-men ; there was also a
company of musket-men, which marched first, they
were two deep and ten abreast ; witness was in the
pistol company ; George Rigg and witness were
ordered to go last and drive them up, and see that
none went back.   They all went in line over Hartshead Moor, and in this manner went to Rawfolds.
Witness said they assembled at a place where there
was an article called the Dumb-steeple.   Witness
said there were hatchet-men, and others who had
sticks, and others who had nothing at all ; there were
also hammers and mauls.   When they got to
Rawfolds they were stopped and formed into lines
thirteen abreast ; Mellor formed the musket company,
and Thorpe formed the next company.   The witness
being desired to look at the bar, and point out all
the persons there, named James Haigh, Jonathan
Dean, John Ogden, James Brooke, John Brooke,
John Walker and John Hirst ; he did not see Thos.
Brook there.   They formed into a line, and then
advanced towards the mill.   There was a good deal
of firing from the inside of the mill ; witness was
amongst the last, when he got up to it they were
breaking the windows and doors ; heard Mellor call
out, " The door is open," " Fire at the bell ; " heard
one call out, " There is a man shot," saw a man
lying on the ground, did not know him.   Witness
fired twice into the mill.   The firing on both sides
continued a considerable time.   The door in the
front was cut through, but not opened.   Witness
only saw one person on the ground ; when the firing
ceased they got away as fast as they could ; he went
through the beck in the direction of Hightown.
Overtook James Dyson.   Saw none of the prisoners
going from the mill.   Did not see any person without a hat.   There was a hat brought to John Wood's

shop by Thomas Brook, who told him to get it to the place it belonged to, if he could, and referred him to George Mellor, as the person who would inform him to whom it belonged. Mellor told witness that he did not know where he was until he got to Hightown, and that he called at Samuel Naylor's. Witness said he did not remember stopping on the road or any of the party stopping, nor heard them ask for anything on the road. Sir George Armytage's field, where they assembled, was about three miles from Mr. Cartwright's mill.

Cross-examined by Mr. Williams: Witness said it was a pretty fair night for seeing, it was not very dark, and he could have known a man at a moderate distance, within a yard or two. He said he saw the prisoners in the field of Sir George; does not know whether he saw them after, he saw them when they were standing together, not in ranks, and had not seen them before they got to this field, which was the place appointed for them to assemble at. Witness knew Mellor and Thorpe before the day on which the attack was made; witness said he had seen Haigh at a public house kept by Robinson, but did not desire a person of the name of Berry, or any other person to point out Haigh to him, and had never said that he did not know Haigh; had known him before; could distinguish a good many persons there by their voices; saw the men he had spoken of in Sir George Armytage's field; did not see them at the place where they halted.

On his re-examination he said, that being ordered to see that none of the persons went back, he could state that only two persons left them, and they let them go because they were sick and would do them no good.

CHAPTER XXVIII.

CONTINUATION OF THE TRIAL OF THE RAWFOLDS RIOTERS.

Guilt is the source of sorrow ; 'tis the fiend –
The avenging fiend—that follows us behind,
With whips and stings.—*Rowe.*

The next witness called was Joseph Drake, who
was examined by Mr. Topping. He said he was a
cloth dresser, and worked at the time of the attack
on Mr. Cartwright's mill, at John Drake's. He
went with John Walker and Jonathan Dean from
Jonathan Dean's house. He set off about ten o'clock
at night. He had been acquainted with them for
some time. They were to meet in a field of Sir
George Armytage's. As they went they overtook
many persons going to the same place, but did not
overtake any of the prisoners. When they arrived
at the place of meeting they found a considerable
number of persons collected, from one hundred and
thirty to one hundred and fifty. He did not see
any of the prisoners in Sir George's field. They were
called over by numbers, and placed two by two.
They were also mustered into companies; could not
say who mustered them. A good number of them
had arms. Witness was in the pistol company ; did
not know how many companies there might be.
There were companies of musket men, companies of
pistol men, and also companies of hatchet men.
When they were put in order they were marched to
Mr. Cartwright's mill. Witness did not go to the
mill, but halted about sixty yards from it. Never
saw the prisoner Dean after they left Sir George
Armytage's field, but did not see him go away.
Witness when he was at the place where they halted

heard a good deal of firing. Many of the party stopped behind. Witness had a pistol part of the way but had not a pistol when they halted; he had then no arms. The main body proceeded to the mill; the firing was loud; could not hear the breaking of the windows for the noise of the firing; the firing continued a quarter of an hour to twenty minutes. Dean had a hammer with him, and was solicited to go by John Walker, who had a pistol with him and a smock frock on; did not know James Haigh; knew Thos. Brook; first saw him at Hightown on their return. The party went off in different directions. Witness went towards Hightown; Thomas Brook had nothing with him when he saw him; had seen him before, his clothes were very wet. Witness thought he said he had been in the mill dam, and he was without hat. George Mellor was with him, they stopped at Samuel Naylor's, and a hat was borrowed there for Thomas Brook. Mellor was the person who borrowed the hat, and he went along with them; they stopped at another place near Clifton, where they asked for some muffins and water; a woman gave them some out of the window. The hat was delivered to them by Samuel Naylor's wife. Witness knew John Ogden (another of the prisoners): had known him before the 11th of April; met with him at Hightown after the attack; had not seen him before; he had a pistol with him and nothing else; he said he had been at the attack at the mill; they parted with him before they got to Cowcliffe.

Cross-examined by Mr. Broughton: He said it was a very dark night before they fell into ranks at Sir George Armytage's field; the field was also near a lane that occupied a considerable space; it was also near a lane that went up by the side of the wood: remained there a quarter of an hour, it was then very dark.

Benjamin Walker (the accomplice in the murder of Mr. Horsfall) stated that he was one of the party

who went to Rawfolds mill on the night the attack
was made upon it; he went with George Mellor,
Wm. Thorpe, and Thomas Smith (the unfortunate
men who had been executed), to Sir George
Armytage's field; saw none of the prisoners there,
nor before they got there; he was No. 13; they were
formed into divisions. Mellor's company was the
first, and was chiefly armed with guns, the next
company was armed with pistols. George Mellor
had the command of the first company, and Thorpe
of the second. Saw the prisoner Jonathan Dean
in going from Sir George Armytage's field, between
that place and the spot where they halted; it was
nearly at the mill; witness continued in the first
company armed with muskets; there was a good deal
of firing; witness fired his piece. Witness saw
Booth, who was wounded, and is since dead; he did
not see any other person wounded. Witness saw
Jonathan Dean, in his own house the morning the
attack was over, about six o'clock in the morning;
he was in bed, and his hand was bleeding; he told
him he had got hurt, but did not tell him where;
said he had got hurt in the finger with a shot, but
witness had no further conversation with him.
Witness stated that they stopped at a place where
they borrowed a hat for Thomas Brook (one of the
prisoners); it was Hightown where they stopped.
Thomas Brook told him he had lost his hat in the
mill-goit; he said he had fallen in; his clothes were
very wet. Saw John Walker between Sir George's
close and where they halted near the mill; he had a
pistol with him, and saw him again some time after
that. Saw James Haigh in the field of Sir George
Armytage; thought he had a maul; saw no other of
the prisoners there. Witness knows the village of
Clifton; they got some muffins there, which were
given them by a woman; was armed with a gun and
pistol; he gave the gun to Varley. Witness had a
mask on that night, and some other persons were also
disguised with masks. Mellor ordered him to burn
his, which he did. The Counsel for the prisoners

did not ask any questions of this witness.

Joseph Sowden stated that he was a workman at
John Wood's shop at Longroyd Bridge; remembers
the attack on Cartwright's mill. Witness knows
Jonathan Dean and John Walker and the three
Brooks. Witness never heard anything personally
from them of what passed at Cartwright's mill;
never saw them for ten weeks after; had some conversation with John Walker at the beginning of the
week following: the conversation happened at John
Wood's shop: he heard him say, not directing his
discourse to witness, that he had a horse pistol;
that he was standing looking in at a window and a
ball came through and struck the crown of his hat,
and that he put his hand into the window, and fired
his pistol at the place the flash proceeded from, and
said, " I was determined it should go if my hand
went with it." Nothing further was said. Previous to the attack, Jonathan Dean and John Walker
were the first that proposed the frame-breaking
system, in imitation of the frame-breaking at Nottingham, and who came with a person to request
them personally to consult, contrive, and adopt plans
for the destruction of machinery. Nothing at that
time was said about Mr. Cartwright's mill; the
application was first made in the way of solicitation,
but afterwards in a threatening way. Nothing was
said in his hearing about the intended attack on
Mr. Cartwright's mill. Witness said, so far from
approving of these proceedings, he always detested
them. Witness never heard anything from Brook
on the subject.

Mr. Hullock: " Detesting as you did these proceedings, why did you not instantly give information
of them?"

Sowden : " Because I did not conceive they would
ever come to the pass they did."

Mr. Hullock: " But when you found they had
come to that pass, why did you not then inform?

Why should you conceal these enormities so long in your breast?"

Sowden: "I acted as every other person in the circumstances, and with my spirit would have acted."

Mr. Hullock: "Pray, sir, what kind of a spirit have you?"

Sowden: "A timid spirit."

Mr. Hullock: "But it seems you timidly at last gave way. How was it you at length summoned up courage to make a disclosure?"

Sowden: "When I was questioned upon oath, I was obliged to speak the truth, and leave the circumstances."

Witness stated that it was the 24th of October that he first disclosed his knowledge of the circumstances he had given in evidence.

Mary Brook lived at Clifton in April last; remembered the night of the Rawfolds stir some persons came to the door that night, and asked to buy some bread; she got up and gave them muffins and a pitcher of water through a pane that was broken, and they gave her threepence for them. Witness did not see any of the persons.

Mrs. Sarah Naylor lived at the top of Hightown, was a married woman; remembered in the night of the attack on Cartwright's mill, that some persons called at her house and asked her to lend a man a hat, which she did; did not know any of the persons who called at her house.

Richard Tattersall, practised surgery, and lived at Lepton, which is about four and a half miles from Huddersfield; remembered some person coming to his house on Sunday, the 12th of April, and saw him again on the Tuesday following; only saw him during the time he dressed his wound. Witness afterwards saw the person at Mr. Radcliffe's and knew him again. Witness was then asked to look at the bar and point him out, if he was there. Witness looked at the bar and pointed out James Haigh. The first

time James Haigh came to his house was about four
o'clock ; he said he wanted a wound dressing. The
wound was on the right shoulder, at the back part ;
it was about an inch deep; it was not a perforation,
but an open wound. His shirt was bloody ; at the
edge of the wound there was some lint; the wound
was more wide than deep, and was a largeish wound.
Haigh said he came from Dalton, and the wound was
occasioned by a stone. Witness said nothing to him,
but dressed his wound ; it appeared to be a bruise,
and it appeared as if it might have been done by a
stone. It appeared to be a fresh wound ; sewed it
up at each end and in the middle, he took three
stitches in the whole. Haigh did not tell his name.
The Judge asked some questions to ascertain whether
the wound was a perforation or an open wound, but
the witness persisted in asserting that it was an open
wound.

Joseph Culpan lived at Penistone Green, in a
lone house ; it was fourteen miles from Huddersfield ;
knew a place called Dalton, which was about twelve
miles from his house. Witness had a relation lived
at Dalton, of the name of Ardron ; saw him in April
last, he came to his house ; there was another person
with him ; it was on the 15th April between twelve
and one at night. The witness was in bed. After
some conversation, his wife and he got up, that they
might lay down ; he had only one bed in the house.
Witness said that the person who was with his
relation was James Haigh. Witness thought that
Haigh said he had been hurt; but the witness seemed
extremely unwilling to give an account of what had
passed. Witness said he got up about five o'clock
in the morning, and after some trifling breakfast, set
off with his relation, Ardron, to go to Ardron's mother,
who lived at Willow Bridge, leaving Haigh at his
house. The purpose of their visit was to prepare
for James Haigh going there. Haigh remained at
witnesses's house until next day in the afternoon.
Ardron's mother lived about a mile from his house

and thirteen from Dalton.   No questions were asked
of this witness by the prisoner's counsel.

Thomas Atkinson went to James Haigh's house
at Dalton on the 23rd of April to apprehend him;
found nobody in the house; there were some brewing
vessels containing liquor which had been in a state
of fermentation, but which had completely gone off.
Witness found the door locked, and broke it.   In
consequence of some information he went to Tattersall, the country surgeon, and from thence to
Penistone to Ardron's mother, from thence to
Wragby, and from Wragby to Methley, where he
apprehended James Haigh; the distance from Methley to Dalton in a direct line was nineteen miles,
but by the circuitous route he went was considerably
more.   Witness found him at his brother-in-law's;
he was wounded in the shoulder.   Witness took
him before a magistrate; asked him no questions
respecting the manner in which he was wounded.
Witness stated that the prisoner's shirt was taken off
at Mr. Radcliffe's, who gave him one of his.   The
shirt being shown to Major Gordon, he stated it as
his opinion, that the rent had been made by a musket-
ball; James Haigh heard this, but made no observations upon it.   The shirt had been mended, the
prisoner said by his wife; it was produced in court.

Mr. Michael Bentley stated, that he remembered
seeing the prisoner, James Haigh, in April last; saw
him first at the witnesss's own house, where he
shaved him; it was the day before he was taken up
—on Sunday; witness said he appeared to be hurt
in the shoulder, he thought it was the left shoulder;
witness asked him no questions about his wound,
but he asked him if he was one of the Ludds, to
which he gave no sort of an answer.

Mr. Allinson, the solicitor, was called upon to
prove the examination of Jonathan Dean, but it
appearing that some expectation had been held out
to him that it might be for his advantage to make a
disclosure, Mr. Park said he would give it up.

The examination of John Hirst being proved, was put in and read, in which he admitted he went to Rawfolds, and heard some firing.

Mrs. Fanny Mills knew James Brook, one of the prisoners, and lived near him; a window only parted the two doors. After the morning of the attack on Mr. Cartwright's mill, witness said she saw nothing particular, heard a deal of whispering. James Brook was telling a very sorrowful tale, as she could tell by the motion of his hands. There were many of the shearmen going to and from the house; they were men who worked at their shop. Witness knowing that if she went in they would give over talking, hung back, and heard James Brook say, "of all the dismal dins that ever man heard, it was the most dismal; they might hear it for half a mile; and he would be clammed (hungered) to death before he would be in such another stir."

On the prisoners being called upon for their defence, James Haigh and Jonathan Dean said they were not guilty, but left their defence to their counsel. John Ogden said he was never in company with them. James Brook said he was not in the affair. Thomas Brook said he was never at the place; and John Brook and John Hirst repeated that they were not guilty.

CHAPTER XXIX.

DEFENCE OF THE RAWFOLDS RIOTERS.

Ranging the waste of desolate despair
Start any hope.—*Southern.*

The following witnesses were examined on the part of the prisoners :—

Abram Berry stated that he knew James Haigh, that he was in his company shortly after the last York Assizes, at a public-house kept by a person of the name of Robinson ; a person whom he did not know, but who said his name was Hall, asked him.— [The Court here said, unless the witness could state that the person who so accosted him was the William Hall who had been examined on the part of the prosecution, it could not be received as evidence.] Wm. Hall and a number of other persons were brought into court, and he was desired to point out the person with whom he had that conversation, but the witness after looking at them, said he could not point him out.

Thomas Ellison said he was a woolstapler, and lived at Lockwood ; knew the prisoner James Brook, who lived with his father at Lockwood ; remembered the affair of Mr. Cartwright's mill ; remained at Huddersfield until nine o'clock, and on his return stopped at a tavern called the Spring Gardens, where he remained until half-past ten o'clock ; from thence to his own house was rather more than a quarter of a mile. In his way home he saw the prisoner ; had some conversation with him : overtook him opposite his own house as he was going home ; this was about a quarter past twelve o'clock. Had known James

Brook all his life, and there was not a man in Lockwood had a better character. Lockwood was about
seven or eight miles from Cartwright's mill. Had
some talk with him. Witness was here asked by
Mr. Park whether Mr. Blackburn, attorney, had not
communicated with him some particulars of the trial.
Witness said he had not; had seen Mr. Blackburn,
but the only question put to him was, whether all
the witnesses were forthcoming.

George Armitage lived at Lockwood; remembered
the evening of the 11th of April; was down at Hud
dersfield, returned at nearly twelve o'clock; saw the
last witness Thomas Ellison. Witness called upon
James Brook at his father's house; got there some
time near twelve o'clock; saw James Brook sitting
near the fire and had some talk with him, his father
called out to him. Rawfolds mill is about eight
miles from Lockwood. Witness heard of the attack
on Rawfolds mill the next morning.

Witness, on his cross-examination, said, he did
not hear of the attack before he went to bed. Had
seen Thomas Ellison at Huddersfield; he repeated
that James Brook was sitting by the fire-side, and
remembers looking at the clock, and it wanted five
minutes to twelve o'clock; it was within five minutes
of twelve; he recollected it from the circumstance
of hearing of the attack on Rawfolds mill next morning. Nothing occurred till he was summoned to
York to draw his attention to it.

Hannah Tweedle knew Fanny Mills; lived very
near her; heard her say she was determined to have
the Brooks distressed before they came from that
place, and that some of them must be hanged before
they left York. This finished the defence of James
Brook.

John Ellis worked for Thomas Brook in the spring
of last year; worked for him at the period of the
attack on Cartwright's mill. Thomas Ellarman and
John Vickerman were working upon his premises at
the same time. Thomas Brook did not work at the

shear-board; they were very busy at this time; saw his master in the evening of that day in which the attack was made; he worked until his master came to the shop and said it was nearly twelve o'clock; he then went into the house and drew his wages, and then the clock struck twelve.

Cross-examined by Mr. Park: He said there was at that time no scarcity of work at Lockwood, they were busy'; the persons he had mentioned and himself were the only persons then employed by the prisoner; cannot remember any particular person coming into the shop in the course of the evening; received a one pound note, this was the sum he usually drew; Saturday was the customary pay-day. Much time was consumed in questioning the witness as to the number of minute circumstances, whether the children were up, where they slept, where the wages were paid, who was paid first, to which his answers were rather confused and inconsistent. He said he had been working upon a piece of plain cloth, but could not recollect the colour of it. In answer to a question from the bench, he said he had been working the whole day except when he went to his dinner.

Richard Lee knew John Walker, of Longroyd Bridge; had lived with him nearly six years. lived with him in April last; went home between eight and nine in the evening of the attack on Rawfolds mill; remained at home the whole night. John Walker came in between ten and eleven at night; when he came home, went to fetch two barrows of coals from Hannah Blakey's, it was then about eleven o'clock. John Walker then shaved Joseph Walker, who then went to his house. John Walker slept in the lower part of the house, and he slept in the chamber over it. Witness in the course of the night occasionally heard him cough and snore in bed. Nothing material came out on his cross-examination. In answer to a question from the Judge, he said that Joseph Walker came in about ten o'clock, and waited

until John Walker came in to shave him, there was
no one else in the house; there was no other person
in the house except his wife, who told him they
wanted coals; John Walker asked Joseph Walker
to go with him for the coals.

Joseph Walker lived at Huddersfield; remembered
the stir at Rawfolds mill; was at Lockwood the
night before; got there about half-past ten at night.
The prisoner, John Walker, asked him to assist him
in getting a few coals from J. Blakey's; the wife's
name was Hanrah; fetched two barrows from
Blakey's, who lived about two hundred yards from
James Walker's. John Walker afterwards shaved
him, and he left his house twenty minutes before
twelve. When he got to Huddersfield he heard the
town clock strike twelve. When he got to his own
door, he saw Richard Lee in the prisoner's house.

Cross-examined by Mr. Topping: Lockwood is
better than half a mile from Huddersfield; there were
barbers in Huddersfield but he always went to
Walker's to be shaved. When he got there he was
sat in his chair and strapping his razor; went for the
coals before he was shaved.

Hannah Blakey stated that her husband was a
mason, and that she sold coals; knew the prisoner
John Walker; remembered Rawfolds stir; saw the
prisoner on that night come to fetch two barrows of
coals; Joseph Walker was with him; it was sometime
about eleven o'clock.

On her cross-examination, she said she was sure
it was that night; always recollected that it was that
night, because next morning she heard of the affair
at Rawfolds mill. She also remembered from
putting the coals down on a slate; did not pay for
them. Never lent the prisoner a smock-frock in her
life, or ever lent one in her life to Drake. Witness
repeated that she had always kept it in her recollection that it was the night of Rawfolds stir. In
answer to questions from the Judge, she said John
Walker had always bought his coals from her ever

since she began selling; that they fetched them when they wanted them, sometimes on Saturdays, and sometimes on other days, but did not take any particular notice of any except the night she had spoken of, which she always kept in her recollection. This witness finished the defence as far as the above was concerned. A number of witnesses were then called, who spoke of all the prisoners as honest, industrious and peaceable men.

SUMMING UP.

Mr. Justice Le Blanc then summed up the evidence with the usual accuracy and precision. He stated that his indictment was formed on a statute of George III., made to supply the omission of a former act. By this act it was made a capital offence to demolish any water, wind-mill, or mill of any other description that was, or might be in future, erected; and it was also made a capital offence to begin to demolish any such mill. There would, therefore, be two questions for the jury to determine. First, whether the evidence given in the trial, and which he should recapitulate, satisfied them that there was a beginning to demolish the mill. A mere breaking of the windows would not constitute that offence; but they would consider whether the breaking of the frames of the windows, and the instruments that were used, did not denote an intention to destroy the mill, and whether they had not, in fact, begun to carry this intention into effect. If they determined this question in the affirmative, and which he could not state to be one in which there could be much doubt, they would then have to say whether all the prisoners, or any of them, were present in this attack. Nor would it be necessary in this enquiry to make out any specific acts of violence committed by any of the prisoners, because every person present on such an occasion, and who thereby contributed to the general strength of the party was in law equally guilty with those who might individually do the acts of violence alleged to have been done.

His Lordship, after stating the law with reference to the evidence of accomplices, and the degree of credit to which it was entitled, proceeded to recapitulate the evidence, making those observations which naturally arose from the facts related by the different witnesses.

His Lordship, in the course of his observations, spoke in warm terms of the firmness and spirit evinced by Mr. Cartwright, in the defence of his property, and said it was an example worthy of being followed by every person placed in similar circumstances; and which would prove the most effective and speedy method of suppressing all tumults and outrages of this description. By this spirited conduct, the assailants were driven away without accomplishing their object. It remained for the Jury to consider whether they had not begun to demolish the mill.

His Lordship, having finished his observations as to the subject matter of the offence, proceeded to comment on the evidence, as it applied to the cases of the respective prisoners, noticing particularly those facts which confirmed the testimony of the accomplices; of these were the wound in the shoulder of James Haigh; the wound in the hand of Jonathan Dean; and the circumstance of Thomas Brook having lost his hat, stated by one of them, and his being seen without one, and having one borrowed for him in their return after the attack.

His Lordship then went through the witnesses called to establish an alibi on the part of the prisoners, and dwelt particularly on the discrepancy between the evidence of Richard Hill, and Joseph Walker, called to prove an alibi for John Walker; and on the inconsistencies of John Ellis with respect to Thomas Brook.

His Lordship concluded with recommending the Jury to weigh the evidence with serious deliberation, and if they saw room for it to discriminate between the prisoners. If they thought the evidence insufficient in any case let them acquit such, and if the contrary it would be their duty to convict.

The Jury retired out of court at six o'clock and returned in an hour pronouncing James Haigh, Jonathan Dean, John Ogden, Thomas Brook, and John Walker, guilty; and acquitting James Brook, John Brook, and John Hirst.

CHAPTER XXX.

THE SENTENCES.

" When a man's life is in debate
The judge can ne'er too long deliberate."
Dryden.

" Though Justice be thy plea, consider this—
That in the course of justice none of us
Should see salvation."—*Shakespeare.*

Perhaps the most notable thing about the trials
of the Luddites is the course pursued by the counsel
of detailing minutely what they were prepared to
make clear by the evidence at their command. This
was carried to an unusual extent and must be regarded as at variance with the principles of justice.
If counsel were permitted to furnish explanatory
notes of the evidence as was done in the cases of
these unhappy men, statements might be interpreted
in such a manner as to entirely misrepresent the
meaning of the witnesses.

The reader will also notice that the alibis set up
in some of the cases, especially in that of the Halifax
Luddites, were treated in a rather irregular manner.
The Jury seem to have heard them and then to have
dismissed the evidence given in their support entirely from their minds, apparently as unworthy of
investigation. If they really thought the witnesses
in support of these alibis were not to be believed,
and that they had deliberately conspired to deceive
the Court, they ought to have been proceeded against.

At the conclusion of the trials, on Tuesday, the
12th of January, Mr. Park, addressing the bench,
said :—" My Lords, there are still remaining in your
calendar, seventeen persons, who stood capitally in-

dicted for different offences. Upon looking through
a list of their cases, with all the accuracy in my
power, assisted by my learned friends, I discover
that three of the ringleaders in all those offences
have already suffered the penalty of the law; two
others of those, who are involved in some of these
indictments, have also been capitally convicted; I
will not state their names because I wish to create
no prejudice. I further observe, that two others of
those persons were acquitted on a former trial, on
Saturday night.   I do not think that that ought to
influence my judgment upon the present occasion,
so as to render it my duty to put them upon their
trial again; but inasmuch as I consider that those
whose cases remain, including the two who were
acquitted on Saturday night, have been, to a considerable degree, the dupes of designing persons,
and that they have been led on by the five persons
to whom I have alluded, I am in hopes that I shall
not be doing wrong, in permitting them to be discharged on giving bail to appear at any time, when
called upon by the crown.   And I do assure your
Lordships, that if they conduct themselves as honest
industrious subjects, they shall never be called upon;
and I trust that I shall very materially benefit this
country by the course I have taken, and that this
lenity and forbearance on the part of the crown
(for so the prisoners must consider it), will have a
powerful effect upon their minds."

The seventeen prisoners alluded to, were accordingly discharged, upon bail, to answer the indictments when required.

Mr. Baron Thompson then proceeded to pass sentence upon the prisoners convicted, beginning with
the minor offences.

Mr. Baron Thompson: "John Eaden, John
Baines, the elder, Charles Milnes, John Baines, the
younger, William Blakeborough, and Geo. Duckworth, you, the several prisoners at the bar, have
been convicted of an offence, which the wisdom of

the legislature had made a felony.   You, John
Eaden, and John Baines, the elder, are convicted of
having administered to different persons an unlawful
oath, an oath tending to bind the persons taking it,
and intended that it should so bind them, to join in
a society of persons to disturb the public peace,
binding them to secrecy in that association and
never to declare what they should know respecting
that confederacy.   You, the other prisoners at the
bar, have been convicted of being present, aiding
and consenting to the administering of that unlawful
oath, by the prisoner John Baines, the elder, and
your offence is the same degree as that of the men
who actually administered that oath.

"In the course of very serious investigations
about which we have been so long employed in this
place, it has but too plainly appeared what have
been the dreadful effects of such oaths so taken.
They certainly have been the means of inducing
many unwary persons to enter into these illegal
associations, and of which engagements in support
of them, has been such as we have unfortunately
witnessed in the evidence laid before us in the course
of the enquiries: they have tended to the disturbance of the public peace in the most populous manufacturing part of this county; they have induced
large bodies of men to engage in the most tumultuous proceedings, to attack the houses, plunder the
property, begin to demolish the mills, and to destroy the machinery employed in the mills—nay they
have had the effect of going much further, and have
even induced persons to proceed to the horrid crime
of murder.   Strictly speaking, the administering of
those oaths does not make you in law accessories to
those offences, but still they must lie heavy upon
your consciences, if you have any sense of right or
wrong left.

"You, John Eaden, seem to have been long practised in so administering this oath.   To the person
to whom you administered it, you gave instructions

to get that oath by heart, that he might qualify himself to be the administrator of it; and to a person who called upon you shortly after you had so administered that oath, you fully explained to what it was intended to bind the parties, not scrupling to admit that the intention of it was to overturn the very government of this country.

"You, John Baines, the elder, have made it your boast that your eyes have been opened for three-and-twenty years, and you also declared your sentiments with respect to government, and with respect to no government, plainly, according to what we have collected from the evidence, preferring anarchy and confusion to order and subordination in society. Such is the offence of which you, the prisoners at the bar, stand convicted, and the punishment which the legislature has provided for that offence is certainly not a severe one, if it is considered only what a profanation of religion it is; such a daring appeal to the Almighty to witness your desperate engagements, as well as the horrid consequences that follow from it. If the offence committed by one of you, that is, John Baines, the elder, of administering this oath, had been committed only two days later than it was, the administering of that oath would have amounted to a capital felony; for the legislature, seeing that the punishment was hardly sufficient for offences of such magnitude, have enacted, that to administer any such oaths, whereby a person is held bound to commit any murder or other capital felony, shall itself amount to a capital offence; that act of parliament, however, did not take place till a day after you had committed the offence.

"Under all these circumstances, we feel it our duty to pronounce that judgment upon you which the law has provided. The judgment of the court upon you, the prisoners at the bar, is, that you be severally transported beyond the seas for the term of seven years."

* * * *

The unhappy persons, FIFTEEN in number were

then brought up for judgment. The bar, though a large one, was insufficient to contain the whole, and a seat in front of it was cleared of the spectators, that all the prisoners might stand at once in view of the Judge, and a more painful and distressing scene was never witnessed. The prisoners were all young and in the prime of life, and of respectable appearance, many of them particularly good-looking men.

They were placed in the following order:—John Swallow, John Batley, Joseph Fisher, John Lumb, Job Hey, John Hill, William Hartley, James Hey, Joseph Crowther, Nathan Hoyle; James Haigh, Jonathan Dean, John Ogden, Thomas Brook and John Walker. The last five were convicted of an attack on Mr. Cartwright's Mill at Rawfolds, and beginning to demolish the same.

The Clerk of the Arraigns then enquired of the several prisoners in the solemn language of the law, why judgment of death should not be awarded against them: who each entreated that their lives might be spared.

Baron Thompson and Mr. Justice Le Blanc having put on the symbol of the awful sentence they were about to pass, Baron Thompson addressed these unhappy men in nearly the following terms:—

" You, John Swallow, &c.—[his Lordship here repeated the names of all the prisoners, in the order we have stated them.]—the unhappy prisoners at the bar, stand convicted of various offences, for which your lives are justly forfeited.

" You have formed part of a desperate association of men, who, for a great length of time have disturbed the peace in the West Riding of this county; you have formed yourself into bodies, and proceeded to the most alarming outrages. The cause of your first associating appears to have been the use of machinery in the woollen manufacture, by which you apprehended that the quantity of labour would be diminished; but a grosser delusion could not have been practised upon you. In the attainment of this you have proceeded to the greatest extremities.

"Your first object seems to have been the possession of fire-arms; and though some of you seem to have confined your depredations to this object, others of .you have taken, by terror, force and violence, property of every description.

" You, the prisoners, Job Hey, John Hill and William Hartley, do not appear, indeed, to have taken anything but arms; but you went armed and disguised in the night-time, and created great terror and alarm. James Hey, Joseph Crowther, and Nathan Hoyle, have been convicted of robbing in a dwelling-house, and putting the persons therein in great fear. You have all of you been convicted on evidence the most satisfactory."

His Lordship, then particularly addressing the last five prisoners, said:—" You have been convicted of one of the greatest atrocities that was ever committed in a civilised country; you have been long practised; you have formed yourselves into companies commanded by different leaders, and armed with guns, with pistols, with axes, and other weapons of offence and mischief, you marched in military array to the mill of Mr. Cartwright, which you afterwards begun to pull down; you kept up a dreadful fire for some time; others of you began the work of destruction, and you were evidently bent on the worst of mischief, intending, doubtless, to demolish the machinery. This attack was accompanied by cries and exclamations.

" The courage and resolution displayed in the defence of the mill, were successful in repelling your attack; but two of your wretched company paid the forfeit of their lives. It was this defeat that afterwards instigated some of your companions to the more atrocious crime of deliberate murder, and they have suffered the penalty which the law inflicts; and a similar fate is about to await you, the prisoners at the bar.

"The jury who tried you, recommended one of you, John Lumb, to mercy; they thought they saw grounds for discriminating between his case and that of the other prisoners included in the same charge. On this ground it is possible that mercy may be secured. For the rest of you, I wish I could have discovered any grounds for mitigating your sentence; but this I have not been able to do. It is of infinite importance to society that no mercy should be shown you; it is of importance that your sentence should be speedily carried into effect; and it is but right to tell you, that you have but a very short time to remain in this world; and I trust, that not only those who hear me, but all without those walls, to whom the tidings of your fall may come, will be warned by your fate, and avoid those fatal steps which have conducted you to it; for they may rest assured, that, when once engaged in lawless enterprises, it will be impossible for them to say ' Hitherto will I go, but no further;' and that they will go on till death will, sooner or later, overtake them in the shape of punishment."

"Prisoners,—I would exhort you to set about the great work of repentance, and to make your peace with God; and that, feeling convinced of your crimes, you will make a full confession of them, as the only reparation you can make to society, and that you will give yourselves up to the admonitions of the Rev. Clergyman whose office it is to prepare you for your awful change; and God grant, that by worthily bewailing your sins, and sincerely forsaking them, you may find mercy of the Lord."

"Prisoners—hear the sentence which the laws of man award your crimes. That sentence of law is, and this court doth award it—That you be taken hence to the place from whence you came, and from thence to the place of execution, and that you severally be hanged by the neck until you are dead, and may Almighty God have mercy upon your souls."

One of the prisoners fell into a fit during the time
the Judge was addressing them; and when he came
to that part of his address in which he spoke of the
certainty and near approach of their execution, involuntary groans of anguish burst from several of
the prisoners. The scene was inexpressibly painful.

The Judges, before they left York, ordered for
execution fourteen of these unhappy persons, on
Saturday, the 17th of January. Lumb was the
prisoner respited.

CHAPTER XXXI.

EXECUTION OF THE LUDDITES.

" Oh God! it is a fearful thing
To see the human soul take wing."—*Byron.*

We now approach the last awful scene of this tragical
assize. After sentence of death had been passed
upon the persons convicted of making the attack on
Mr. Cartwright's mill at Rawfolds, and of stealing
arms, all of them (except John Lumb, to whom
mercy was extended), were removed to the condemned
ward, and their behaviour in that place was very
penitent. They confessed they had offended against
the laws of God and of their country, but on the
subject of the offence for which the sentence of death
was passed upon them, they were unanimously silent
and reserved. All of them, except one, tacitly
confessed that they stood convicted, and when they
were asked if any of them could say they were not
guilty, they all remained silent, except James Haigh,
and Nathan Hoyle, the former of whom said, "I am
guilty," and the latter, "I am innocent." This was
the day before the execution; but Hoyle did not
make any declaration to that effect when brought
to the platform. Their minds for the most part had
attained a wonderful degree of composure, except
the mind of John Ogden: he appeared for some
time to be much disturbed, but on the question
being put to him whether his agitation arose from
and discovery he had to make, and with the weight
of which his conscience was oppressed, he answered
no, his agitation arose from the terrors of his situation.

And here we may note the striking fact, that if any of these unfortunate men possessed any secret that it might have been important to the public to know, they suffered it to die with them. Their discoveries were meagre in the extreme. Not one of them impeached any of his accomplices, nor did they state, as might reasonably have been expected, where the depot of arms in the collection of which some of them had been more practically engaged, was to be found. When interrogated on this point, some of them disclaimed all knowledge of the place, and others said Benjamin Walker, the informer, against Mellor, Thorpe, and Smith, could give the best information about arms, as he had been present at the most of the depredations. On the question being put to them whether they knew who were concerned in the robbery of a mill (now Rawfolds) near Cleckheaton, James Hey said "I and Carter, the informer, were present at that robbery." It was observed to James Hey, that it was very extraordinary that he who had had the advantage of a religious education, his father being of the Methodist Society, should have come to such a disgraceful situation; to which he replied, in a manner that shewed that his vices, however flagrant, had not extinguished in his bosom the feelings of filial affection, "I hope, said he, "the son's crimes will never be imputed to his father."

Most of the ill-fated prisoners were married and had families. William Hartley, the poor tailor with whose pitiful case the reader will be quite familiar, had left behind at his poverty stricken home, seven children, of whom Mary was the eldest. The broken-hearted mother expired it will be remembered at the time when the officers of the law came to apprehend Hartley. On the morning before the execution, Rayner, who had obtained permission to see him visited him in his cell. Hartley received his old friend in the cold and apathetic manner which had of late become habitual with him, exhibiting indeed no satisfaction in his company, and showing no desire to enter into conversation with him. When, however, Rayner began to talk of his much loved daughter, and to tell him, after a time, that she was in the city—nay, just outside the prison walls waiting anxiously for a parting interview the fountain of tears was unsealed, the vacant, stolid look left Hartley's face, and he bowed his head in deep anguish. Rayner, who was not displeased to witness this change in his friend's demeanour, next endeavoured to obtain Hartley's permission for Mary to visit him in his cell. At first the poor man's eye brightened at the thought of seeing his darling child again, but by-and-bye he realised his sad condition as a condemned criminal who had but a short time to live, and harshly blaming Rayner for disturbing his closing hours he refused to listen to his entreaties, and almost angrily asked his visitor to leave him alone in his misery, and not disturb his last hours. But Rayner dared not face the sorely stricken girl who was so anxiously waiting his return without having wrung the consent for a meeting from her father. Poor Hartley would fain have been spared the anguish of this closing interview, but Rayner's pleadings were seconded by the yearnings of his own heart, and he yielded at last to Rayner's strong importunities. The latter, fearful that the sadly distraught man would withdraw the consent he had so reluctantly given, left the prison at once to bring in the anxious daughter who was waiting at a house at the gates. When Rayner ushered the poor trembling girl into the cell Hartley tottered on to his feet, a shudder swept over his frame, and the tears from his bloodshot eyes rolled slowly down his cheeks. As he folded her in his arms and mingled his tears with hers the very turnkeys were moved with deep compassion although they were used to such painful scenes, and their eyes were wet with tears as after a time they drew her half-fainting from the cell and gave her into the care of Rayner. The heart-broken father would fain have been spared the anguish of this parting interview, but after it was over it was noticed that the stolid expression of hopeless despair seemed to give place to one of calm resignation.

At eleven o'clock on Saturday morning, the Under Sheriff went to ·demand the bodies of John Ogden, Nathan Hoyle, Joseph Crowther, John Hill, John Walker, Jonathan Dean and Thomas Brook. They were all engaged in singing the well known hymn :—

> Behold the Saviour of mankind
>   Nail'd to the shameful tree !
> How vast the love that Him inclined
>   To bleed and die for me !
>
> Hark, how He groans ! while nature shakes,
>   And earth's strong pillars bend :
> The temple's veil in sunder breaks ;
>   The solid marbles bend.
>
> 'Tis done ! the precious ransom's paid ;
>   " Receive my soul," He cries ;
> See where He bows His sacred head !
>   He bows His head, and dies !
>
> But soon He'll break death's envious chain,
>   And in full glory shine :
> O Lamb of God ! was ever pain,
>   Was ever love, like Thine.

One of them dictated the hymn in a firm tone of voice : and in this religious service they continued on their way to the platform, and some time after they had arrived at the fatal spot. They then joined the ordinary with great fervency in the prayers appointed to be read on such occasions ; and after that gentleman had taken his final leave of them, ejaculations to the throne of mercy rose from every part of the crowded platform.

Joseph Crowther, addressing himself to the spectators, said, " Farewell, lads ; " another whose name is not known, said, " I am prepared for the Lord ; " and John Hill, advancing a step or two on the plat-

form, said, "Friends, all take warning by my fate;
for three years I followed the Lord, but about a year
since I began to fall away, and fell by ...le and little
and at last I am come to this; persevere in the ways
of goodness, and O! take warning by my fate."
The executioner then proceeded to the discharge of
his duty, and the falling of the drops soon after
forced an involuntary shriek from the vast concourse
of spectators assembled to witness this tremendous
sacrifice to the injured laws of the country.

The bodies, having remained suspended for the
usual time, were removed, and while the place of
execution was yet warm, the remaining seven, namely,
John Swallow, John Batley, Joseph Fisher, William
Hartley, James Haigh, James Hey, and Job Hey,
were led, at half-past one o'clock, from their cell to
the fatal stage; their behaviour, like that of their
deceased confederates, was contrite and becoming.
James Haigh expressed deep contrition for his
offences. John Swallow said he had been led away
by wicked and unprincipled men, and hoped his fate
would be a warning to all, and teach them to live a
life of sobriety and uprightness. They all united in
prayer with an earnestness that is seldom witnessed
in the service of devotion, except in the immediate
prospect of death. A few moments closed their
mortal existence, and placed them at the bar differing
from all earthly tribunals in this infinitely important
particular—here, owing to the imperfectness of human
institutions, repentance, though sincere, cannot procure forgiveness:—there, we have the authority of
God himself for saying, the cries of the contrite and
broken-hearted shall not be despised. "Charity
hopeth all things."

The criminal records of Yorkshire do not, perhaps,
afford an instance of so many victims having been
offered, in one day, to the injured laws of the country.
The scene was inexpressibly awful, and the large
body of soldiers, both horse and foot, who guarded
...e approach to the castle, and were planted in front

of the fatal tree, gave the scene a peculiar degree of terror, and exhibited the appearance of a military execution. The spectators, particularly in the morning, were unusually numerous and their behaviour on both occasions was strictly decorous and becoming.

CHAPTER XXXII.

AFTER THE BLOODY ASSIZE.

Frail creatures are we all ! To be the best
Is but the fewest faults to have.—*Coleridge*

At the time the Luddites were executed, the law
had not come into existence requiring that the bodies
of such criminals should be buried within the precincts
of the prison, and unless it was part of the sentence
that the corpse of the culprit should be delivered
over to the surgeons for " anatomization "—as was
done in the case of Mary Bateman, the abominable
person known as the " Yorkshire witch," and many
others—it was given up to the relatives for interment. This appears to have been the case with the
bodies of most of the culprits from Huddersfield and
the neighbourhood, and there are many old people
still living who remember the carts that contained
the coffins passing through Millbridge on their way
to that town. The vehicles were of course followed
by crowds from this neighbourhood, and when they
arrived at the precincts of Huddersfield an immense
number of people were waiting for the melancholy
procession. As might be expected, the excitement
was intense and universal, both when the bodies
arrived and at the funerals that followed, and the
few aged people now living who were old enough at
that time to remember the mourful scenes, speak of
them as being unprecedented in their experience. As
we have already said in the previous chapter,
Luddism did not by any means die spark out when
its leaders were put to death. The more ignorant
and headstrong portion of the generation never indeed seems to have wholly lost the feeling, and it

came again and again to the surface during the bitter days that followed the great war, when the unhappy wretches were confronted by the grim spectre of starvation. The intelligent portion of the working classes, however, became gradually alive to the advantages of machinery, and as the trade of the country revived, the unquiet spirit of Luddism was at last laid at rest. It is beyond all question that this result was materially hastened by the writings of the famous William Cobbett, which at this time became widely diffused througout the whole country and were eagerly bought by the working classes, who hailed with enthusiasm their fearless, warm-hearted champion, who, springing from the people and knowing their sufferings, pitied them in their misery and was proud to suffer for and with them. In his "Letter to the Luddites," Cobbett displayed his fine, vigorous Saxon common sense and doubtless convinced many an ignorant enthusiast of the folly of destroying that which was destined to prove itself his most beneficent helper. He says :—

"To show that machines are not naturally and necessarily an evil, we have only to suppose the existence of a patriarchal race of a hundred men and their families all living in common, four men of which are employed in making cloth by hand. Now, suppose someone was to discover a machine by which all the cloth wanted could be made by one man. The consequence would be that the great family would (having enough of everything else) use more cloth ; or if any part of the labour of the three cloth makers were much wanted in any other department, they would be employed in that other department. Thus would the whole be benefited by this invention. They would have more cloth amongst them, or more food would be raised, or the same quantity as before would be raised, leaving the community more leisure for study or recreation. See ten miserable mariners cast on shore in a desert island, with a bag of wheat and a little flax seed. The soil is prolific, they have fish and fruits : the branches or bark of trees would make them houses, and the wild animals afford them meat. Yet what miserable dogs they are ! They can neither sow the wheat, make the flour, nor catch the fish or animals. But let another wreck toss on the shore a spade, a hand-mill, a trowel, a hatchet, a saw, a pot, a gun, and some fish hooks and knives, and how soon the scene is changed ! Yet they want clothes : and in order to make their shirts, for instance, six or seven out of the ten are constantly employed in making linen. This throws a monstrous burden on the other three who have to provide the food. But send them a loom and you release six out of the seven from the shirt making concern, and ease as well as plenty succeeds immediately. In these simple cases the question is decided at once in favour of machines."

These arguments of Cobbett are irrefutable and may be thus summarised : Improved machinery lowers the price of production. The cheaper a fabric is the greater is the demand for it, and it at once undersells that produced by hand. Where the demand for it increases more hands are of course employed. Younger persons can work by machinery than at handicrafts where strength is required. Suppose machinery abolished in Yorkshire, what would prevent its use elsewhere? The wives and children would be thrown out of work by the stoppage of the lighter machinery. The husband and father having now to support his family alone requires higher wages. Prices are raised to meet this extra demand, and trade again flows into the cheaper market. The trade in the progressive places dwindles. Fewer workmen are required ; down go wages : and poverty, famine, and death, those cruel teachers of political economy, creep into the half-deserted factories, and push the workmen from their seats into the graves that have been long gaping at their feet.

There were, as the reader will hardly need to be told, many capital punishments, many were transported and imprisoned, and a few were acquitted.

Of those whose lives were spared, and who remained
in the country, it is singular to note that many of
them seem to have been all the rest of their lives
mixed up with all the political and social movements
which followed, and which were to some extent under
the ban of the law. Many of the foremost men of
the bands led by Cobbett, Cartwright, and Hunt,
in the Radical movement, and many of the leaders
of the Chartists under Feargus O'Connor and others
had been in their earlier days connected with the
Luddite movement. They lived in hard times,
when as Thorold Rogers makes abundantly manifest
in his great work, the bulk of the labouring classes
were ground down to the very dust. They were
miserably poor and wretched; society had dealt
very hardly with them, and all their lives they were
more or less at war with the established institutions
of the country.

John Hirst, the head of the Liversedge Luddites,
had a narrow escape of suffering the fate of Mellor
and others. There is no doubt that William Hall,
of Parkin Hoyle, the informer, was the chief means of
this being brought about. He knew well enough
that the Liversedge leader was really more guilty
than many of the unfortunate men who suffered the
extreme penalty of the law, but he seems to have
recoiled from bringing his old shopmate, under whom
he had worked for seven or eight years, and who had
often concealed his irregularities from the foreman,
to his doom. When therefore the conduct of Hirst
came to be enquired into, Hall's memory became a
blank especially with regard to Hirst's proceedings on
the eventful night when he acted as guide to the body
who attacked Cartwright's mill. After his acquittal
at York, he came back to Liversedge, but finding
himself so noted a man that he could hardly walk
through the village without bringing crowds at every
corner to gaze at him, and being also pestered and
annoyed with inconvenient questions, he soon removed
to a thinly populated part of Mirfield. Knowing

that he had only escaped the hands of the hangman by the skin of his teeth, he would never discuss Luddism with anyone or give any information about it. Years afterwards when he fell into dotage, he seemed to live over again that eventful period of his life and was constantly muttering mysterious passwords, administering to imaginary neophytes the secret of the oath, or going through some Luddite ceremony, drill, or attack. During his closing years, he lived with a married daughter, and when engaged in rocking his grandchildren to sleep he invariably soothed them by crooning out an old Luddite ditty, every verse of which, a neighbour, who was greatly interested in listening to him, remembers,. ended with the refrain :—

"Around and around we all will stand,
  And sternly swear we will,
 We'll break the shears and windows too,
  And set fire to the tazzling mill !"

With regard to Bob Wam or Witham, he disappeared from Liversedge after the night of the attack on the mill, but he is said to have been in after years a prominent figure in the Radical movement at Oldham, and afterwards, when a grey headed old man, was imprisoned for taking part in some chartist physical force demonstration. He returned to Liversedge and died there. Jonas Crowther and Robert Naylor, both escaped apprehension by disappearing from the neighbourhood. The latter never returned to the locality, but Crowther, after many years came back to live at Moorbottom. In after years he was connected with all the strikes and physical force movements but managed to keep out of prison. He was as we have said a morose and silent man, and like John Hirst, would never talk about the Luddite movement or acknowledge that he had been prominently connected with it. Some years after his death a person who had taken the cottage at Hightown where he lived during the time he worked at Jackson's shop, found in digging a deep trench in the garden a rusty pike head and an old gun. These weapons had no doubt been buried by Hirst when he returned from the attack on Cartwright's mill, and took his flight to escape the consequences.

There is but little more of the Luddite band we need mention before proceeding with our narrative. Those of our readers who have followed with interest the fortunes of Rayner, who had such a miraculous escape, and of his sweetheart Mary the daughter of Hartley the poor broken-hearted tailor, will be pleased to learn that the sun of prosperity brightened in some measure the remainder of their lives. After the closing interview with her father the poor girl was carried in an unconscious state to her lodgings, where she had a serious relapse, and her life for some time hung in the balance. She at last, however, slowly recovered and was removed to her native village, where she eventually regained her health. In Rayner's absence his grandmother sickened and died suddenly. He lived in his cottage about a year alone, and then brought home to it as his bride the beautiful daughter of his old friend Hartley. Here they lived in happiness all the remainder of their lives, but Mary never forgot the tragic fate of her parents, and years after, when she was old and feeble herself, her eyes would fill with tears as she told of their hard and undeserved fate.

CHAPTER XXXIII.

COMFORTING FRIENDS.

" Pure religion and undefiled before God and the Father is
this : To visit the fatherless and widow in their affliction, and
to keep himself unspotted from the world.—*St. James.*

When the horror occasioned by the wholesale
execution at York of the starving wretches, whose
lives had been appraised as Lord Byron said in his
famous speech, as of less value than a cropping frame,
had died away somewhat, enquiries naturally began
to be instituted respecting their wretched widows and
poor innocent children. This feeling, though
naturally strongest in the Huddersfield district, where
these objects of public sympathy chiefly resided, was
widespread, extending to Brighouse, Elland, Halifax,
and also as far as the Spen valley. No one, it
will have been seen, suffered death from the last
named locality, but the feeling referred to evidenced
itself in an intense outburst of dislike towards Cartwright and William Hall the informer.

In the interesting journal of Thomas Shillito, a
devoted member of the Society' of Friends, we have
evidence of this widespread feeling of sympathy. When
this worthy evangelist was journeying in this part
of the country, he tells us in quaint Quaker phraseo-
logy, that his mind was brought into such feelings of
sympathy with the widows and fatherless children of
the sufferers that he believed he should not stand
acquitted in the sight of the Divine Master unless he
visited them. Finding that Joseph Wood, another
friend " was under a similar exercise," they went
together. He says :—We first proceeded to the
house of Jonathan Dean, who had been hanged for
rioting at Rawfolds mill. (This was the man it will

be remembered who used his great hammer with such tremendous effect on the mill door). The widow's mind appeared to be under very great distress with her helpless fatherless children; the oldest child being about eight years old, and the youngest about as many months. All that was alive in us and capable of feeling for her, plunged as she was into such accumulated distress, we felt to be brought into action. We next visited the house of John Walker (rollicking John Walker, who sang the Luddite song at the Shears Inn, Liversedge), who also suffered for rioting at Cartwright's mill. One of the children was an infant at the breast. The feeling of distress awakened in my mind in sitting down with this family were such that I was tempted to conclude human nature could hardly endure to proceed with the visit before us. We endeavoured in both cases to impart such counsel as came before our minds, which we had reason to hope was well received and had a tendency in some small degree to add a ray of comfort to their deeply tried minds."

"After tea, feeling my bodily strength recruited, and my resolutions afresh exerted, we proceeded to the mournful house of George Mellor, a single young man, and a leader of those concerned in the murder of the master manufacturer. We sat down with the parents, who are living in a respectable line of life. In this opportunity we had fresh cause to acknowledge holy help was near. We endeavoured to be on our guard that nothing escaped our lips that should be the means of unnecessarily wounding their feelings. Our visit was thankfully received by both parents, and, as we afterwards understood, was like a morsel of bread to those ready to famish. The father acknowledged that the melancholy circumstances had brought their minds into such a tried state that they had concluded to move to some other part of the country; but our visit had tended to settle them down again in their present place of residence."

" The second day we bent our course to Lockwood
and sat with the widow and three children of Thomas
Brooke (this is the man who accompanied John
Walker on his visit to the Liversedge croppers). We
also had the company of his parents and two brothers.
His two brothers were in York Castle with him, but
were discharged. This proved a heart-rending opportunity to us all. Being willing, as I may
humbly say we were, to sit where the surviving
sufferers sat, we were helped to go down into suffering with them. Our minds were clothed with feelings of campassion for the widow, and the afflicted
parents. The sufferer, we were informed had only
been out once with the rioters, at which time he
lost his hat which caused his apprehension. At our
parting they endeavoured to make us sensible that
our visit had been like a cordial to their minds, and
they expressed the thankfulness they felt for it.
We proceeded to Huddersfield, visited the widow
of James Haigh (another of the Rawfolds rioters).
He left no children. We found the widow under
deep affliction. She appeared to have a clear view
of our motives for taking the step which we did,
expressing in strong terms the gratitude she felt for
our visit."

" Our next visit was to the house of William
Thorpe, who was a single man, and who suffered for
the murder of the master manufacturer. We felt
deeply for the afflicted parents. It appeared a
time of precious visitation to the sisters. In the
afternoon we proceeded to Cowcliffe to visit the widow
of John Ogden, who had also suffered for rioting at
Rawfolds. We proposed to visit here at her
husband's parents, in order to have their company,
and that of two of the sufferer's sisters ; but we were
given to understand that the parents spurned at
the idea of sitting with us. As it did not appear to
me that we should be warranted in so easily giving
up this prospect, we took the widow and family with
us into their cottage, and took our seats amongst

them. The parents were both confined to the house in consequence of the melancholy event that that had occurred in respect to their son, and from their appearance with one of their daughters, they were smarting under the weight of their afflictions. The parents, at our parting expressed in a very feeling manner their thankfulness for our visit.

" On the third day, accompanied by James King and James Lees, friends of Brighouse meeting, we proceeded to Sutcliffe Wood Bottom, to sit with the parents of Thomas Smith, the companion of George Mellor and William Thorpe in the murder of Mr. Horsfall. At the time I was engaged in addressing the company a young man opened the door, came in ; and immediately left again ; on which I felt a stop against proceeding, and was obliged to request the young man might be sought for, to give us his company, which taking place, I was enabled to proceed . . . . After the opportunity, the young man walked with us a short distance ; his mind appeared much broken under a remarkable visitation. He told my companion he had been apprehended with the rest of the prisoners and confined in the castle, but was discharged on bail ; that he knew nothing of our being in the cottage, nor could tell what brought him there, as he had no business with the family. " In the afternoon we went to Skircoat Green. Our first visit was to the widow and five children of Nathan Hoyle, who suffered for robbery of arms. They lived with her aged father and sister, who sat with us and who appeared under great difficulties to procure the necessaries of life. Their situation appeared to us very pitiable indeed. We next proceeded to the house of James Hey who left a widow not twenty years of age and two children. The sufferer's parents gave us their company ; we were favoured with a comfortable time together."

" On the fourth day we went to Sowerby Bridge. Our first visit was to the widow of Joseph Crowther, who suffered for the same offence as the two fore-

going.   He had left three children, the widow near
being confined of her fourth.   We were enabled to
labour with her to persevere in an endeavour after
a steady reliance for help on that divine power
which alone would be sufficient to support her mind
in her future tossings and temptations."

The next visit of Mr. Shillito and his friends was
to the house of the poor tailor, William Hartley, to
whose hard lot we have referred so often.

We next proceeded to the house of the parents of
William Hartley.   With them resided his eight
children bereft of both parents, the mother having
been deceased about three weeks.   The neighbours
observing us go into their cottage followed us, quietly
taking their seats.   The opportunity proved to many,
especially to some of the children, a heart-rending
scene, and one I believe that will long be remembered
by some present.

" Our next visit was to North Dean, to the widow
of John Hill, Hartley's leader in the raid for arms.
He had left one infant.   His widow presented us
with an interesting letter received from him on the
day before his execution, manifesting the peaceful
state of mind he had been favoured to attain to
under the evidence that he had been enabled to
forgive all mankind and himself experiencing Divine
forgiveness for all his sins..   She informed me the
night he was taken he was forced out of bed by the
gang; that she ran after him half-a-mile without any
of her upper garments, until they obliged her to
return, threatening to blow her brains out if she
followed them.   A brother of Hill's was also im-
plicated in these riotous proceedings the same night,
his neighbours say, not from inclination but overcome
by threats, he being always considered a religiously
disposed young man, and he was much esteemed, but
he escaped being taken with the rest.   His mother
was maintained by the produce of a small farm, and
he was her sole dependence in the management of it.
The loss of the other son by such an untimely' end

with the continued fearful apprehensions she laboured under of her other son being taken—there being a warrant out and search being made for him—appeared almost to drive her to despair. We endeavoured to console her all in our power. Before we left her I felt it laid upon me to assure her on account of the good character we had received of the young man, and the manner of his being led away, we would lay his case before the magistrates who granted the warrant, and use our influence to obtain permission for him to return home with safety.

" Our next visit was to the widow of Job Hey and her seven fatherless children. We found her in a state of mind bordering on despair. She recovered somewhat as ability was afforded after that quietude and submission to the dispensation permitted to be her lot ; but her poor mind was so overcharged with the prospect of her great poverty, her numerous fatherless children without any visible means for their support, we were ready to fear that what we had to offer obtained but little entrance."

The next visit of Mr. Shillito was to no less notorious a person than Benjamin Walker, the in-former ; and it will be observed that, like everybody who came into contact with this ignoble individual, he was very unfavourably impressed. " On the fifth day', agreeable to our request, Benjamin Walker met us. On entering the room he appeared to us raw and ignorant ; with so much apparent self-condemna-tion in his countenance as we thought we had never before witnessed : as if he thought himself an outcast and thought a mark of infamy was set upon him ; newly clad, as we supposed, from the money he had recently received as the reward for having betrayed his accomplices in the murder for which the latter had suffered. We could not but admit the deplorable situation he would find himself in when the means of keeping up his spirits were exhausted. On taking his seat his mind appeared to be much agitated, and during the opportunity he was unable to sit with

ease to himself on his seat. After a time spent with
him in quiet, a door of utterance was opened whereby
we were enabled faithfully to relieve our minds towards him, although he did not manifest a disposition to resent what we offered to him, but little, if
any, appearance of tenderness was manifested. The
opportunity was the most distressing to us we had
experienced; feeling, as we were enabled to do,
deeply on his account lest his mind was getting into
quite a hardened state, and that his case would become a hopeless one: yet not without some reason for
believing that in the opportunity we had with him,
things had been brought home so closely to him that
he would not be able to cast them away again.
When we went away those who were in the room
through which he had passed, observed to us that his
countenance was pale and ghastly, and his joints, as
it were, so unloosened as if they were scarcely able
to support his body. We advised him not to go
into company, but to return directly home; advice
which we afterwards heard he attended to. The
feelings of suffering we were introduced into on his
account will not, I believe, soon be forgotten.

" When the friends at Paddock heard of our intended visit to the families of the sufferers it appeared
to them advisable to wait upon Joseph Radcliffe, the
magistrate, who had been so active in putting a stop
to these riotous proceedings, to inform him of our
intentions lest any unfavourable construction should
be put upon our conduct. Being now come nearly
to the close of our visit, and having found drawings
in my mind, at times, to make a visit to Joseph
Radcliffe. I opened my prospect to my companion,
but he not appearing to feel much, if anything, of
such a concern, it occasioned me close exercise, but
as it appeared clear to me my own peace of mind
was involved in it I laid the subject before my kind
friend John Fisher, requesting him, if he felt nothing
in his mind against it to inform Joseph Radcliffe
therof: which, being done, he gave for answer that

our company would be acceptable next morning.

" On seventh morning my companion accompanied me and John Fisher as proposed. The magistrate and his wife received us very courteously and we had with them a free and open conversation for an hour and a half. I gave him as far as memory furnished me therewith an account of our proceedings in the visits, and the state of mind in which we found the poor widows and those we met with who had been liberated on bail. On assuring him that we heard nothing from any one we had visited in the least degree reflecting on him, or on anyone who had taken part in apprehending the sufferers he appeared to receive it as satisfactory information. I then laid before him the suffering situation of the widow Hill, against whose son his warrant was issued, detailing the good character the young man uniformly bore in the neighbourhood where he had resided before his escape : and that it was the first and only night he had been out with the rioters, and then more by constraint than by inclination. Our remarks exciting in his mind feelings of tenderness towards the young man, we requested him to consider his case, and the case of his mother, and to afford him all the relief in his power, to which he replied " The young man must come before me and surrender himself," at the same time giving us authority to inform his mother that if he thus proceeded he should not remain in custody, but have his liberty to return home, and shouldn't be disturbed so long as he conducted him-self in a quiet and orderly manner. His mother being informed to this effect the young man sur-rendered himself, and was liberated. Since that time he has married and is comfortably settled in life ; and we understand from good authority con-tinues an exemplary religious character. I felt truly thankful this point was so far gained ; but there was another which appeared to me of equal importance and which I also laid before the magistrate, namely the deplorable situation of the widows and children ;

there appearing no prospect but that they must by degrees sell their household furniture to procure subsistence, they informing us that none would employ them; some refusing through prejudice, and some through fear of being suspected of countenance the proceeding of their husbands; whereby the parish workhouse would soon be their only resourse if no speedy remedy were applied. This, from the view I had of the subject was to be dreaded; the children from the company they must associate with being likely on every slight offence to have reflections cast upon them on account of the conduct and disgraceful end of their fathers. Thus, held in contempt, the danger was that the minds of the children would by degress become hardened, and they thereby become unfitted for usefulness in society. After thus expressing my views, and that some mode should be adopted to educate and to provide for the children until they attained to an age fitted for servants and apprentices, and to aid the earnings of the widows whilst they remained single; and proposing for his consideration a plan for these purposes, which had suggested itself to my mind almost daily of late, I felt discharged from these subjects which had pressed very heavily upon me. At our departure he took us by the hand and in a very kind manner bade us farewell."

"We proceeded to Berrisfield, where the widow of Joseph Fisher, and other families of the sufferers lived They, having no regular place of settlement were collected into one cottage. The opportunity with them was a favoured one, leading us to hope the labour would not all prove in vain. The state of mind of a woman whose husband was transported called for much sympathy; she believing her own case to be more trying than that of the poor widows who, she said, had seen the end of their husbands' suffering in this life. The scenes of distress this opportunity presented to our feelings is not to be described.

"We then went to Elland Moor, and sat with the
widow and six children of John Swallow who suffered for robbery of arms.   Her mother, brother and a
sister of the sufferer sat with us.   Words would fall
short to attempt to describe the state of distress her
mind appeared to be in.   We had largely to hand
out to her encouragement to look for support where
alone it was to be found, and where we had reason
to hope the poor mind found a centring.   She received our visit with expressions of gratitude, and
with it our services of this nature closed."

It is pleasant to read that the kind hearted friends,
while doing their best to comfort the minds of the
disconsolate widows and their sorrowing children,
also did their best to inaugurate a movement to secure
their temporal benefit.   What may have been the
after fate of these bereaved ones we know not, but
we hope the beneficent plans of Mr. Shillito for
their welfare were carried into effect.

We have said that the sympathy which was evoked
in Spen Valley towards the bereaved families
evidenced itself in revived dislike towards Cartwright.
With regard to that gentleman, it must be said in
simple justice, that although he was a hero in the
estimation of his brother manufacturers throughout
the West Riding, who had presented him with a
handsome sword and the sum of three thousand
pounds as practical proofs of their admiraiton of the
noble way he had stood forth in defence of the rights
of property, he never expressed himself as feeling in
any way but sorry that he had been the means, even
in carrying out his clear duty of defending his mill,
of depriving any of its assailants of their lives.

We have it on the authority of an old dame who
lived as nursemaid in Mr. Cartwright's house, that
although some of his friends when visiting there
would fain have heard from his own lips a recital of
the tragic incidents of that awful night, when his
mill was surrounded by a mob of desperate men, he
would never gratify them, but at once changed the

subject. The topic was evidently distasteful, and distance of time did not make the retrospect more inviting. Once indeed, our informant states, and only once, so far as her observation went, he said a few words to a near relative on the subject, to the effect that he could not derive any pleasure from his reminiscences of that tragic event, although he felt no doubt in his mind respecting his right to take the course he did in defence of his property. This public feeling of dislike showed itself so unmistakably in Cartwright's case that it must have been a constant source of pain to him. Naturally stern, silent and self-contained, he mixed less and less with his neighbours as the years passed by. If he went to church it is said no one spoke to him. He was ostracised, and such being the case, one cannot wonder that he eventually absented himself for lengthened periods from public worship and contented himself by sending for the Rev. Hammond Robinson's sermons Sunday by Sunday as that gentleman delivered them, and reading them aloud to his family and servants, who were all summoned into the room to hear them, and also a selection from the Church Service which he devoutly recited.

As we have already said, it must not be concluded that this dislike of Mr. Cartwright arose from sympathy with the objects or methods of the rioters. That was only the case to a very limited extent. The true reason was that public feeling was outraged by the spectacle of men, many of whom were positively starving, being shot down or hanged by the score for outraging laws which had been expressly framed to compass their destruction.

CHAPTER XXXIV.

THE   NOTTINGHAM   CAPTAIN."

Although the condition of the working population of this district was a little more tolerable in the year 1813 than it had been during the black year of the first Luddite risings, employment still remained scarce, provisions very dear, and taxation very heavy. Such being the case it is hardly to be wondered at that the mobs of half-starved wretches often invaded the markets in large towns and compelled the dealers to sell their produce at prices that were within their reach.   One of the most serious riots of this kind took place about the time the authorities were beginning to break into the Luddite organisation. The dealers in Leeds market were demanding the astounding price of nine pounds per quarter for wheat, and a serious riot consequently occurred. Headed by a virago who assumed the title of " Lady Ludd," the desperate populace furiously assailed the dealers in the market.   Not contented with dictating the price at which wheat should be sold, they seized upon a considerable quantity and threw it about the streets. Then they repaired to the works of a miller at Holbeck, who had made himself obnoxious to them by what they considered to be unfair efforts to keep up the price, and did considerable damage to his premises.   The labouring classes of this district were indeed at this time in a most depressed and unhappy condition ; they could with difficulty procure the necessaries of life, and the spirit of outrage need not therefore be wondered at, however we may condemn it.

The record of the Luddite riots is a black and warning page in the social history of England.   It is a melancholy picture of ignorance, of useless crime,

and of cruel vengeance; but we should be wanting
in fairness if we did not take into consideration the
social condition of the wretches who were, in many
cases, goaded by starvation to commit deeds which
they would have shrunk from in their calmer moments. The wholesale execution of the leaders
seemed to crush the movement to a great extent in
the West Riding, but though it never afterwards
made much headway, leaders being wanting, and
many of the better class of workmen holding aloof
still the movement was not finally crushed. The
old spirit existed and woke up on many occasions,
and had not the lot of the labouring population
gradually become better Luddism would not have
died out so soon. Agents of the organisations of the
various towns in the locality and also at Nottingham
still flitted about, and meetings were still held
occasionally. The idea of a general rising to redress
the grievances of the working classes continued still
to be advanced by the Nottingham centre, and arms
were still collected with that object over a wide area,
but the organisation proved again and again a rope
of sand, and many led away by the promise of the
asasistance of great bodies of working-men from other
localities, which never came, found themselves deceived and utterly ruined.

Perhaps the most formidable of these abortive risings
took place about three years after Mellor and his
companions had been hanged at York. The great
war had come to an end at last, and the restless
ruler of the French nation was safely chained on the
barren rock of St. Helena. The nation was doubtless
covered with glory, but France did not thank us for
thrusting upon her her old imbecile line of Kings.
Byron, apostrophising the Duke of Wellington in one
of his satirical verses, exclaims:—

"But I should be delighted to learn who
Save you and yours, have gained by Waterloo."

Doubtless there was some gain to the aristocratic
class, who had combated so fiercely against the

Corsican parvenu, but to the working population the result was loss, and loss only. The Corn Bill, which prevented foreign grain from coming into England so long as the price of wheat averaged under eighty shillings per quarter, had been passed amidst execrations of the starving populace, the House of Commons being protected from their fury by the bayonets of the soldiery during the discussions. The population of the manufacturing districts was also angry and restless. To drive this discontent into some tangible shape, Lord Liverpool sent amongst those ignorant, turbulent, but sincere men, spies who were paid to urge them on to rebellion so that they might be dealt with by the sword and bayonet of the military!.

Of the "Nottingham captain," Brandreth, who led the rising of 1817, very little positive seems to be known, but he was a man of great energy and determination. This rising seems to have taken place on Sunday, the 8th of June, on the borders of Derbyshire. On the morning of that day the parlour of the White Horse, at Pentbridge, was taken possession of by a mob of about two score stalwart men. Near the window was seated the "captain," a stern-looking man in a brown coat and grey trousers, who had a map spread out before him. Next to him was a young man whose face would be familiar to the Luddites of the West Riding, for this was the notable George Weightman, the "Nottingham delegate," who attended the meeting at the St. Crispin at Halifax, and many other gatherings, to urge on a general rising. On the other side of Brandreth was another sanguine and notable leader, who was afterwards hanged and beheaded. The Captain talks undisguised treason, declares that the Government is to be overthrown, and points out on his map the routes of the various armed bodies that are hastening, he says, to the general rendezvous. "A cloud of men" are coming from the north, "he states," and bodies from other quarters will, he adds, "fall in"

at various points he is tracing out on the map. Lists
of pikes and guns are gone through and the readiness
of the contingent in the immediate locality discussed,
then Brandreth addresses them in a wild fashion,
concluding with some rhymes composed by himself—

> "Every man his skill must try
> He must turn out and not deny';
> No bloody soldier he must dread
> He must come out and fight for bread
> The time has come you plainly see
> When Government opposed must be!"

The missive is sent off to Nottingham by a trusty
messenger, and leaders are called to whispered con-
ferences with the chief, after which they leave the
room to carry out their orders. "At Nottingham,"
Brandreth promised, "there will be plenty of men
and a hundred guineas for each of them. A band
of music and thousands of friends will meet us at
Sherwood Forest; the roofs of the churches we pass
will furnish lead for bullets and at Nottingham there
will be bread, beef, and half-a-pint of rum for every
man." He then went on to announce that England
and Scotland were to rise that night at ten o'clock,
and "the northern clouds would come down and
sweep all before them."

The march of the little band which was to swell
into such a grand army, according to the Nottingham
captain, commenced. On their way they pressed
farm labourers, pitmen, and ironworkers into their
ranks, and cleared out the arms from the houses.
After an episode at the Butterly Iron Works where
Brandreth found himself opposed, the rebel band
made for Ripley Town-end, where they shouted as
a signal for the Henge and Belper detachments to
join them. At Langley Mill, a little further, they
met George Weightman returning from Nottingham.
He reported that all was going on well; the soldiers
kept quiet in barracks; the town was in possession
of their friends, and all they had to do was to march
forward.

A little before midnight, William Roper, keeper of
the racecourse stand, three quarters of a mile from
Nottingham, was returning to his home from the
town, when to his amazement he saw a crowd of
men armed with guns, pikes, etc., marshalled in
line. As he and another man were hurrying to escape
ten of them followed in pursuit. Roper and his
friend managed to reach his house, but their pursuers
followed and demanded arms at the closed door.
Roper owned that he had some but told them that
he would not deliver them up, and they then
threatened to break down the door and take them by
force. Roper threatened to blow out the brains of
the first that entered. Brandreth, infuriated at this
threat, shouted for the men with the firearms to
come forward. The men came, but they could not
force the door. After a brief conference the band
left the house and marched on towards Nottingham.

The news of the advancing host had reached Nottingham, and crowds of people congregated in the
streets. The faces of the well-to-do classes wore a
pale and anxious expression. As time passed on,
however, the scouts brought in reports of the numbers,
arms, and discipline of the "liberators" the confidence of the friends of the order grew stronger,
and preparations were made for resistance. Mr.
Robertson, a magistrate, rode early on the morning
of that day on the road the mob were said to be
coming, to reconnoitre and ascertain whether they
were really so numerous and so formidable as some
alarmists reported. When about a quarter of a
mile from Eastwood he saw in the distance a body
of working-men, armed with pikes, guns, poles, and
scythes, and turning his horse he galloped to the
nearest barracks for the soldiers. With these he
again advanced on the road, but the news of the
coming troops appears to have gone before them.
The people on the way informed them that the rioters
were dispersing, and as the Hussars dashed through
Eastwood they found the road littered with guns and

pikes, which the alarmed rioters had thrown down when they took their flight. At a short distance to the left they saw a band of thirty or forty labourers who were throwing away their rough arms and running for their lives. They captured a few and rode onwards. Beyond Eastwood they came on another body of armed men. Brandreth was at the head of these and was trying to put them in line and encourage them to march forward, but the men lost heart at the sight of the soldiers and fled in all directions. The Turners and several other insurgent leaders were taken prisoners, but Brandreth escaped and was not captured till more than a month after. George Weightman also escaped, but was traced to Sheffield, and was some time after taken into custody by the constables.

The leader of this ill-started movement, Jeremiah Brandreth, alias John Cook, alias " The Nottingham Captain," was tried with about a score of the captured insurgents at Derby, on the 16th of October. Brandreth displayed a resolute and undaunted spirit during the proceedings, and the spectators were greatly impressed by his calm and collected manner. This feeling seems to have been shared by the counsel, the celebrated Denman, for he quoted apropos of Brandreth, Byron's well-known lines in the " Corsair," which were thought very applicable to the insurgent leader.

" But who that chief? His name on every shore
Is famed and feared, they ask and know no more.
With these he mingles not but to command—
Few are his words, but keen his eye and hand.

    *   *   *   *

His name appals the fiercest of his crew,
And tints each swarthy cheek with sallower hue;
Still sways their souls with that commanding art
That dazzles, leads, yet chills the vulgar heart.
What is that spell that thus his lawless train
Confess and envy yet oppose in vain?
What should it be that thus their faith can blind!

The power, the nerve, the magic of the mind!
Link'd with success—assumed and kept with skill
That moulds another's weakness to his will—
Wields with their hands—but still to these unknown,
Makes even their mightiest deeds appear his own.
Unlike the heroes of each ancient race,
Demons in acts, but gods at least in face.
In Conrad's form seems little to admire,
Though his dark eyebrows shade a glance of fire;
Robust but not Herculean—to the sight
No giant frame sets forth his common height;
Yet on the whole, who paused to look again,
Saw more than marks the crowd of common men.
They gaze and marvel how, and still confess,
That thus it is, but why they cannot guess.
Sunburnt his cheek—his forehead high and full,
The sable curls in wild profusion veil;
There breathe but few whose aspect could defy
The full encounter of his searching eye;
There was a laughing devil in his sneer,
That raised emotions both of rage and fear;
And where his frown of hatred darkly fell,
Hope withering fled, and mercy sighed farewell ! "

The evidence against Brandreth, Turner, and
Ludlam was too strong to be gainsaid, and they were
all sentenced to death. Brandreth appears to have
caused much excitement and aroused great curiosity
throughout the country. To the last he maintained
that he had fallen a victim to the machinations of
Oliver, the Government spy, the same who had so
nearly entrapped some of the local politicians at the
gathering at Thornhill Lees. He would answer no
questions likely to incriminate anyone. As for himself, he acknowledged he was responsible for any
wrong committed, and hoped he should die as became
a christian. He was at all times calm and answered
questions with a certain quick abruptness. The
tones of his voice were deep and sonorous. He received visitors continuously, but he did not like to
be made the object of idle curiosity.

The execution of Brandreth took place opposite Derby gaol a few days after the trial; the law gave short shrifts in those days. He entered the prison chapel with his customary indifference of manner. Meeting Turner in the passage, he kissed him affectionately, saying, "We shall soon be above the sky, where there will be joy and glory for ever."

"Yes," responded Turner, with enthusiasm, "there will be no sorrow there; all will be joy and felicity."

Brandreth said he had no fear of death. When he stood upon the scaffold, he said, God bless all but Lord Castlereagh. This is all Oliver's work."

"The Lord have mercy on my soul," cried Turner.

Ludlam prayed for the king and for all within the realm, high and low, rich and poor.

After the bodies had been suspended half-an-hour, the platform was covered with sawdust, and a bench, block, two axes, and two sharp knives were placed upon it. The bodies were then cut down and placed on the bench and their heads on the block. The executioner then proceeded to chop off the heads of the criminals. As the head of the "Nottingham Captain" fell, he held it up to the three sides of the scaffold, and called out, "Behold the head of Brandreth, the traitor!"

This he also did with the heads of Turner and Ludlam, and the three bodies were then placed in their coffins, their names being written on the lids with chalk, and they were deposited in a deep grave at St. Weyburgh's Church.

After this Luddism died out in Nottinghamshire and the adjoining counties. Weightman was acquitted with about thirty others and we hear of him no more.

CHAPTER XXXV.

OLIVER, THE SPY.

"Low breath'd talkers, minion lispers
Cutting honest throats by whispers."—*Scott.*

"I will be hanged if some eternal villain,
Some busy and insinuating knave . . .
Hath not devised this slander.—*Shakespeare.*

"God bless all but Lord Castlereagh! this is all Oliver's work," cried poor John Brandreth as he stood with undaunted mien on the scaffold in front of Derby goal, prepared to suffer the fearful sentence to which the savage law of that day had doomed him.

Who was Oliver the spy'? It is our intention in this chapter to answer this question, and in doing so we shall endeavour to lift the veil which covers one of the most loathsome biographies that ever was written. Had the judge who sentenced poor Brandreth, Turner, and Ludlum but set them at liberty and executed the vile tempter who led them step by step to their doom in order that he might pocket the blood money, justice would then have been done. Oliver was a paid spy in the employ of the Government—only one of a great number—but the most wicked, unscruplous, and infamous of the whole vile troop. He had had many splendid jobs during the troubled year 1817, and had grown fat and scant of breath. The times indeed were rife for the informer and the detective. General distress continued to prevail, and the people after the immemorial habit of the Anglo-Saxons, were desirous of expressing in public meeting assembled the sense of wrong and their general misery. But the Government of the day had no faith in large gatherings, and spies spread throughout the land with the ubiquity and loathsomeness of locusts. Mysterious delegates attended the

peaceful meetings of the Hampden clubs, which were
planted thickly in the large towns of Yorkshire and
Lancashire, and dropped their poisoned words into
the ears of the simple-minded men who met to
strengthen one another in the struggle for political
reform, but who had never dreamt of adopting any
but peaceful means to accomplish their objects.
They were told that other centres were disgusted
with their foolish apathy, that to expect the Government to submit to moral force was simply absurd,
and that the only means of gaining their ends was to
march to London and demand their rights, pike and
sword in hand.   If it happened that words of wicked
and wild resolve were heard at public meetings,
those incitements to deeds of violence came almost
invariably from the base hirelings of the ministry,
as was too often discovered afterwards when it was
too late.   It has been demonstrated beyond all
question that the wild and foolish movement of the
Blanketeers was not originated by local men.   It is
well known indeed that Bamford and all the other
intelligent leaders in the neighbourhood of Manchester exposed its folly, and did their utmost to prevent
it.   There are, however, always some headstrong
individuals connected with every onward movement
who can be worked upon by evil and designing men,
and these proved too strong for the more cautious
of the fraternity.   At the famous meeting held at
Manchester, from which the Blanketeers started on
the foolish expedition to London, many wild speeches
were made, but there was one which capped all
others in absurdity and violence, and that was uttered
by a "Delegate from London," who had been for
weeks before inflaming the passions of the starving
population at meetings held in and around Cotton-
opolis.   The base wretch, who stood up in that
surging crowd and incited the working classes to
make another Moscow of Manchester if the employers of labour and the capitalists did not find them
work and wages, was no local man.   It was the

THE RISINGS OF THE LUDDITES.

" Delegate from London," better known afterwards
by the name of " Oliver the Spy," the same that
incited the men of Nottingham to rise, and led the
captain and his companions to their doom upon the
scaffold. Edward Painter, the pugilist, detecting
the base rascal through his disguise, waxed furious
as he watched the effect of his infamous speech on
the poor deluded wretches around him, and did his
best to expose him, but his voice was drowned by
the clamours of the excited crowd. Painter determined, however, to punish the vile miscreant who
was so fatally misleading so many men whom he
well knew would never have themselves dreamt of
violent measures. Quietly watching him as he
dropped from the waggon and skulked through the
surging crowd, Painter followed him until he had
got into a quiet lane outside the town, when he fell
upon him and thrashed him until the sneaking ruf-
fian literally howled in agony. From that moment
Painter was to the spy a marked man, and he swore
that if ever the opportunity came, Mr. Edward
Painter should end his days in the hulks or on the
gallows. Without entering into further particulars
touching this private feud, we may say that Oliver
nearly proved as good as his word. He dogged
Painter's footsteps like a sleuth ..ound, and although
entirely innocent the pugilist had subsequently some
difficulty in escaping from the diabolical spy.

Lancashire becoming too hot for Oliver, he soon
after migrated to the West Riding, which was also
in a state of great political agitation at this time. He
was introduced into Yorkshire by a prominent reform delegate of the name of Mitchell, of Liversedge.
It was thought at the time that this Mitchell had
been duped by Oliver, and that he was not aware
of the real character of the man for whom he stood
sponser, but facts that were made known justify us
in concluding that though such might possibly have
been the case at the commencement of their acquaintance, it was not so at a later period. The first

evidence that Oliver was at work in this locality
appeared in the Mercury of June 7th, 1817 ; in the
shape of the following mysterious announcement : -
" Rumours of a threatened insurrection have been
circulated in this town with great confidence.   The
meeting took place at Thornhill Lees, near Dewsbury, when ten persons were taken into custody by
General Byng.   The examination took place at
Wakefield, to which place the prisoners were taken
in carriages, escorted by the police.   Information
leading to the arrests was given by' one of their number, who stated that fifty stands of arms would be
found in a barn near the place of meeting.'

As the meeting of the so-called " Conspirators "
had only taken place the day before the Mercury was
issued, we need not wonder that the news was not
of a more explicit character.   Before the next issue
of the paper, however, information of a startling
character began to leak out.   On the 13th of June,
Mr. Edward Baines received a letter from his friend
Mr. James Holdforth, which led him to determine
to investigate the matter thoroughly.   He at
once took a chaise, and went to Dewsbury.

In the issue of the Mercury of the following day
there appeared a more detailed account of the apprehension of the delegates.   After stating that on the
suppression of the Union Societies some of the members associated together in a private and clandestine
manner, the writer proceeds to say that Oliver was
introduced to the ultra-reformers of this locality,
by Mitchell, a delegate who had been taken into
custody with the rest.   He was vouched for by
Mitchell as a person deserving their countenance,
and not only disposed to communicate information
as to the state of the country, but able also to afford
the most effective assistance.   Thus recommended by
one who was well known as a prominent reformer,
Oliver was heartily welcomed to all the meetings of
the various organisations, and soon possessed himself of their unbounded confidence.   At every

gathering within a wide circle the spy invariably made himself conspicuous, and dropped poisonous seeds on every suitable occasion. He represented to these credulous men that all the people in the metropolis were longing for the downfall of the Government; that everything was organised and absolutely settled to obtain that result. He stated that it had been arranged that on the 9th of June a general rising would taken place, and that as a consequence of this movement all the public offices were to be seized, and the state prisoners were all to be set at liberty. A plan had been arranged for securing all the military, he further stated, by which means a change would be effected without any bloodshed. His object in coming to the manufacturing districts, he said, was to apprize the political organisations in the country of this arrangement, and urge them to act simultaneously with the London brethren by carrying out a similar plan, so that a bloodless revolution might be effected.

The central committees, he said, urged that on the night agreed upon, namely Sunday, June 8th, all the military in England should be secured in their quarters, their arms seized, and that all magistrates and other civil officers should be arrested and placed under restraint.

Having by such representations as the above excited the passions of a few headstrong men, he thought his scheme sufficiently ripe, and acquainted the magistrates that secret meetings were being held in the neighbourhood, and that one was to be held at Thornhill Lees, at which delegates would attend for the purpose of inaugurating a revolution. . These delegates, he states, were representatives of the Leeds, Wakefield, Bradford, Huddersfield, and other societies, and they had pitched upon Thornhill Lees because of its central and retired position. The truth was that the organisations in question had not agreed to send any delegates, the men apprehended being simply a few headstrong individuals who had been led by various representations to meet Oliver at the place named, none of whom, however, had any idea that they were about to initiate a general rising. The object of Oliver in bringing these men from the towns all round was to show the magistrates and the Government that the conspiracy was wide-spread, and that he was placing them under very great obligations by exposing such a dangerous plot. As will be seen as our account proceeds, Oliver failed to induce the man he had pitched upon as the Dewsbury "delegate" to attend the meeting, and only brought in a Leeds "delegate" by a singular and daring stratagem.

On the morning of Friday, the 16th of June, the meeting arranged by Oliver took place at Thornhill Lees, but no business was transacted, for they were no sooner assembled than the house was surrounded and those present were taken into custody. The following are the names and places of residence of the "delegates" apprehended : —John Smaller, shoemaker, Horbury ; James Mann, cloth drawer, Leeds ; Thos. Wood, cloth drawer, Wakefield ; Miles Illingworth, carpenter, Manningham ; Benjamin Whiteley, cloth drawer, Holmfirth ; Edward Fletcher, cardmaker, Hightown ; Josh Midgley, clothier, Almondbury ; Wm. Walker, clothier, Thornhill Lees.

These men were, as has been before stated, immediately conveyed to Wakefield, where they were examined by Sir F. L. Wood, Benjamin Dealtry, Esq., and other magistrates. The examination was private. It was asserted by Oliver that in a barn at Whitley, near the place of the meeting, there were deposited one hundred pikes and fifty stand of arms ; and at the house of John Smaller, at Horbury, would be found a quantity of ball cartridges. Messengers were despatched to search both places. The straw in the barn was carefully examined, but not a single pike nor firearm could be found, in fact it was plain that the straw had not been disturbed for some time. The evidence relating to the ball cartridges was also falsified, nothing of the kind being found in the house of Smaller.

This was as the matter stood when Mr. Edward Baines commenced his investigations. Calling upon Mr. Willans, a printer, at Dewsbury, he learned from him that a person named Oliver had waited upon him and introduced himself as a Parliamentary reformer sent from London to ascertain the disposition of the people in the country. This man, Willans describes as of genteel appearance, and of good address, nearly six feet high, of erect figure, light hair, red and large whiskers, and full face pitted with the smallpox. His usual dress was a light, fashionably made, brown coat, black waistcoat, dark blue mixture pantaloons, and Wellington boots. He called upon Willans several times, and during one of his visits said it was quite evident the Government would not listen to the petitions of the people, it had therefore become necessary to compel attention to their demands. These insinuations Willans silenced by the observation that he could not engage in any proceedings that implied the use of force or the shedding of blood. On another occasion Oliver told him that he was one of a committee of five who effected the escape of the man Watson, who led the absurd attack on the tower of London, and added that if Thistlewood had had equally prudent counsellors he would also have escaped. In fact the whole tenor of his discourse was to show that he was in league with traitors. These conversations aroused Willans' suspicions, and the intercourse had almost ceased when, on the morning the arrests took place at Thornhill Lees, Oliver again called at Mr. Willans' shop between ten and eleven o'clock, and Mr. Willans being absent from business, he begged his wife to tell him that a meeting of delegates was to be held at Thornhill Lees that day, and earnestly requested she would use her influence to get him to attend it. Before Oliver quitted Dewsbury, he called once more at Mr. Willans' shop and found he had returned,

when he renewed his solicitations, telling him the
friends in London were almost heart-broken because
the people in the country were so quiet.   At the
same time he told him he had walked from Leeds,
and that the person he had with him was a Leeds man.
Unmoved by Oliver's solicitations, Mr. Willans refused to attend the meeting, and thus Dewsbury was
prevented from swelling the number of "delegates."

When the so-called "delegates" were seized at
Thornhill Lees, Oliver was taken amongst the rest,
but was suffered to escape.   While the examination was going on, Oliver had repaired to his quarters
at the Stafford Arms, at Wakefield, and here to his
consternation he was seen and recognised by a Mr.
Dixon, a draper, of Dewsbury, who immediately
addressed him—"How does it happen that you, who
have taken a leading part in the recent meetings, are
at liberty, while your associates are in custody?"

"Because," replied Mr. Oliver, "no papers were
found on me, and being a stranger, the persons who
apprehended me were obliged to set me at liberty."

This reply was made in a very hurried and confused
manner, and Mr. Oliver at once withdrew and took
a seat on the Wakefield coach to Leeds.   As soon
as he had taken his seat a person in livery stepped up
to him, and, moving his hat, entered into conversation with him.   On the departure of the coach Mr.
Dixon went up to the servant, and asked him if he
knew that gentleman, to which he replied that he had
seen him at Campsall, and had driven him a few
days before in his master's tandem to catch the coach.
Mr. Dixon went and asked who his master was, to
which question the servant replied, "General Byng."
Mr. Dixon then left the man and asked Mr. Lyles,
who kept the Stafford Arms, if he knew Oliver, to
which he answered that he had been there several
times—that he believed he was from London, and
that several London letters had come directed to him
at the Inn.

Mr. Baines published these and other disclosures
in the "Mercury," and they created great excitement
throughout the country. So impressed were the
magistrates with them that they at once released
Oliver's dupes from custody. The Government was
also questioned on the matter, and Lord Liverpool
was obliged to admit that Oliver was an agent of the
Government. As Oliver was only one of a large
number of spies, the people awoke to the fact that
it was such vile instruments as those by which scores
of innocent men were led to the scaffold, and a strong
petition against the iniquitous system was made.

The way in which the "delegates" were brought
together may be seen from a statement made by
Murray, who was said to represent the Leeds society.

Murray says that he was walking in the neighbourhood of Leeds, when Oliver met him, and asked him
the road to Dewsbury. He then further asked him
to accompany him as guide, promising to pay his
expenses. When they had left Dewsbury for Thornhill, and had arrived at a lane about a hundred
yards from the Spoortsman's Arms, he saw three
gentleman, one of whom being General Byng, riding
up to meet them at full speed. On their approach,
Sir John advanced up to Oliver and said, "I think I
know you, sir?"

Oliver, affecting to be overcome with fright, made
no reply.

"I have an accurate description of you from
London," continued Sir John, "is not your name
Oliver?" Oliver remained silent, and by the orders
of Sir John he was now surrounded by the cavalry
and taken prisoner. Murray, who was amazed at
this, attempted to walk away, but he was soon
stopped and dragged into the Sportsman's Arms,
where he found five or six more in custody. He did
not know any of the men, and was not aware why
he or they had been apprehended. A carriage was

shortly brought up and they were conveyed to Wakefield.

What a fearful light is thrown by this statement on poor Brandreth's dying cry—"This is all Oliver's work."

Oliver, the spy, was soon afterwards rewarded with a pension, and retired to an obscure part of the country to finish his ignoble life.

CHAPTER XXXVI.

PETERLOO.

Man, proud man !
Dressed in a little brief authority . .
Plays such fantastic tricks before high heaven,
As make the angels weep.—*Shakespeare.*

Notwithstanding all that could be done either by
Government spies or Government officials, political
agitation amongst the working classes in the West
Riding, and throughout Lancashire, continued to
grow.   Hampden clubs became as plentiful as black-
berries, and the agitation for a reform in Parliament
waxed stronger and stronger, helped on as it now
was by the notable democrat, known as " Orator
Hunt." This remarkable man, who, for some years
was the chief idol of the working classes, was of a
very different stamp from the pureminded patriot,
Major Cartwright.   His appearance was very striking ; standing upwards of six feet in height, and well
proportioned, his figure was a prominent one on the
platforms of the great reform gatherings.   His expression was pleasant and agreeable, except, when he
became excited in his oratory, at which times the
kind smile would be exchanged for the sneer or the
curse, his mellow tones gave way to sonorous bellow-
ings, his doubled fist was uplifted defiantly, and his
whole manner showed the wild passions that were
struggling for utterance.   It had been arranged that
a great reform gathering should be held at Manchester, and that " Orator Hunt," and other well-
known democrats should be the speakers.   As the
authorities seemed to take alarm at the formidable
preparations that were being made to accommodate
the immense multitude to be present, it was deter-

mined by the leaders that no excuse should be given
for the threatened interference of the magistrates,
they therefore forbade their followers to carry any
arms in the procession, and as the time grew nearer,
it was ordered that even ordinary walking sticks
should be laid aside.

When the morning appointed for the meeting
arrived, immense processions of working men, dressed mostly in their holiday attire, filed through the
streets of Manchester to the central meeting place,
St. Peter's Square, accommmpanied by bands of music,
and carrying hundreds of gay banners. When the
great space was filled with some 80,000 reformers,
a tremendous shout from the surging multitude
announced the arrival of Hunt and a number of
other well-known leaders. It was proposed that Mr.
Hunt should preside, and the motion being carried
the great demagogue took off his white hat—then a
recognised symbol of radicalism—and proceeded to
open the meeting; he had scarcely uttered a score
sentences, however, when an uproar was observed
to take place at the outskirts of the crowd. It was
said at first that it was the procession from Blackburn
that was coming in, but it soon became evident that
a body of cavalry had arrived, and were forming in
line with their drawn swords ready for action. The
soldiers were received by the people with a hearty
shout of goodwill, the idea apparently being that
they had come to preserve order. It soon became
plain, however, that such was not their errand, for
shouting wildly in reply, they waved their sabres
over their heads and striking spurs into their horses,
began to slash and strike down the helpless crowd
before them. Then ensued a scene of wild confusion. The multitude would fain have fled, but
flight to the great bulk was plainly impossible, and
in their efforts to escape they only wedged themselves into a still more dense mass. The cavalry,
with all their weight of man and horse, could not
for a time penetrate into the crowd, and they plied

their swords to hew themselves a way to the platform, and chopped off limbs, and bleeding heads and
faces were soon visible all along the disordered line.
Groans and cries were mingled with the wild shout of
the mad soldiery, and from ten thousand throats cries
of "Butchers! Shame! Shame!" were heard above
the horrid confusion. With a heavy rush and a
sound like thunder, the imprisoned crowd burst
through the line of soldiers, but scattered though
they were by this desperate movement, the military
still stuck wildly around them in blind fury, and
piteous spectacles of maimed men and even women
were scattered all round the feet of the prancing
horses. Finding themselves widely separated by
the desperate efforts of the crowd to escape from the
confined space, the soldiers wheeled about and dashed into the people wherever they saw an opening,
disregarding the piteous cries of the women, old men
and striplings, who formed so large a proportion of
the gathering. Bye-and-bye the flags attracted their
attention, and they made sallies in all directions so
long as one remained flying. In less than a quarter-
of-an-hour the enormous assembly had dispersed, and
the great square was deserted, except by groups of
good Samaritans here and there, who were carrying
off the dead, and ministering to the necessities of the
wounded, while the ground was covered with hats,
bonnets, shawls, and other articles of dress, trampled,
torn and bloody.

In addition to the soldiers who cleared St. Peter's
Field, others chased and harrassed the fugitives as they
escaped. In Deansgate several pieces of artillery
were stationed, and a large number of special constables paraded the streets in the immediate vicinity.
Hunt and the other speakers left the platform at the
beginning of the melee, but were recognised as they
passed through the streets, taken into custody, and
lodged in the New Bailey prison.

As might naturally be supposed, this savage and
unexpected attack on an unarmed multitude, who

had met with no hostile intent, but simply to discuss their political grievances in a peaceful and constitutional manner, excited great indignation throughout Lancashire and also throughout all England, and the Radical press indignantly denounced the crime and demanded that those who had instigated the attack, as well as those who had carried it out, should be brought to justice. In the neighbourhood of Manchester itself the people were goaded to fury, and there was much talk of a bloody revenge. Smiths were busy all night long in the villages making pikes; rusty old guns were cleaned and repaired, scythes were fixed upon poles, and everything that could be made to cut or stab was got ready. Had not the Radical leaders been nearly all of them opposed to physical force, it is possible that the Manchester soldiers would have had reason to rue their cowardly attack, but sober counsels fortunately prevailed, the rougher spirits were restrained, and the people relied upon Parliament to do them justice.

As soon as the news of this riot, as the ministerial papers styled it, reached London, a Cabinet Council was held, and instead of the military who had committed these outrages being called to account, they received the formal thanks of the Government for their prompt and valorous conduct. The friends of reform in London, however, were determined that the truth should be made known, and at a large meeting, held in Palace Yard, Westminster, at which Sir Francis Burdett and John Cam Hobhouse were the chief speakers, the affair at St. Peter's Field was denounced as a massacre and a foul attempt to destroy the liberties of the English people. The Government was too strong, however, to be affected by any resolutions passed at public meetings, and the well-known "Six Acts" were introduced and carried by large majorities through both Houses.

These tyrannical acts took away the right of traversing in cases of misdemeanour; punished those found guilty by imprisonment for life; required the

names of seven householders to the requisition calling
any meeting for the discussion of any subject connected with church or state, and gave the magistrates
the power of entering any man's house by night or by
day. Thus not only were the people cut down by
the military, but when they complained of the outrage their liberties were further restricted by this
despotic House of Commons. The misrepresenta-
tions of Lord Castlereagh respecting the conduct of
what he called "the mob" are simply astounding. It
has never been proved that the Riot Act was read,
but Castlereagh not only states that it was read
publicly from a window, but goes on to aver that a
man who went to the hustings to re-read it was
trampled under foot. With regard to the "unarmed multitude" as it had been called in a petition
for justice, the same noble Lord astonished the nation
by informing it that they commenced the riot and
that the military exercised great forbearance. This
unarmed multitude," said the noble Lord, "though
the place had been cleared of stones that were calculated to hurt human beings, assailed the military
with so many that the next day two cart loads were
found upon the ground, so that the parties had come
with stones in their pockets. It was also evident
there were men amongst them armed with pistols, for
they fired at the troops."

These false statements were received with great indignation by the Radicals, and their gagged press did
its best to refute them by pointing out that they were
sheer inventions. None of the astounding events
named by Lord Castlereagh had been so much as
hinted at the state trials which had taken place, and
as Mr. Edward Baines, in an article in the
"Mercury," said, "They will stand recorded for
ever as having been solemnly averred in the House
of Commons, although they were found in a court of
justice to be wholly untrue." Not content with
exposing the vile conduct of the authorities in his
paper, Mr. Baines contributed largely by his state-

ments as an eye witness to put the public in possession
of the actual facts touching this notable demonstration.

CHAPTER XXXVII.

THE RISING AT GRANGE MOOR.

Better that they awhile had borne,
E'en all those ills that most displease,
Than sought a cure far worse than the disease.
Buckingham.

About nine months after the Peterloo massacre it was shown that the Luddites in this neighbourhood had not forgotten their old place of meeting. The labouring classes were still suffering great privations, and a disposition to tumult still prevailed. On the night of Friday, the 31st of March, 1820, another simultaneous rising was appointed to take place throughout the West Riding. Emissaries from the various clubs and other political and trade organisations had been flitting about for a long time previously, most of them hailing from Barnsley and the neighbourhood, which may be regarded as being the headquarters of this rising. It was arranged that the meeting place for Dewsbury, Heckmondwike, Birstall, Brighouse, and other towns and villages round Mirfield should be the old Luddite meeting place, near the Dumb Steeple, Cooper Bridge. The capture of the town of Huddersfield seems to have been one of the first objects of this rising, and it was arranged that the detachments from the surrounding places should approach the town simultaneously. In order to prevent their plans from being prematurely divulged, all the stage coaches were stopped, and horsemen and pedestrians were prevented from continuing their journey. Toward the hour of midnight considerable bodies of men marched in small detachments towards the appointed place and committed

some excesses on a few pedestrians who refused to
stop when ordered and fall into rank. After waiting
some time for the signal to march agreed upon, the
leaders became apprehensive that something had gone
wrong and they advised the men to disperse. The
be paid spies like Oliver, were busy flitting about on
the day following. They explained that the central
body had found that owing to unexpected difficulties
the united movement could not take place on that
evening, but it had been arranged that the various
bodies should meet on Grange Moor on the Wednesday following and march on Huddersfield in a compact army. The malcontents in this immediate
locality being either disgusted with their failure
or afraid of the consequences of their rash
action, do not appear to have mustered in
large numbers, and when the "grand army"
as it had been beforehand named was assembled, it was found to consist of a mere handful of
men, principally from Barnsley and its neighbourhood, many of them workmen out of employ'ment
and none above the rank of labourers. The little
frightened band waited some hours in the momentary
expectation of reinforcements, but when morning
approached and they found that the triumphant
"army of the north," which was to march on London,
did not appear, they began to disperse to their
homes. The Huddersfield authorities who were duly
apprized of the state of matters on the moor sent out
a few soldiers to reconnoitre, but when they arrived
they found nothing to tell of the whereabouts of the
rebel army, except a few score pikes and sticks which
the insurgents had abandoned in their flight, for fear
of being compromised if they were captured before
they reached home.

During the next day a strict search was made in
the surrounding towns and villages, especially in the
neighbourhood of Barnsley, and twenty-two of the
ringleaders were apprehended. An immense number
of pikes were also discovered hid in haystacks and

outhouses, and also in draw-wells. The suspected persons were committed to York Castle until Monday, the 11th of September, when an adjourned assize was held for the purpose of trying them.

Mr. Baines, the editor of the "Leeds Mercury," had, at intervals since the apprehension of the rioters, been urging upon the authorities that the extreme punishment of the law should not be inflicted upon these misguided men, but that a long period of imprisonment should be substituted. Their miserable, half-starved condition was dwelt upon, and any circumstances likely to tell in their favour were brought forward week after week. On the Saturday following the opening of the assize, the editor was in a position to make the following gratitfying announcement : —

"The special assize at York has terminated more abruptly and more favourably both for the interests of humanity and the interests of the country than was expected. All the prisoners captured during the late unhappy affair at Grange Moor, to the number of two and twenty, have pleaded guilty, on the understanding that whatever punishment it may be judged proper to award them, their lives at any rate shall be spared. This is a course which, as our readers well know, we have from time to time taken the liberty to recommend, and without presuming to suppose that the recommendations in question have had any influence whatever in deciding the conduct of the government and their law officers, we may now state that soon after the paragraph appeared, we had the satisfaction to learn that the sentiments it expressed met with favour amongst persons of considerable power and authority in the state. The time for making the offer with which the prisoners closed, was very appropriate and well chosen; it was the night of Sunday before the opening of the commission, and the commencement of the trials. On the arrival of Mr. Williams, the leading counsel for the prisoners, at York, it was made known to him if the prisoners thought proper to plead guilty and in that way cast themselves upon the clemency of the crown, the sentence awarded for the crime with which they all stood charged, would not be executed upon any' of them.　This offer the learned gentleman (accompanied by Mr. Starkie) communicated to his clients, without any recommendation or dissuasion whatever, whether to accept it or reject it.　The proposal was made about eleven o'clock at night, and soon after twelve the counsel returned to know their opinion on it, at which time they found a paper, drawn up we believe by Comstive, bearing the names of all the prisoners, those from the neighbourhood of Huddersfield as well as those from Barnsley and neighbourhood, in which they all consented to accept of clemency on the terms proffered to them.　We shall not attempt to describe the change which an hour had produced in the minds of these unfortunate men ; from the contemplation of death as near at hand and in its most hideous form, the prospect of life continued to its natural duration, and of a speedy return to their families had burst unexpectedly upon them, and rendered a night which had commenced in horrors, the happiest in their existence.　On the following morning, sensations equally pleasurable were imparted and confirmed in the minds of their friends, who, instead of the awful denunciation of the law, pointing at death as immediately at hand, heard the compassionate judge cast the spectre to a distance, and address the prisoners in the eloquent and cheering language—And whenever death shall come upon you, may God Almighty', whose mercy is infinite, extend to you that mercy which your situation may require."

An investigation into the circumstances of this extraordinary treason would, we apprehend, have shown that the great bulk of its infatuated perpetrators had been led into crime by the persuasions of designing men, who had themselves abandoned them in the hour of trial, and that many of them in joining the rebel army, as the rabble rout was somewhat

pompously called, had acted under a momentary
impulse, and not from any deliberate purpose to
overthrow the government. In adjudging the punishment which will, we apprehend, be imprisonment for
different periods, these circumstances will be taken
into consideration, and a line of distinction be drawn
between the exciters and the excited. We are not
in the habit of complimenting the government on
the wisdom or moderation of its measures, but in
the present instance we have no hesitation in saying
that their clemency has been dictated by sound
policy, and that more will be effected by mercy
than could have been accomplished by severity. To
the prisoners themselves, and to their connections,
the jeopardy into which their lives have been brought
by listening to the counsel of desperate men, will
have read them a lesson which they will never,
we hope, forget, and will have added another tie
to the obligations under which they were before
placed to hold the laws, and respect the institutions
of the country."

Comstive, the ringleader, referred to in the above
extract, was a native of Kirkham, in Lancashire, but
had been a resident in Barnsley for a few years before his apprehension, where he was employed as a
weaver. He had served in the 29th regiment of
foot under Captain Longbottom, under whom he
attained the rank of sergeant more than once, but
was broken through unsteady conduct. He was at
Waterloo, where he again proved himself to be a
brave and reckless soldier. He was the captain
of the Barnsley rebels, and the soul of the movement. He was a good penman, and having a fair
knowledge of military matters, drew up a plan for
attacking Huddersfield, and arranged the general
plan of rebellion. He gave the plan he had drawn
up to Craven Cookson and Stephen Kitchen, who
had been appointed a deputation to go to Huddersfield, and these men turning traitors the document
came into the hands of the authorities. After the

arrangement, the counsel for the prosecution showed Comstive this document, which made him feel very nervous, as he had no idea that the delegates had betrayed him, and that so damnatory a proof of his guilt was in possession of the crown. Had the trial proceeded his fate was inevitable, he therefore naturally exerted himself greatly to persuade all his friends who had been apprehended to throw themselves on the mercy of the government, when the promise was made that if that were done all their lives should be spared. He was transported for life. Another Waterloo veteran, who had been Comstive's right hand man, was also transported for life, as were many of the others. His name was Richard Oddy, and he was a small linen manufacturer. His wife and children went with him into exile, as did nearly all the near relatives of the others who were sent out of the country.

From the report of a gentleman who had been out to Van Dieman's Land in 1836, sixteen years after the Grange Moor rising, it seems that all the men transported from this district did well in their new homes except poor Comstive. Many of them rose to be large dairy and sheep farmers, and one was sitting on the Launceston bench as a magistrate. Comstive's ill-luck followed him. He might have done well, but the old reckless spirit could not be kept under. He was finally concerned in the forging of a will, and was transported once more to Norfolk Island.

The informers, Craven Cookson, Stephen Kitchen, and Thomas Morgan were always treated with much contempt during the remainder of their lives, and if one of them entered any company in a public-house or elsewhere, all conversation ceased at once.

CHAPTER XXXVIII.

CHARTIST RISINGS.

Men of England ye are slaves,
Though ye " rule" the roaring " waves,"
Though ye cry from land to sea,
" Britons everywhere are free!"

Disraeli, in his younger days, once wrote to Hume
to ask him to introduce him to some Radical con-
stituency as a candidate, and concluded his letter
with the exclamation, " My forte is sedition!"
Whatever may be the verdict about the Conservative
chief it is curious to note how truly this exclamation
might have been uttered by many Yorkshiremen of
the last generation. It is notorious that thousands
of working men, made desperate by their hard lot,
joined every movement whose aim was opposition
to the government. Some of them were Luddites
when that faction was in existence, Radicals afterwards, and finally as old men joined in the Chartist
risings.

When Queen Victoria ascended the throne trade
remained still very bad, and provisions being dear
discontent was rife amongst the half-starved operatives of the great industrial centres. Only a few
weeks after the coronation day a great Radical meeting was held at Birmingham, and from this gathering
may be said to have originated the movement which
by and by developed into Chartism—a disturbing
influence in political life in England for ten remarkable years, whose record has never yet been fully
written.

The Reform Bill of 1832 had not satisfied the
working classes. The well-to-do portion of the
middle classes had certainly secured some represen-

tation under it, but the great body of operatives
who, when they were rejoicing over its safe passage
thought they were inaugurating the millenium, soon
found out that they were as much left out in the
cold as ever.   The Chartists, we need hardly say,
were so named from the famous document, called
the People's Charter, which appears to have been
drawn up by William Lovett, and after being revised by Roebuck and others was finally adopted
with great enthusiasm, and upwards of a million
men were speedily enrolled under the green banner
which was their political symbol.   The name of
the manifesto—which was certainly a happy one—
seems to have been given to it by Daniel O'Connell,
the great repeal agitator, who speaking at a meeting
where it was adopted in 1838, exclaimed "There's
your charter; agitate for it, and never be content
till you get it."

The want of a newspaper to advocate the claims
of the new movement was soon felt, and the
"Northern Star" was speedily established in Leeds,
Mr. Joshua Hobson being the publisher and Mr.
Hill the editor.   Although the paper could not be
sold at less than 4½d. per copy, owing to the heavy
stamp and paper duties with which the government
then crippled all efforts for the political education
of the people, it soon secured a large circulation,
and it is said to have eventually reached 60,000
copies weekly.   The movement had not been long
in existence before it was divided into two sections,
one of which advocated moral suasion and the other
physical force.   The majority of the Chartists of
Lancashire and the West Riding, like those of
Birmingham, belonged to the more violent section.
Moral suasion amongst these was openly scoffed at
and the people were counselled to provide themselves
with guns, pikes, and knives in order to force the
upper classes to grant to them what they considered
to be their rights.   Dear bread and bad trade
fanned the discontent into a flame, and during the

year 1839 the working classes were in a desperate
state, especially in Lancashire and the West Riding.
Unsound corn was 76s. per quarter, and the best
reached 10s. more, and every other necessary of
life, excepting butchers' meat, was equally dear.
Wages had fallen very low, and in Leeds alone
upwards of 10,000 people were walking the streets
in enforced idleness, other Yorkshire towns being
equally as bad. Great meetings were held on the
moors and commons in central localities, the chief
orators at which were poor, poverty-stricken men
who, driven to desperation, spoke with extraordinary vehemence and recklessness, and as a natural
sonsequence riots broke out everywhere. It was
recommended that a general rising should take place,
but it was resolved that the state of the country
should be first brought before the legislature. A
chartist convention was with this view assembled
in London, which comprised representatives of almost every important town in England. At this
great gathering a petition to the House of Commons
was adopted, which was speedily signed by more
than a million and a quarter people. In it the
legislature were asked to take into consideration the
six points of the charter, but this, by a majority of
189 in a house of 281, was refused. On this being
made known great indignation meetings were held
everywhere, at which the people were advised to
purchase arms and march on London. The advice
was acted upon; vast quantities of weapons, especially pikes, were secretly collected, until the
authorities, alarmed at the threatening aspect of
affairs, instituted a search and seized all they could
discover. Riots of a formidable character occurred
at Birmingham, Manchester, Oldham, Preston, and
Newcastle, and the whole of the West Riding was
in a ferment. In some of these places attempts
were made to stop the factories and bring all labour
to a standstill, the object being to show capitalists
how helpless they were without the working classes.

At Birmingham the rioters were exceedingly violent, and when resisted attempted to fire the town. In Bradford and Leeds fierce fights were waged in the streets with the constables and the military, and in Lancashire, where the mobs had almost the mastery, bakers and provision shops were broken into and looted in all directions. At Birmingham the loss of property, and from damage was estimated to reach £40,000, and the Lancashire towns suffered in equal proportion. As the authorities got the upper hand many of the Chartist leaders were arrested, and the disturbers of the peace were gradually overawed.

It would be unjust to represent the leaders of this new political crusade as mere violent demagogues whose whole aim was disturbance and sedition. Some of them were men of great ability, and their political speeches were often characterised by rare eloquence. Amongst them were able writers like Thomas Cooper, poets of genius like Ernest Jones, and great orators like Julian Harney and Bronterre O'Brien, who could sway large crowds with their impassioned oratory as the corn is swayed by the autumn wind. The head of the movement, Feargus O'Connor, who was a man of great stature and tremendous strength, had considerable oratorical gifts, and his rough humour and "bonhommie" endeared him to his humble followers. Thomas Cooper, in his interesting autobiography, gives an amusing description of an election scene at Nottingham, where Feargus O'Connor, irritated by a crowd of jeering Tory butchers, leaped down from a waggon into the midst of them and "fought his way through them, flooring them like nine-pins." "Once the Tory lambs got him down," Cooper adds, "and my heart quaked, for I thought they would kill him, but in a few minutes his red head emerged again from the rough human billows, and he went on fighting as before. Feargus O'Connor had education, had mixed in good society, belonged to an old and wealthy family, and with good warrant boasted his descent from a line of Irish kings. His sincerity was proved by the sacrifices of time and money which he made to help on what he regarded as the people's cause, and though his faults and errors were great and manifold, he was for many years the idol of the working classes, who flocked to hear him in thousands in all parts of the country.

On Whit-Monday, in this year, there was an immense gathering of Chartists at Peep Green, a large stretch of waste land between Hartshead and Roberttown, which is said to have been the largest political meeting ever held in England. This great historical gathering was organised at the Old Yew Tree, at Liversedge, by some of the principal local Chartists, of whom Mr. Pitt Keighley, of Huddersfield, and Mr. Luke Firth, of Heckmondwike, were the leading spirits. When the day arrived processions miles in length came from all the great towns around, and a sight was witnessed such as will probably never be seen again. Each detachment had flags innumerable, and as they were each accompanied by two or three brass bands, they attracted almost the entire population along the route. As they marched on to the great common where the meeting was held, with bands playing and banners flying overhead for hour after hour, the enthusiasm was indescribable. In appearance those joining in this memorable demonstration seemed to be operatives of the more intelligent class, and their demeanour throughout the proceedings was sober yet determined. When the immense masses of people had taken up the positions assigned to them by the marshals, it was calculated that a quarter of a million people were present. The spectacle of that ·sea of upturned faces as seen from the platform was, we are told by an old veteran who witnessed the sight, one which could never be forgotten. The meeting was opened by the singing of Wesley's fine lyric:—

"Peace, doubting heart! my God's I am;
Who formed me man forbids my fear;
The Lord has called me by my name,
The Lord protects, for ever near.

The singing of which from such a vast multitude
had an indescribable effect, accompanied as it was
by thousands of musical instruments. A touching
prayer was then offered up by Mr. William Thornton,
of Halifax, a man of superior intelligence. When
the popular idol, Feargus O'Connor, stood up to
address the meeting, the enthusiasm of the assembly
was tremendous, and it was a long time before the
cheering, which volleyed like thunder, could be
stilled sufficiently to allow his stentorian voice to
be heard. O'Connor's harangue was warm and impassioned, but in wild fervour it fell far behind that
of Bronterre O'Brien, who was one of the most
eloquent of perhaps the most remarkable band of
orators that ever stood on a political platform in this
country.

Amongst the early apostles of Chartism was Henry
Vincent, an enthusiastic young printer, full of fire
and energy, who was considered one of the best
speakers in England at that time. He had been
put into prison at Newport, Wales, along with other
Chartists for his violent speeches, much to the indignation of the stalwart miners there, who were
nearly all physical force Chartists. As winter drew
on a scheme was devised amongst these men to
liberate their leader, and Mr. Frost, a Newport
magistrate, aided by his neighbours, Messrs.
Williams and Jones, agreed to head the rescue
party. The prison was to be assaulted on four
sides simultaneously by four divisions numbering
10,000, or according to some accounts 20,000, who
thought they would be able by attacking it
on all sides to distract its defenders, but as often
happens in such enterprises, owing to cowardice or
miscalculation, the junction was not made at the
time agreed upon, and when Frost began the attack'

with his division, he found to his dismay that they were alone. He had thus to bear the whole brunt of the defending forces of military and policemen, and his little troop were soon driven back with the loss of ten killed and fifty wounded. In their flight they met or saw the lagging divisions, but nothing remained for all of them but a speedy flight. Frost, and his assistant leaders, Williams and Jones, were apprehended, and after a time were tried and found guilty of high treason. Death, under all the revolting circumstances which attended the end of Brandreth, the Nottingham captain, would have been the finish only a few years before, but public opinion would not allow another barbarous exhibition of that sort, and their sentence was commuted to transportation for life. Even this was not carried out, for when the Chartist movement had collapsed, Frost was allowed to return home. He found on settling again at Newport that a great change had come over the scene. The abolition of the corn laws inaugurated the era of cheap bread, and free trade had unloosened the springs of commerce so that the working men, being better fed and better clothed, had ceased to agitate against government, except by constitutional methods.

After and about the time of the Newport riots there were riots and turmoils everywhere. The Chartist leaders were hauled up before the magistrates by scores, no less than five hundred of them being in prison at one time. Amongst them was Thomas Cooper, the well known author of the "Purgatory of Suicides," which able work he in fact wrote when in confinement. Cooper, in his "Autobiography," gives a very graphic sketch of the state of the country at this troubled period, and tells a little anecdote which strongly illustrates the feeling amongst workmen at this time. "Wild and infidel notions," he says, "were proclaimed by many of the leaders. I was holding a meeting one day in Leices-

ter, when a poor, religious stockinger said, 'Let us
be patient a little longer, surely God Almighty will
help us soon.' 'Talk to us no more about thy
Goddle Mighty' was the savage cry that came from
the audience, 'there isn't one! If there was one
he would not let us suffer as we do.'" Next day
a poor stockinger rushed into his house, and throwing himself wildly on a chair, exclaimed "I wish
they would hang me out of the way! I have lived
on cold potatoes that were given to me two days,
and this morning I have eaten a raw potato from
sheer hunger. Give me a bit of bread and a cup
of coffee or I shall drop to the ground." Benjamin
Wilson, of Salterhebble, says rightly that he was
not surprised that people were so much in earnest
about Reform when he saw how they had to live.
His own mother was engaged in the laborious occupation of "braying sand," really a strong man's
work, and her only remuneration for it was a few
potato parings, which she boiled for the family
dinners.

CHAPTER XXXIX.

CHARTIST RISINGS.

Onward! while a wrong remains
To be conquered by the right;
While oppression lifts a finger
To affront us by his might;
While an error clouds the reason,
Of the universal heart,
Or a slave awaits his freedom,
Action is the wisest part.—*Mackay.*

During the whole of 1839 the Chartist movement waxed greatly in strength, and the alarmed authorities began to concoct means to check it. Finding that they did not succeed very well they soon resorted to their old discreditable weapon, paid spies. This led to the capture of scores of the local leaders of chartism throughout the country, many of them being imprisoned on the very doubtful testimony' of the hired informers who joined the organisations for the express purpose of hounding men on to violence so that they might land them in prison and then draw the wages for their villainous work. The abortive attempt at Newport, and the heavy punishment that had been meted out to those who had been captured in arms against the authorities so far from stopping the agitation seemed to increase and strengthen it, and as fast as one batch of "martyrs," as they were always called, were immured in prison there was another eagerly contending for the privilege of suffering for the people's cause. As great demonstrations celebrated the liberation of every prisoner, at which some of the most fervent apostles of the new political faith defended its methods and enforced its claims, the whole country rang with their eloquence and working men

joined its standard in large numbers, especially in
Yorkshire and Lancashire. The operative classes
grew more and more bitter against the Whigs whom
they denounced at one time as being worse than the
Tories, and whose defeat afterwards was doubtless
contributed to by the angry fire of Chartist denunciation and criticism. With a contemptuous
hatred of the upper classes, who were ridiculed un-
sparingly in all the Chartist publications, there
was conjoined a profound distrust of the middle
classes and their leaders. One would have thought
that the movement for the repeal of the Corn Laws
was one which would have secured at once the enthusiastic support of the artizans of all the large
towns who had suffered so much from them, but
so strong was their distrust of the middle classes
and the commercial men who took the lead in that
movement that they met the agitation for cheap bread
with coldness or downright hostility. "When we
get the charter," said one of their chief speakers,
"we will repeal the Corn Laws and also all other
bad laws, but don't be deceived by the middle
classes again. You helped them to get the Reform
Bill and what fine promises they made you then!
Don't be humbugged by them again. Stick to your
charter—without votes you are slaves !"

During the pleasant summer months large meetings were held in all the great centres of population,
which were often addressed by wild orators, whom
starvation or poor fare had made desperate, and
who took little trouble to disguise their treasonable
sentiments. Moral force was ridiculed and physical force was openly advocated. "Provide yourselves with knives," said one, "good long knives,
and then when the beef comes you will be ready."
A month of complete abstention from work—called
"the sacred month"—was now the chief burden of
the harangues. Without the labour of the toilers
it was pointed out the social pyramid would inevitably collapse, and to avoid the destruction that

would follow, the upper and middle classes would gladly concede their rights. Alarge gathering to help on the agitation for the sacred month was held at the end of July, at Barnsley, the chief speakers at which were Joseph Crabtree, Peter Hoey, and William Cowling. Government spies were present and careful note was made of the violent language used, the result being that the three men just named were speedily lodged in prison and tried at the succeeding assizes at York, when it was shown that physical force had been advocated strongly by all of them. Hoey, it was shown had used some very inflammatory language, and his companions were equally violent. In advocating the sacred month they said that a national holiday would be a national revolution, and before the month had expired the charter would be the law of the land. The possession of arms was declared to be the inalienable right of Englishmen, and hints were given that the poorest should possess themselves of pikes, which they were told were now being almost openly produced at Sheffield, Bradford, &c., in large numbers. Hoey said that up to that time he had been a moral force man, but the sight of so much destitution and misery had driven him into the ranks of the advocates of physical force. Joseph Crabtree declared the government to be bloodthirsty and tyrannical, and he emphasised the advice to procure arms and use them if necessary to secure their just rights. The weavers were already acting on this sanguinary advice so far at any rate as securing arms, and the miners now began to follow their example. Crabtree urged the latter to bring their picks out of the pits, and said they would soon have something softer to use them upon than the coal face. He said that at Birmingham the working men had produced a greater effect by trying to set fire to the town and had advanced the cause more than they could have done by a whole year of agitation, and that if the government did not grant their demands they would

light a fire in Yorkshire that would not soon be put
out—large enough in fact to warm the whole country
—they were indeed determined to have the charter
or England should be a heap of smoking ruins.
William Cowling's speech was equally violent and
withal of a practical sort, for he urged them to follow
the example of Sheffield, where hundreds were
sharpening their pikes ready for action, and told
them where they could be had. As a result of all
this plain speaking the three orators were sentenced
to be imprisoned, but the seed they had sown sprung
up and the whole district was disturbed for some
years after.

Partial outbreaks took place also at Leeds, Wakefield, Dewsbury, Halifax, and Bradford, and in
almost every instance it was found on investigation
that the men who had been most active in bringing
the discontent to a head were government spies.
One of these minions, named Harrison, who ingra-
tiated himself with the Bradford Chartists, while
bringing some of the leaders into trouble prevented
by his action, perhaps unintentionally, what would
otherwise have been a formidable rising by the non-
delivery of missives to other centres, which were
entrusted to his care. It had been arranged that
a rising of the West Riding towns should take place
on the 26th of January, 1840. The plan was to
take possession of the populous centres simultaneously by the local chartists, after which the cannon
at Lowmoor Ironworks was to be seized, and the
united forces were to march on London. The rising
was to begin at Bradford, and the Chartists at
Liversedge, Heckmondwike, and Dewsbury were to
join with a strong reinforcement, as were also Halifax
and Leeds : but Harrison threw the whole movement into confusion by destroying or not delivering
the orders sent from the centre at Bradford, and the
succours consequently never arrived there as expected. The leaders in this affair at Bradford
were Robert Peddie, who seems to have come from

·THE RISINGS OF THE LUDDITES.

Edinburgh to take the chief command, William Brook, Thomas Duke, Paul Holdsworth, and James Holdsworth. Before taking the control of the operations, Peddie visited all the West Riding towns and exhorted them to hold themselves in readiness for rising when he should give the signal. The chief witness against the insurgents at these trials was James Harrison, the government spy already named, of whom it may be said that he performed his dirty work in a less blamable manner than many of his colleagues. How he came to thwart the movement at the last moment by the non-delivery of the signals has never been satisfactorily explained, but it has been suggested that he was himself alarmed by the magnitude of the plot and was startled at the task of involving such a large number. The arrangements on the eve of the fateful day were complete. To avoid suspicion the leaders had met at Lidget Green, an outside village which stands away in the fields. There the leaders sat, after sending away orders to all the surrounding centres, and at two o'clock in the morning went forth to inaugurate what they expected was going to be an overpowering manifestation against constituted authority. There were less than two score of them all told, but they knew that thousands had promised to rally round them when the signal was given, and they therefore confidently marched into the town to the Green Market, which they had decided to make the centre of their operations. As they walked through the silent streets they encountered two constables, and these they captured and took with them to their rendezvous. A shed, at one corner of the market near the inn, served as a place of confinement for their prisoners, who having been dispossessed of their rattles were thrust into it, and a couple of pikemen were told off to act as warders over them. Brook was, it appears, employed at the Lowmoor Ironworks, where much cannon was then made for the government, and he

had on the previous Sunday taken Peddie round the
works to show him where the guns were. Although
it was intended that the bulk of the cannon should
form the equipment of what was grandiloquently
called the "Army of the North" in its march on
London, Peddie seems to have had an idea of also
fortifying the buildings round the Green Market.
The bazaar, a long building surrounding three sides
of the square behind the old Manor House, was to
be taken possession of, and in this and a large news-
room adjacent the various bodies of men were to be
put until all were assembled. A number of colliers
had also been engaged, who with their picks were
to make holes in the walls of these buildings through
which the guns from Lowmoor were to frown defiance on the enemy. Why this should be done is
not plain, as the whole army was to march immediately on London, but it may have been that it
was intended to leave a detachment here to overawe
Bradford. Peddie marched impatiently about the
Green Market armed ready for the fray, and wondering much, no doubt, how it was that the men
who were to come in hundreds east, west, north,
south were so slow in arriving. In the missives he
had sent out he had strongly exhorted them all to be
as near the time as possible. Those who were in
command of 100 must bring 50 if only that number
had mustered at the time and so on, but there was
to be no delay or the whole arrangements would be
spoiled. They were exhorted to seize all constables
on the route, and if they refused to come he significantly advised that they should be left so that
they would make no noise. The men were told
that though their numbers might not be large at
starting they would gather strength as they marched,
and two thousand at starting would speedily grow
into twenty thousand. When they had stormed
London this extraordinary commander stipulated
that he must have a day or two's leave of absence,
and he promised he would leave one as good as him-

self in command.   He would himself take a post
chaise and go to meet Dr. Taylor, who would be
marching at the head of the men from Durham,
Newcastle, &c.   He further instructed his men that
they were to take anything they wanted on the way.
The "army of deliverance" was to want for nothing,
but the sufferers were to be indemnified for all losses
after the Republic, which they should proclaim in
London, had been fully settled in power.

After Peddie had vapoured round the Green
Market for an hour or so he began to feel uneasy.
Not a score of men had joined him instead of the
thousands he had been expecting with so much confidence, and he began to fear that something had
gone wrong.   He sent scouts out in all directions,
but those who returned at all came but to tell him
that there were no signs of any reinforcements in
any direction.   There were signs, however, that
the authorities were waking up.   Messengers had
been despatched to the barracks at Bradford Moor,
and the echoes of horses'hoofs could be heard in the
streets.   The military and the special constables
by and by formed a cordon round Peddie's position,
but by the time it began to close round the Green
Market nearly all Peddie's men had dispersed, and
a sudden descent being made upon them the nucleus
of the "Grand Army of the North" was speedily
lodged in durance vile.

Although this rising ended so ingloriously there
were ferments and disturbances throughout the
whole of England for some time after, and the
military and special constables were kept at work
almost night and day.   Many of the Chartist
leaders were taken into custody, and Feargus
O'Connor, the chief disturber, shared the same fate.
The Chartist chief was tried on the 17th day of
March, 1840, before Mr. Justice Coleridge, at York,
the Attorney General prosecuting on behalf of the
government.   Mr. O'Connor, who defended himself
in person, made an extraordinary speech extending

over five hours, which seems to have greatly impressed the Judge, who treated the arch-agitator
with marked courtesy.   Boldly addressing the jury,
he declared that he stood up in defence of the working men of England, who had been all their lives
oppressed and ground to the very dust by laws
made by their more fortunate countrymen and which
they had no means of opposing but by the means
they had adopted, and though they might find him
guilty in court they could not find him guilty in the
secrecy of the closet.   He avowed himself a Chartist—a democrat if they liked—in the fullest sense
of the word, and declared that if his life hung upon
the abandonment of his principles he would scorn to
hold it on so base a tenure.   He then in the same
bold and defiant manner criticised the speech of the
Attorney General, and with wonderful ingenuity
explained away its most formidable charges, concluding his eloquent defence amidst loud applause,
which was with difficulty suppressed.   The Judge,
in summing up, testified his great admiration of Mr.
O'Connor's abilities, and regretted that he did not
more respect his own high acquirements and talents
than to use them for the purpose of exciting an
illiterate audience by a caricature of the other
classes of society.   The jury retired and in about
ten minutes brought in a verdict of "Guilty."   The
Attorney General pressed for immediate sentence,
but the Judge refused the application.

The action of the authorities so far from checking
the Chartist movement served only to cause it to
spread all the more widely and swiftly.   The
leaders throughout the country seemed rather to
court prosecutions than to avoid them, and as they
stood on their defence before the magistrate, which
they almost always conducted in person, the result
was that what were virtually Chartist meetings were
held in scores of court-houses with the presiding
magistrates in the chair.

CHAPTER XL.

THE PLUG RIOTS.

A crouching dastard sure is he,
Who would not fight for liberty,
And die to make old England free,
From all her load of tyranny.—*Bamford.*

Trade in 1842, the year of the plug riots, was worse than ever, and the sufferings of the working classes throughout Yorkshire and Lancashire were very great. It was hoped that as summer came on matters might improve, but they grew gradually worse, and at the beginning of August the distress was at its height. The corn laws were then in full operation, and the ports being closed the people throughout the country were starving. In the north it was reported that a fourth part of the population was dying of famine. At Stockport half the masters had failed, and five thousand work-people were walking the streets, nor were they much better in any of the towns in Lancashire. The Chartist movement had gathered much strength during the past year, and the working classes in all the large towns were in a state of great discontent and disaffection. The masses of the people were still persuaded that the " People's Charter " would enable them to secure higher wages and better food, and that for that very reason the "aristocrats," against whom they inveighed so furiously would not grant it. Another immense petition in favour of the charter was presented in the House of Commons in May, and great meetings were of almost nightly occurrence in all the large towns of Yorkshire. At Leeds the pauper stone heaps now amounted to one hundred and fifty thousand tons, and the guardians offered 6s. weekly for doing nothing rather than 7s. 6d. for stone breaking. Poor rates swelled to with dismay the heavy drain on their resources. Towards the end of June a meeting of tradesmen and shopkeepers was held in the Bradford court-house, "to enable them publicly to make known the unparalleled distress which prevailed, and the decay of trade consequent thereon, and to adopt such measures relative thereto as might be deemed advisable with a view to avert impending ruin."

Disturbances of an extraordinary character and on a large scale took place in Lancashire, which speedily assumed an alarming character. They commenced at Stalybridge. On Sunday, August 7th, a large meeting was held at Mottram Moor, which was attended by eight or ten thousand people. The disturbances originated in this way:—Some of the manufacturers of Stalybridge finding, as they stated, that others in the vicinity were paying lower wages than they were gave notice of a reduction. The workmen consented at one mill at the expiration of the notice to take the lower price. At another place, however, they refused to submit to the change. The workpeople of the firm last mentioned waited upon their employers, Bayley Brothers, and spake roughly on the proposed reduction, on which one of the masters said if they took the matter up in that spirit they had better play until they thought differently of it. On hearing this the deputation set up a loud shout, when all hands left the mill, without waiting for any formal answer to the demands of their representatives. Proceeding to the different mills in the town, the workpeople nearly all turned out and joined them, and their number soon swelled to more than 5,000, of whom one-third were females. Day by day they extended their march and emboldened by their numbers they determined to put an end to all work until their political demands were met. In accordance with this resolve they stopped all the collieries, and insisted upon men of all trades participating in the general holiday. Finding that all were not willing to join in the mad enterprise, they did not hesitate to overawe and coerce them, and procuring a number of formidable bludgeons, they tried to intimidate any workman who resisted them. Proceeding to the print works of Thomas Hoyle and Son, who had made themselves' very obnoxious, they spoiled a great many of their goods, and then went on to Ashton, where they were joined by fresh crowds. An immense meeting was held there, when the passions of the mob were inflamed by the fiery oratory of reckless demagogues. They next proceeded to Oldham and Manchester, where, however, they found the military drawn up to check their excesses. As the mob did not at once commit depredations the military were withdrawn, but a scene of pillage and disorder soon followed, the chief sufferers being the provision dealers and bakers. The military again marched out and fourteen of the ringleaders were taken into custody. At Birley's Mill a determined struggle took place. The rioters were first deluged with water, but as this did not compel them to disperse, some of the workpeople ascended the roof and threw pieces of iron, stones, and other missiles upon them. Many persons were very seriously hurt, and a young girl killed on the spot. From Lancashire the disaffection speedily spread into Yorkshire.

The Halifax Chartists were on the "qui vive" on Saturday, August 13th, the leaders having received word that large detachments of turnouts were on their way from Lancashire. Groups of suspicious-looking people with bludgeons were seen entering the town. Evening came on, and about eight o'clock the bellman went round the town calling a public meeting to be held next morning at five o'clock. The gathering took place, and was well attended. About six o'clock, while Mr. Ben Rushton, a well known local democrat, was speaking, the special constables, who had been sworn in on the previous day, were seen approaching the gathering, headed by two magistrates, Mr. George Pollard and Mr. William Brigg, and were received with groans. Mr. Pollard at once rode in front of the platform and declared the meeting to be illegal. He advised that the proceedings should be immediately brought to an end, and that all should depart in quietness to their homes. Mr. Rushton attempted to resume his speech, but he was not allowed to do so by the special constables, and, eventually, the assembly formed into procession and perambulated the district. Ere they dispersed it was arranged that another gathering should take place early next morning.

On the afternoon of that same Sunday (August 14th) a large gathering took place on Bradford Moor, under the presidency of George Bishop. Mr. Ibbotson, a well known news vendor, whose place of business was on the Bowling Green, addressed the gathering, which was estimated to number 10,000, and was followed by other speakers, stirring up the enthusiasm of the surging crowd, who received their treasonable utterances with wild cheering. The alarmed authorities summoned the chief inhabitants to meet the same evening at the Talbot Inn, when it was resolved that steps should be taken to put down the outbreak. Special constables were sworn in in large numbers, and troops were sent for from Leeds. Next morning another Chartist meeting was held in front of the Odd-Fellows' Hall, Thornton Road, at the early hour of seven, when it was resolved that the people should never relinquish their demands until the Charter became the law of the land. The immense crowd then formed into military order, marched up Manchester Road towards Halifax, stoppng at the mills on the way. The arrival of the Bradford contingent at Halifax was preceded by that of J. W. Hird, Esq., a magistrate, who announced to the startled authorities that thousands were on the way there, that the rest of the Bradford magistrates and a troop

of the 17th Lancers were coming to the assistance
of the Halifax authorities. As news had just been
received in Halifax that a large body was also on
the march from Todmorden, the alarmed outhorities
held at once a hurried consultation, and it was
resolved to move the civil and military forces to
New Bank, it being thought that the aim of the
rioters would be to stop Messrs. Ackroyds' and
Messrs. Houghs' mills. The cavalry, under the
command of Captain Forrest, and a body of infantry,
under Major Byrne, accordingly proceeded to the
spot, and arrived at New Bank just as the rioters
were seen coming over the brow of the hill. The
first action of the lancers was to range themselves
across the road in order to prevent the rioters from
going further. Behind the cavalry were ranged
the foot soldiers and the special constables. The
rioters, pressed forward by the surging mass behind, came marching on until the two bodies met,
but eventually the mob, seeing their way was
effectually barred, got over the walls, ran across the
fields, and formed again in Range Bank, where they
encountered the Bradford contingent and joined
forces, forming a compact mass of 25,000 men and
women—for no inconsiderable number of the insurgents and women—and strange as it may seem the
latter were really the more violent of the body.
The mob thus reinforced proceeded down Crown
Street towards North Bridge, and were met at the
top of Park Street by the military and civil forces.
Here the Riot Act was again read, but the magistrate who read it was jeered at by the crowd.

The thousands of female turnouts were looked
upon with some commiseration by the well-disposed
inhabitants, as many were poorly clad and not a
few marching barefoot. When the Riot Act was
read, and the insurgents were ordered to disperse
to their homes, a large crowd of these women, who
stood in front of the magistrates and the military,
loudly declared they had no homes, and dared them
to kill them if they liked. They then struck up

THE UNION HYMN.

Oh! worthy is the glorious cause,
　Ye patriots of the union;
Our fathers' rights, our fathers' laws
　Demand a faithful union.
A crouching dastard sure is he
　Who would not strive for liberty,
And die to make old England free
　From all her load of tyranny.
　　Up, brave men of the union!

Our little ones shall learn to bless
　Their fathers of the union,
And every mother shall caress
　Her hero of the union.
Our plains with plenty shall be crowned,
The sword shall till the fruitful ground,
The spear shall prune our trees around,
　　To bless a nation's union.

Singing this stirring hymn they defiantly stood in
their ranks as the special constables marched up,
but their music did not save them, for the constables
did not hesitate to strike them with their staves,
and a "melœ" ensued which ended in the disper-
sion of the mob in considerable disorder.

After stopping Messrs. Haigh's mill the crowd
proceeded to Haley Hill, where they did the same
at Mr. Dawson's mill letting off the steam. They
then went forwards to Messrs. Ackroyd's mill where
they stopped the works and turned the hands out.
They forced the boiler plug, and, while this was
being done, a party proceeded towards Booth Town
to stop Atkinson's silk mill, and another branched
off into Mr. Ackroyd's grounds for the purpose of
letting off the reservoir.

At two o'clock in the afternoon, a meeting of ten
to fifteen thousand people was held on Skircoat Moor,
when resolutions were passed touching the "people's
rights," and a deputation despatched to the Mayor
to demand the release of the prisoners that had

been captured by the authorities during the day's "melees." The women were very excited and were heard urging the men to attack the prisons in which the rioters were confined. Another gathering was held on Tuesday morning, and opened with singing and prayer, as was customary at most Chartist gatherings. The speakers were far more temperate in their language than on the day before. After the meeting they divided into bands and left for Greetland, Elland, Brighouse and other places to continue the work of stopping the mills. At Brig house they seem to have first attacked Samuel Leppington's mill at Brookfoot, where they drew the plugs; and from thence they proceeded to John Holland's, Slead Syke; Perseverance Mill, and Victoria Mill (Rev. Benjamin Firth), Upper and Lower Mills; Robin Hood and Little John Mills, were all visited. At the latter place a local man, Joseph Baines, drew the cloughs in connection with the water wheel, and was tried at York for the offence afterwards, being sentenced to six months imprisonment. Thornhill Briggs Mill was also visited, and part of the crowd then went to Bailiffe Bridge. and drew Holdsworth's plugs. Several local ringleaders at Brighouse and Elland, who made themselves conspicuous, were afterwards punished, some, however, judiciously absented themselves until the storm had blown over.

The great pressure brought to bear on the Halifax authorities with respect to the prisoners, and the strong manifestations on their behalf, led them to think it would be better to remove them to safer quarters, and it was decided to convey them to Wakefield. For this purpose two omnibuses were procured, and six police officers being told off to escort the eighteen men in custody to Elland railway station, a band of eleven hussars accompanying them. Upon arriving at the bottom of Salterhebble hill the party encountered a large mob, who made way for the omnibuses, but sent a volley of stones after them. The soldiers, however, escaped without much injury, passing through Elland Wood in safety, and the prisoners were duly placed in the train. Upon returning, Mr. Brigg wisely resolved that the troops should proceed up the higher road by Exley to Salterhebble, as he feared another encounter with the mob in Elland Wood. In coming down Exley Bank the soldiers were observed by the mob, who rushed out of the wood in vast numbers. Mr. Brigg, who was a little in advance of the hussars, motioned them forward. This magistrate appears to have been a special object of attack, and the first stone that was thrown hit his horse a severe blow on the head. The soldiers galloped forward, but, when opposite the Elephant and Castle, they encountered the mob in force congregated on the rising ground. Scores were also on the tops of the houses. The mob had all large stones, and it was evident from the number that they must have accumulated them. These missles they hurled with fearful violence upon the devoted soldiers in the road beneath. Mr. Brigg was hit in several places, his left arm being broken; his groom was hurt, and three of the hussars were unhorsed and taken prisoners. The soldiers fired upon their assailants, but the shots took little or no effect. Deeming that to continue the conflict would mean certain death, the hussars wisely retreated to a position on the brow of the hill, where they were joined by the remainder of the troop from Halifax, who had fortunately gone to meet them, expecting that their help would be required. Reinforcements were immediately sent for from Halifax, and the infantry with ten hundred special constables were shortly on their way to Salterhebble to disperse the mob. At another meeting held at Skircoat Moor, it was agreed to proceed to Haley Hill, which was now defended by the authorities, the entrance being protected by wool packs, &c. About four o'clock the turn-outs began to arrive, a large number of the malcontents being as usual, women. A shot was fired from the crowd at the

military massed at the bottom of Haley Hill, and
the bullet or slug struck one of the officers, but
did him no great injury. Several stones were then
thrown, whereupon the soldiers received orders to
fire upon the mob, which they did, and several
persons were wounded. The hussars also dashed
up the hill at full speed and several sabre blows
were administered to the flying crowd. The mob
gave way, and then made for Bankfield, the residence
of Mr. Ackroyd, but were met by a well directed
fire from some defenders of the mansion, and about
thirty persons were captured. After this the mob
made no further headway in the town, and on the
day following order was restored.

The Lancashire turn-outs commenced operations
in the Huddersfield district by stopping two manufactories at Milnes Bridge. They met with a slight
resistance at Armitage Bros'. Mill; and one still
more determined at Starkey's at Longroyd Bridge,
the gates being closed against them, but they had to
be opened or soon would have been broken down by
the enraged mob who congregated round them. At
Folly Hall ,a very extensive factory, the workpeople,
being apprized of the approach of the rioters, left the
mill to avoid any collision. At places where the
mob encountered any opposition they threatened to
return next day, when, if they found the mills
running, they would pull them down. The first
halt they made in the town was at Joseph Schofield's
Scribbling Mill in New-street, where, meeting with
some resistance, they drew the plug and let out
the water. The crowd then divided, parties proceeding to Paddock, Marsh, &c., the main body
next visiting Lockwood's factory in Upperhead Row.
Thence they proceeded through the town to the
factories of Messrs. Roberts and Mr. W. Brook. At
the latter place Mr. Brook hesitated to turn his
workpeople out, and endeavoured to reason with the
mob, but they refused to listen to him, threw him
While this was progressing, other parties proceeded

down into the engine house, and drew the boiler plug. to every mill in the neighbourhood, stopping them all. A meeting was then held at Back Green. The speakers were chiefly Lancashire men, and their utterances were resolute and determined. After the meeting, a raid was made upon many of the shops and houses for eatables. Mr. Brook, a magistrate, attempted to harangue the people at a meeting on Back Green, but the crowd refused to disperse and would not listen to him. The streets were by this time filled with people. In front of the George Hotel the mob was specially demonstrative, brandishing their bludgeons, and shouting and gesticulating wildly. Here some of the leaders were captured by the military, and taken into the inn. Rescue was attempted, but the result was that several others of the more prominent mob leaders were taken into custody. At this time the Market Place, New-street, Kirkgate, and Westgate presented one dense mass of human beings, and the aspect of affairs was very threatening. The military were commanded to clear the streets, and an awful scene took place as the trumpets sounded and the lancers dashed into the crowd, cutting down or riding over all who stood in their way. The crowd, thus assailed, ran in all possible directions, screaming dreadfully in their terror. Every street and corner was soon speedily cleared, the mob rushing wildly into the open country to escape the soldiers, and by eight o'clock on Monday evening the town was comparatively quiet.

When these stirring events were occurring I was a lad of some ten years of age, but I well remember the savage appearance of a huge crowd of men as they marched through Horton to Bradford, at the close of their day's work at Halifax. The sight was just one of those which it is impossible to forget. They came pouring down the wide road in thousands, taking up its whole breadth—a gaunt, famished-looking desperate multitude, armed with huge bludgeons, flails, pitch-forks and pikes, many without coats and hats, and hundreds upon hundreds with their clothes in rags and tatters. Many of the older men looked foot sore and weary, but the great bulk were men in the prime of life, full of wild excitement. As they marched they thundered out to a grand old tune a stirring melody, of which this was the opening stanza:—

"Men of England, ye are slaves,
    Though ye "rule" the roaring "waves,"
    Though ye shout, 'From sea to sea
    Britons everywhere are free.'"

As the wild mob swept onward, terrified women brought out all, their bread and other eatables, and in the hope of purchasing their forbearance, handed them to the rough-looking men who crowded to the doors and windows. A famished wretch, after struggling feebly for a share of the provisions, fell down in a fainting condition in the doorway where I was standing. A doctor, who lived close at hand, was got to the spot as soon as possible, but the man died in his presence. One of his comrades told us that the poor fellow had eaten raw potatoes at Ovenden after being without food two days; these the doctor said had killed him, "raw potatoes on an empty stomach being poison."

By this time all the towns and villages in Yorkshire were in a state of great excitement and confusion. On Tuesday, the 16th of August, a considerable mob entered Cleckheaton, and met with much oposition from the people at work in the mills. They succeeded in stopping one mill, and then went on to the works of Mr. George Anderton. Here they were gallantly opposed by the workmen within the mill, who with the assistance of a large number of the inhabitants drove them out of the millyard, and pelted them with stones, until they finally expelled them from the town. On the same day mob law was put in force at Dewsbury. A large meet-

ing was held at the Market Cross at six o'clock in
the evening, after which a procession was formed,
and the crowd proceeded to Batley Carr, Batley,
Birstall, Littletown, and Heckmondwike. They
tapped all the boilers on the way and turned out all
the hands, after which another meeting was held at
the Cross, at which it was stated that thirty-six
boilers had been "let off." The Dewsbury' shops
were closed as soon as word came that the rioters
were returning, and the public-houses closed at six
o'clock. Next morning another gathering took
place after which the mob marched through Earls-
heaton, and Horbury Bridge, coming back by way of
Thornhill Lees. They had some time to wait at
the colliery of Joshua Ingham, Esq., to get out the
men and horses before they tapped the boilers. Here
a field of turnips belonging to the Rev. Henry Torr,
the rector, was nearly stripped of its produce. Another meeting was held at the Cross on their return
and it was arranged that the next muster should be
held at Birstall. The shops were again closed
although it was market day. The men, who were
all armed, went from house to house begging, and
in many instances, if refused and only women happened to be in the house, force was resorted to.
The magistrates, J. B. Greenwood and John Hague,
Esqs., attended from early in the morning till late
at night to swear in special constables, and many
hundreds from Dewsbury, Batley and Heckmondwike offered their services.

On Thursday' morning all the factories and collieries
round Dewsbury were stopped by a mob 5,000
strong. The same mob than visited Batley and
stopped Bromley's and Ellis and Sons' mills, where
they drew the plugs without any opposition. They
then resolved to pay a second visit to Cleckheaton,
to do the work they had been unable at their previous
visit to accomplish, and strong parties were told off
to stop the mills, collieries, etc., at Gomersal, Millbridge, and Heckmondwike. It does not appear

that any opposition was offered at any of those places, and as the various mobs passed rapidly through the towns to rejoin the main body of their comrades at Cleckheaton their ranks were swelled by a large number of local chartists, who, deceived by the apparent impotence of the authorities, were persuaded that they were about to inaugurate a revolution. The time for redressing their grievances had, they were persuaded, at last arrived. The long-suffering people had risen in their strength, and by stopping all production were going to teach "the aristocrats" how completely they were dependent on the classes beneath them in the social scale, to whom they had so long denied their just political rights. Many of the men had coarse grey blankets strapped to their backs, their idea being that when they had stopped all the mills and turnel out the workpeople they would march in immense bodies to London, and there put the affairs of the nation on an equitable basis. "And what would you have done?" one of them was afterwards asked, "when you had got to London?" "Done," replied the simpleton in amazement, "why we sud a taen t' nation and sattled t' national debt." Amongst the prominent local men who joined the movement was the late Isaac Clissett, a man who, however he might be misled by his political opinions at the time, proved himself afterwards a peaceful and worthy citizen. At first Clissett did not throw himself heartily into the movement, and joined at last with an honest desire to restrain the mob, but, carried away by the enthusiasm of his companions, he entered Cleckheaton in the front rank of the Heckmondwike detachment.

The first attack of the mob at Cleckheaton was on the mill of Mr. Sutcliffe Broadbent, where they were suffered to draw the plugs without any serious resistance being offered, and being joined by some of the other detachments, they proceeded in a body numbering some five or six thousand to St. Peg mill, and had withdrawn the plugs from two of the boilers when an alarm was raised that the soldiers were coming. As soon as it became known that the rioters were approaching Cleckheaton in strong force, the late Mr. Jas. Anderton, of Upper House, then a young man, rode, it is said, from Cleckheaton to Bradford in the incredibly short space of half an hour to fetch a troop of the Lancers then stationed there, but before they arrived a troop of the Yorkshire Hussars came from Leeds, where Prince George of Cambridge was acting against the insurgents. When the Yeomanry reached Cleckheaton they were joined by some hundreds of special constables, and then proceeded in a body to Peg Mill. The mob had, as we have stated, withdrawn the plugs from two of the boilers, and were proceeding to the third when they saw the soldiers defiling down the lane. Hastily massing themselves, those who were unarmed proceeded to pick up all the loose stones in the yard, while those who were armed with bludgeons, scythes, &c., were thrust to the front. The appearance of the rioters, as they somewhat unsteadily waited for the arrival of the troops, was certainly formidable, but the discipline of the little band who came to attack them more than counterbalanced the disadvantage of the great disparity of numbers. The leader of the friends of law and order called out for a halt as they neared the mob, and addressed to his men a few simple words of encouragement, appealing to their sense of duty to the throne and the peace of the realm. He then waited for the reading of the Riot Act. Before this could be done the mob advanced in disorderly fashion and threw pieces of dross at the compact mass before them, and several men were knocked senseless and bleeding from their horses.

The moment was critical, as the mob, taking advantage of the confusion occasioned, were advancing with stones in their hands once more, Clissett, who was in the front rank, excitedly waving his arms and crying, "Follow me, my brave boys!"

when orders were given to fire. Though this and a
second volley was fired in the air, the crowd fell
back in disorder, and the Yeomanry, taking advantage of the confusion, rode rapidly upon them,
flourishing their sabres over their heads and striking
them with the flat sides. The special constables
followed up the advantage thus gained and drove
the rioters towards the beck, on reaching which they
scattered in all directions, some crossing the stream
and others rushing into a neighbouring corn field,
where they hoped by lying flat to hide from their
pursuers. In a few minutes about twenty or thirty
were taken into custody, and all the fields and lanes
in the neighbourhood were black with wild struggling
masses of human beings trying to escape from the
horsemen, who rode after them flourishing their
weapons. The following is a list of those taken into
custody:—Charles Leighton (18), farmer, Gomersal;
Richard Thomson (26), clothier, Gomersal; Thomas
Barber (22), collier, Gomersal; David Walker (17),
clothier, Batley Carr; Charles Brierley (32),
machinist, Batley Carr; John Hey (18), collier,
Hightown; Matthew Parkinson (30), dyer, Dewsbury; Josh. Holdroyd (20), raiser, Dewsbury; David
Brooke (34), sawyer, Dewsbury; Joseph Farnhill
(35), weaver, Dewsbury; W. Allport Bell, Dewsbury; Robert Waterson (16), no trade, Birstall;
Matthew Mawson (26), collier, Birstall; J. Hodgkin-
son (30), weaver, Birstall; Samuel Newsome (14),
clothier, Hanging Heaton; Josh. Blakeborough (39),
weaver, Batley; Edward Exley (22), weaver, Earls-
heaton; Wm. Wild (17), collier, Alverthorpe; and
Matthew Castle, hawker, Bradford.

CHAPTER XLI.

LAST STRUGGLES OF CHARTISM.

Last scene of all
That ends this strange, eventful history.
Shakespeare.

The suppression of the Plug Riots left the country still in a sadly disturbed state owing to the scarcity of work and the dearness of provisions, and great meetings and riots such as those already chronicled continued at intervals during several years. The prisons all over the country, in the clothing districts especially, were crowded with chartist leaders, no less than fifty of the principal agitators being imprisoned at one time. Amongst these were the wary leader of the movement, Feargus O'Connor and his trusty lieutenants, George Julian Harney and Dr. McDouall, who were tried together before Baron Rolfe, at Lancaster. Hundreds of the leaders of the plug rioters in Yorkshire and Lancashire were also put upon their defence, and some of the accounts given by these men of the circumstances which had led them to engage in that desperate undertaking were of a very pathetic character. Benjamin Wilson, of Salterhebble, who was himself mixed up with the chartist movement, refers to a man named Pilling, who was one of the originators of the great strike which resulted in the plug riots. In his defence, Pilling stood forward and thus addressed the jury:—" Gentlemen, I am somewhere about 43 years of age. I was asked last night if I was not 60. At first, when I went to Ashton, my two sons and myself worked at the mill for 12½d. per cut. Our work was thirty cuts a week, which

made £1 11s. 3d., this would be 10s. 5d. each.   In
a little over twelve months we had to submit to
three reductions in wages, bringing them down to
7s. 11d. each per week.   These were starvation
wages, and on another attempt being made soon
after to reduce us still further, flesh and blood re-
belled and we struck.   In Ashton not one penny-
worth of damage was done to property, although we
were slowly starving for six weeks.   My lord and
gentlemen, it was a hard case with me and mine.
My second son fell into a consumption from insufficient nourishment and hardship.   Before we
struck our united wages had sunk to 16s. per week,
and that was all nine of us had to live upon, and
3s. of that had to go for rent.   During this time
the son I have named laid helpless before me.   I
have gone home night after night and seen that son
on a sick bed and dying pillow, having nothing to
eat but potatoes and salt and no medical attendance.
Someone who knew my sore straits went to a gentleman's house to beg a bottle of wine for my son, and
the answer was, ' Oh, he is a chartist, he must have
none !'   Mr. Rayner, of Ashton, had given notice
a day or two before that he would reduce wages
25 per cent.   That aroused the people's indignation
and the strike was the result.   The people first rose
in desperation because they could not live, and that
was why I joined the movement."

Poor Pilling's reason was doubtless the reason of
thousands besides—it was not so much the desire
for a vote as a desire for food that impelled multi-
tudes to join the great movement which reached at
last such portentous dimensions.   The country continued in much the same disturbed state up to the
remarkable year of revolutions, 1848, when the fall
of Louis Philippe, the French king, caused a wave
of revolutionary feeling to ripple throughout Europe
and a serious sifting time began for the rulers of the
continent.   The Chartists hailed this time of po-

litical earthquakes with wild enthusiasm, being convinced that the long looked for period had come at
last when kings and aristocrats were to be swept
for ever out of existence, and the "long-suffering,
down-trodden people were to come into their rights."
Everywhere the Chartist leaders who believed in
physical force called upon the people to rise in their
strength and demand that the Charter should be at
once made the law of the land. Others of a milder
type contented themselves with demanding the dis-
missal of the ministry and the immediate dissolution
of parliament. "The Charter and no surrender,"
was the cry everywhere, and at an immense gathering held throughout the country delegates were
elected to form a National Convention, which was
to sit in London, and take control of the great movement which many Chartists believed was at last
about to be crowned with success. The result of
all this wild commotion was that the sober-minded
men, who had hitherto succeeded in keeping the
Chartist movement moderately well in hand, found
themselves in a discredited minority. The excited
people, intent upon inaugurating forthwith the political millennium which seemed to them at hand,
would listen no longer to what they deemed timid
counsels, and the cry went forth that the Charter
must now be conceded or the government would be
over-thrown and a republic erected on its ruins. In
order to give Parliament what was ostentatiously
called a "last chance," a monster petition was commenced, which it was resolved should be signed by
millions, and should be presented by an immense
procession, which should convey it to the very doors
of the House of Commons. The central gathering
place was to be Kennington Common, and April
10th was fixed upon as the date. From that place,
after an address by Feargus O'Connor, who though
his popularity had waned somewhat, still held his
post at the head of the Chartist movement, the
crowd was to march in military order to overawe

the House which had so long disregarded their pro-
tests and derided their threats.   Perhaps the great
bulk had no other desire than to impress parliament
with their numbers, but there was a strong contingent of desperate physical force men present, who
would undoubtedly have been too glad to have forced
on a conflict with the authorities in the hope that,
as in France and other countries, the Government
might have been overturned.   The physical force
section began as the day drew near to use language
of such violence in their wild speeches and manifes-
toes that the moderate men took the alarm, and
when the meeting took place many of them stayed
away and the leaders were all disputing amongst
themselves.

The convention which was sitting in London up
to the eve of the day looked forward to with so
much hope by some, and so much apprehension by
others.   It dawned at last, and the meeting was
held amidst a great conflict of opinion amongst the
Chartist leaders, but it was plain the bulk of them
were much sobered by the danger which they saw
was imminent and by the preparations the Government was making to meet it.   Feargus O'Connor
was one of the first to realise the grave situation
and had the good sense to oppose these mad counsels
with all his strength.   The result was a further
commotion in the gathering, which ended in the
withdrawal of the violent spirits who were so de-
terminedly bent on mischief from the National Convention.   These disputes were fortunate for the
physical force men themselves, for these soon found
they had been greatly misled by the apparent fervour which their declamation had evoked.   When
those who sympathised with them so far as supporting their theories was concerned found that the
theories were to be translated into action they began
to scent danger, and so insignificant did the physical
force section become that the police had little difficulty in dispersing their demonstrations.   Even-

tually, when Mr. G. W. M. Reynolds, the proprietor of "Reynolds's Newspaper," and a few other rabid politicians of the same stamp, assembled in Trafalgar Square and attempted to inaugurate a revolution by shouting out in wretched French "Vive la Republique!" in imitation of their Paris compatriots, the British public laughed consumedly, and the police entering into the spirit of the fun allowed the little band to hide their diminished heads in the nearest tap room.

On the morning of the famous 10th of April, the Chartists assembled at Kennington Common in immense numbers, but it was simply to hold a peaceable open air meeting, and the alarmed shopkeepers found at the close of the day' that the goods and chattels behind their strongly barricaded shutters remained intact. Feargus O'Connor and the principal Chartist leaders knew well enough that the Iron Duke was ready for them, and though there was no ostentatious display of military in the streets the old tactician had a strong force well in hand and all prepared to grapple with any disturbances that might arise. The end of the matter was that no procession was formed, O'Connor, who saw the danger, insisting upon that part of the programme being given up. The physical force men denounced the moral force leaders as humbugs, and the quarrel that ensued resulted in thousands of working men withdrawing from the movement in disgust.

The great Chartist petition which was to astonish the House of Commons and carry conviction to the minds of the most obtuse members of the Government was presented in the House, or rather rolled into in, for it was of the dimensions of a cart wheel. Mr. O'Connor, in the inflated harangue he made on the occasion, boasted that it contained five millions seven hundred thousand signatures. Had he been content to have claimed a more moderate number he might have been doubted, but no investigation

would probably have taken place; the statement he
made seemed, however, so absurd, that a committee
was appointed to examine the monster document,
when it was found that the actual number of names
fell short of two millions, and that very many of
them were evidently fictitious. Amongst the rest
of the signatures appeared that of the Queen, Prince
Albert, the Duke of Wellington, Sir Robert Peel,
and, to crown all, Colonel Sibthorpe, a very violent
Tory, who would gladly have seen the leaders of
the Chartist movement transported out of the country.

The absurd ending of this last great rising and
the consequent ridicule with which the Chartists
were now assailed on every hand, owing to 'the
damaging disclosures made by the committee who
examined the "great national petition" had much
to do with discrediting the party, but what gave this
remarkable and once powerful movement its finishing stroke was doubtless the abolition of what John
Bright called the "thrice accursed Corn Laws."
Under a free trade regime the lot of the working
classes was wonderfully changed for the better. They
gradually acquired a position and comforts to which
as a body they had hitherto been strangers, and with
increasing prosperity the old hatred for the classes
above them in the social scale was moderated or died
out, and ultimately constitutional agitation took
the place of the physical force methods, with which
they had so long been familiar.